A Taste *of* Canada

A Taste *of* Canada
a culinary journey

ROSE MURRAY

foreword by ELIZABETH BAIRD

whitecap

Design by Mauve Pagé
Edited by Elaine Jones
Proofread by Naomi Pauls
Food photography by Shawn Taylor
Food styling by Jennifer Stamper
Additional photo credits on last page

Printed in China.

**Library and Archives Canada Cataloguing
in Publication**

Murray, Rose, 1941–
　　　A taste of Canada : a culinary journey /
Rose Murray.

Includes index.
ISBN 978-1-55285-911-7

　　　1. Cookery. 2. Cookery, Canadian. I. Title.

TX715.6.M863 2008　　　　641.5
C2008-901237-2

The publisher acknowledges the financial support
of the Government of Canada through the Book
Publishing Industry Development Program (BPIDP)
and the Province of British Columbia through the
Book Publishing Tax Credit.

08　09　10　11　12　　　5　4　3　2　1

for MITCHELL

CONTENTS

Foreword ~ *viii*

Acknowledgements ~ *xi*

Introduction ~ *xii*

Starters ~ *1*

Soups ~ *24*

Breads & Brunches ~ *42*

Mains

    Fish & Seafood ~ *62*

    Poultry ~ *76*

    Pork ~ *93*

    Beef & Veal ~ *102*

    Lamb ~ *117*

    Pasta & Vegetarian ~ *126*

Vegetables, Sides, Sauces & Preserves ~ *140*

Salads ~ *165*

Desserts & Cookies ~ *186*

Other Menus ~ *250*

Index ~ *253*

FEATURES

Jerusalem Artichokes ~ *14*

Tourtière ~ *18*

Bread-Making ~ *51*

Pork ~ *94*

Dried Beans ~ *100*

Lamb ~ *118*

Ukrainian Christmas Eve ~ *133*

Potatoes ~ *143*

Sweet Potatoes ~ *144*

Fiddleheads ~ *147*

Corn ~ *150*

Cranberries ~ *159*

Preserving Pleasures ~ *161*

Great Greens ~ *166*

Wild Rice ~ *171*

Liquid Gold (Maple Syrup) ~ *188*

Plums ~ *205*

Pumpkins ~ *206*

Fruitcakes ~ *209*

Blackberries ~ *218*

Rhubarb ~ *220*

Pies ~ *224*

Apples ~ *229*

Christmas Dainties ~ *240*

REGIONS AND MENUS

British Columbia ~ *21*

   A Picnic in Stanley Park ~ *22*

The Prairies ~ *59*

   A Prairie Brunch ~ *61*

The North ~ *75*

   A Midnight Sun Supper ~ *75*

Ontario ~ *123*

   A Midsummer Grill ~ *125*

Quebec ~ *183*

   A Sophisticated Supper ~ *184*

The Maritimes ~ *244*

   A Maritime Company Buffet ~ *246*

Newfoundland and Labrador ~ *247*

   Christmas Dinner ~ *249*

Other Menus

   Two Easy Festive Dinners for
     Close Friends ~ *251*

   A Cross-Canada Thanksgiving ~ *252*

   Canada's Birthday Party ~ *252*

FOREWORD

Over the generations, there have been many cookbooks about Canadian food. And much discussion as we Canadians seek to define the culinary threads that bind us together. We can butt heads forever arguing, first whether there is such a thing as Canadian cooking, and then if there is, *what* it is. Could our cuisine be the sum of our native ingredients—salmon, game, fiddleheads, wild berries, maple syrup and corn, for example—and the dishes that have evolved out of them? Is it the recipes that waves of immigrants have brought to our shores, to be kept intact or mixed and mingled with the traditions of groups who arrived before them as well as with First Nations traditions? Is Canadian cuisine one created by recent generations of chefs, raised and trained in Canada and devoted to in-season and locally grown ingredients?

Take a deep breath. Canadian food is all of the above. It's what we eat. And we eat from many tables, dipping our spoons into just as many pots and relishing every bite. We eat at upscale white tablecloth restaurants, we eat at tiny mom-and-pop eateries, we eat street food. We can do Italian one night, and order in Thai the next. And as you might expect in a vast country like ours with its many climates and geographic variations, we don't all eat the same.

Rose Murray takes this real approach to Canadian food and builds on decades of culinary travel across Canada and years in her kitchen perfecting recipes for magazine articles, television and radio appearances and award-winning cookbooks. The result? *A Taste of Canada*, a cookbook lush with recipes that taste as good as they sound, recipes that work and won't fail you in your kitchen. These very practical and laudatory aspects of cookbook writing are too often neglected, but not by Rose Murray. Her recipes have the feel of someone who shares your kitchen as she guides you through the various steps. You can tell Rose loves flavours, tinkering as she does with cumin in carrots, curry with beets, roasted asparagus to elevate a soup from the everyday to a special occasion. It's these inspirations that turn a classic but expected dish into something with a spark of new interest. She has bolstered her recipes with anecdotes that link her family, friends and travels to the food, with ingredient lore as well as bites of culinary history, region by region. Of immeasurable help to cooks everywhere, she has also fashioned menus that celebrate Canadian holidays—Thanksgiving and Canada Day, for example—and that celebrate regional flavours, such as the Midsummer Grill featuring Ontario provisions. Food photography by Shawn Taylor with styling by Jennifer Stamper adds a whole other layer to the pleasures of *A Taste of Canada*.

It could be that I am prejudiced, having counted the blessings of having Rose as a friend for over 30 years. But I'll deny even a hint of prejudice. I like to tell people that Rose is one of the most welcoming and generous hosts I have ever met, and when you are invited to the Murrays', the food will always be outstanding, and around Rose, there will always be laughter and fun.

You couldn't be tasting Canada with a better person.

Elizabeth Baird

ACKNOWLEDGEMENTS

Thanks to—

Robert McCullough, publisher of Whitecap, for his faith in my doing such an important book.

Elizabeth Baird for helping to decide what it should include.

Sharon Boyd and *Donna Rowe* for their help in testing and retesting the recipes.

My family and many *friends* who were taste-testers.

My good friends *Julia Aitken, Elizabeth Baird, Pam Collacott, Anne Lindsay, Monda Rosenberg* and *Edna Staebler* (through her estate) for sharing some of their best Canadian recipes.

The remarkable team at *Whitecap*, including Elaine Jones, Naomi Pauls, Mauve Pagé, Claire Philipson, Michelle Mayne, Grace Yaginuma, Meghan Spong, Amanda LeNeve, Nick Rundall, and especially Taryn Boyd for allowing me freedom of style.

My computer guy, my son, *Allen Murray.*

My husband, *Kent Murray*, for his help, support and tireless proofreading.

INTRODUCTION

When our children were young, we spent our family holiday in a different province each year. We would either fly and rent a car or drive there and spend days exploring as much of the province as we could. In the few weeks we had, there wasn't time to discover every corner, but we hoped to give the children a "taste of Canada" before they set off to see the rest of the world.

Similarly, this book takes you on a culinary journey across the country. In such a vast country, we won't go down every lane or visit every kitchen, but you'll get a glimpse of what grows in various regions and how that affects the cooking of the area. Bordered by three oceans and abundant in freshwater lakes and rivers, rich farmlands and great forests, Canada has attracted immigrants for over four centuries. A distinctive Canadian cuisine developed from interweaving the products of these fertile resources and the food traditions brought by each newcomer.

In Canada, everyone has roots in some other place—even First Nations, whose forebears may have been Northeast Asian hunters who followed mastodons across the Bering land bridge or sailed along the ice-free Pacific coast. Some hypothesize the earliest arrivals were ice age Europeans (*Solutreans*) who sailed to eastern North America. However they came, they spread across the country and developed foods and cultures based on the natural resources: caribou hunters in the Arctic; Micmac (*Mi'kmaq*) fishermen on the East Coast; agricultural peoples like the Iroquois and Huron nations in parts of southern Quebec and Ontario; nomadic tribes like the Plains Cree and Assiniboine in the Prairies, who depended on bison; and on the West Coast, interior and coastal nations thriving on abundant marine life and wild plants.

By the time the first Europeans arrived, they found many indigenous societies well adapted to local climates and food supplies. First Nations foods like pemmican, corn and dried salmon saved the first explorers and fur traders from starvation; later, early settlers across the country survived in part because Native people shared not only their knowledge of our natural food supplies, but also their cooking and preservation methods. Foods, depending on

the area, included a wide array of fish, fowl, and mammals, saskatoon berries, blueberries, bakeapples, maple syrup, fiddleheads and wild rice. Regional cooking was born.

With their contrasts in geography, climate, history and the backgrounds of people who inhabit them, today's regions all have their own gastronomic personalities, though there are also many similarities across the country.

But how have we made the journey from boiled buffalo hump (see page 59) to supermarket sushi? By the end of the 18th century the dominant groups in Canada were British, French and American Loyalists. Immigration of Eastern Europeans peaked on the Prairies in the second decade of the 20th century. Right after World War II came Italians and another wave of Eastern Europeans. Even in the 1950s and 1960s, most immigrants (with the exception of the Chinese in British Columbia) came from European countries with a predominantly meat-and-potatoes diet. Following Canada's new multicultural policy in the 1970s, immigrants (some of whom were refugees) have streamed here from places like Hong Kong, South Africa, Latin America, Vietnam, Somalia, Ethiopia, Croatia, Serbia, India, Pakistan, Sri Lanka, the Caribbean and the Middle East. Each decade since then has brought new flavours and food customs. With this ever-expanding multiculturalism and the ability to travel, our palates grow more adventurous.

Immigration has indeed left the biggest imprint on our food culture. But other factors, such as new processing techniques and the coming of railways, helped change the eating habits of the nation. As in clothing, however, there are fads and fashions in food. Some are brought on by necessity. The Depression years meant ingenuity in the kitchen and dishes like bread pudding. With the war years came lots of home gardens. Sometimes, so-called new inventions led the way: pudding mixes, sliced bread and canned cream of mushroom soup in the 1930s and myriad time-saving appliances in the 1950s. That decade also brought the first written reference to regional roots in cookbooks such as Savella Stechishin's *Traditional Ukrainian Cookery* as found in the Prairies. With the 1960s came a whole new wave of packaged convenience foods like fake whipped cream, but there was also a hint that organically grown food should replace that full of additives. And so the 20th century carried on with new technology like microwave ovens and food imported from around the world, but still more regional cookbook authors like Madame Benoit, Edna Staebler and Marie Nightingale extolled the virtues of local food and real food. In the late 1980s, West Coast cuisine led the way in championing local indigenous ingredients.

Before the arrival of airplanes, fast freezing and modern storage, we did enjoy the fleeting pleasure of seasonal cooking

and looked only to local foods. Right now, there is a growing trend once more to eat foods grown locally, even within a 100-mile radius. On the self-sufficient mixed farm near Collingwood, Ontario, where I grew up, our food came from just a few yards away. We grew all our own fruit and vegetables, raised our own meat, had our own eggs and made our own bread and butter. Eating only nearby food in such a situation is easy. These days, it is a bit harder to accomplish, but I still appear on television regularly to commend the virtues of local food, much of which I find at neighbourhood farms or at our farmers' market. We have to be realistic, however, since we are unable to grow certain things. We should enjoy our unmatchable local produce when it is in season, support our farmers, but know there are many wonderful ingredients we would miss if we didn't embrace some imported food, especially when we set about making an exciting dish brought by a newcomer to this part of the world.

A Taste of Canada celebrates the best dishes that are firmly established in this country's cuisine. Some of the recipes reflect ethnic cultures in relatively recent dishes like Pad Thai and beef curry, which have become familiar to most and are here to stay as part of our cooking. Most of the recipes, however, are Canadian classics like pea soup and tourtière that originally helped form the framework of Canadian cuisine and have been passed down from one generation to another. To most of these familiar dishes I've added exciting new ingredients or updated the method.

Many of these dishes can be found in every part of the country, but scattered throughout this book you'll find a description of each major region in Canada along with a menu that highlights some of its specialties—salmon in British Columbia, bread in the Prairies, Arctic char in the Far North, lamb in Ontario, the wonderful chèvre of Quebec on a salad, dessert from the Annapolis Valley in the Maritimes—and when we get to Newfoundland, we'll celebrate Christmas, which has been a welcome respite in our cold winters right across our country since the 19th century. While we acknowledge the other important festivals recently brought from other cultures, Christmas, our most important family holiday, was part of the country's building process and is, indeed, celebrated by other faiths as a secular holiday. At this time of the year, too, many other faiths celebrate their version of the winter solstice.

Canadians have always had a strong tradition of hospitality. The first social gourmet club in America was "The Order of the Good Time" at Port Royal in 1606, when Samuel de Champlain had each of the 15 gentlemen of the company take turns hosting a dinner to distract the members from discontent with the long winter months. Later, even the pioneers found time to socialize, though formal suppers, balls and picnics were more apt to be the fashion in cities. At the end of the book, look for four special menus to share with others: two classic Canadian dinner parties for close friends and menus for two celebrations enjoyed right across the country by long-time Canadians and recent immigrants alike, Thanksgiving and Canada's birthday. New Englanders who settled in Nova Scotia probably brought the idea of a traditional Thanksgiving with them, while Canada's birthday commemorates the creation of the Dominion of Canada on July 1, 1867.

STARTERS

SMOKED SALMON AND CHEESE BROCHETTES
WITH CITRUS GREENS ~ *3*

COD AND POTATO OVALS WITH SPICY
LEMON MAYONNAISE ~ *4*

WINE-PICKLED SALMON ~ *5*

STILTON AND PECAN SHORTBREAD ~ *5*

SPICY SHRIMP WITH FRESH CORIANDER
AND LIME ~ *6*

SPICY LAMB TURNOVERS WITH CURRIED YOGURT ~ *8*

GRILLED TOMATO AND CHEESE QUESADILLAS ~ *9*

QUICK CHÈVRE AND ROASTED PEPPER TARTS ~ *10*

JERK WINGS ~ *11*

CARAMELIZED ONION PIZZA WITH ANCHOVIES
AND BLACK OLIVES ~ *11*

ROASTED TOMATO AND CHEESE TART ~ *12*

LEMON-PARSLEY HUMMUS ~ *12*

GORGONZOLA FOCACCIA ~ *13*

WILD RICE PANCAKES WITH SOUR CREAM
AND CAVIAR ~ *15*

QUICK BRANDIED CHICKEN LIVER PÂTÉ ~ *15*

TOURTIÈRE TURNOVERS ~ *16*

WILD MUSHROOM AND BACK BACON RISOTTO ~ *19*

BRITISH COLUMBIA ~ *21*
A PICNIC IN STANLEY PARK ~ *22*

SMOKED SALMON *and* CHEESE BROCHETTES *with* CITRUS GREENS

The brochettes look pretty spectacular on the salad, but if you wish, omit the greens, garnish the brochettes with lemon slices and serve with sliced baguette as pre-dinner finger food. You'll need 16 (8-inch/20 cm) wooden skewers for the brochettes.

BROCHETTES

2	pkg (5 oz/150 g each) herbed cream cheese (not light)	2
1	pkg (5 oz/150 g) smoked wild salmon, thawed if frozen	1
1 tsp	grated lemon zest	5 mL
½ tsp	black pepper	2 mL
•	Fresh parsley, chopped	•

CITRUS GREENS

¼ cup	olive oil	50 mL
1 tsp	grated lemon zest	5 mL
4 tsp	fresh lemon juice	20 mL
1 tsp	Dijon mustard	5 mL
¼ tsp	granulated sugar	1 mL
Pinch	each of salt and pepper	Pinch
10 cups	lightly packed mixed, washed, dried and torn salad greens or mesclun	2.5 L

BROCHETTES: Divide the cheese into 16 portions, then roll each into a ball; set aside. Cut the salmon into ¾-inch-wide (2 cm) strips, cutting longer strips in half if necessary so you have a total of 32.

Carefully thread 1 strip accordion-style onto a skewer, followed by a cheese ball, then another strip of salmon; wipe the end of the skewer with a paper towel to remove any cheese residue. Repeat with the remaining ingredients and skewers. Arrange in a single layer on a platter; sprinkle with the lemon zest, pepper and parsley. (The brochettes can be covered and refrigerated for up to 6 hours. Let stand at room temperature for 30 minutes before serving.)

CITRUS GREENS: In a small bowl, whisk together the oil, lemon zest, lemon juice, mustard, sugar, salt and pepper. (The dressing can be prepared ahead and stored at room temperature for 2 hours.)

Just before serving, whisk the dressing. In a large bowl, toss the greens with the dressing. Divide the greens among 8 plates; arrange 2 brochettes on each and serve at once.

Makes 8 servings.

COD *and* POTATO OVALS *with* SPICY LEMON MAYONNAISE

This recipe goes full circle. When Portuguese fishermen took salt cod back to their home country, it became one of their traditional foods. The recipe for these little appetizers came from Portuguese immigrants who set up a grocery business in Cambridge, Ontario.

1¼ lb	salt cod, preferably fillets	625 g	¼ tsp	ground nutmeg	1 mL
5 cups	riced or finely mashed mealy potatoes, cooked without salt	1.25 L	¼ tsp	pepper	1 mL
			3	eggs, beaten	3
½ cup	finely chopped onion	125 mL	•	Canola oil for deep-frying	•
⅓ cup	finely chopped fresh parsley	75 mL	•	Spicy Lemon Mayonnaise	•
4 tsp	fresh lemon juice	20 mL		(recipe follows)	

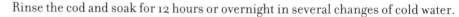

Rinse the cod and soak for 12 hours or overnight in several changes of cold water.

Drain and place in a large saucepan. Cover with cold water; bring to a boil. Reduce the heat and simmer until the fish flakes easily when tested, about 15 minutes. Drain and let cool; remove the skin and all bones if not using fillets. In a food processor or by hand, chop the cod very finely until no chunks remain.

In a large bowl, combine the cod, potatoes, onion, parsley, lemon juice, nutmeg and pepper; stir in the eggs to form a firm but malleable mixture. Use a dessertspoon to scoop out a heaping spoonful of the cod mixture. Cup a second dessertspoon over the first, and press and form the mixture into a rounded oval, letting any excess fall back into the bowl. Place the oval on a large baking sheet lined with waxed paper. Repeat with the remaining mixture.

In a deep fryer, heat 3 inches (8 cm) of oil to 375°F (190°C); fry the ovals, about 8 at a time, until golden and crisp, about 2 minutes. Drain on paper towels. Serve immediately or keep warm until serving. Accompany with the Spicy Lemon Mayonnaise. *Makes about 60 appetizers.*

SPICY LEMON MAYONNAISE

1 cup	mayonnaise	250 mL	1½ tsp	hot pepper sauce (like Tabasco) or more to taste	7 mL
2 tsp	finely grated lemon zest	10 mL			
2 tbsp	fresh lemon juice	25 mL	¼ tsp	salt	1 mL

In a small bowl, whisk together the mayonnaise, lemon zest, lemon juice, hot pepper sauce and salt until smooth. (The mixture can be made up to 1 day ahead, covered and refrigerated.) *Makes 1 cup (250 mL).*

^ *Cod in bucket in Bay d'Espoir, Newfoundland*

WINE-PICKLED SALMON

I once served pickled salmon at my Canada Day July 1st party, and it was such a huge hit that double this recipe disappeared in minutes. We often have a jar of pickled herring in the refrigerator for snacking; this is even better. It is lovely tossed with minced yellow pepper, diced cucumber and chopped fresh coriander, then stuffed inside cooked jumbo pasta shells as part of a salad plate. Or, for an appetizer, serve with sturdy crackers or cocktail pumpernickel slices with or without a dollop of crème fraîche or sour cream.

1 cup	white vinegar	250 mL
½ cup	water	125 mL
2 tbsp	granulated sugar	25 mL
1 tbsp	coarse pickling salt	15 mL
½ cup	dry white wine, preferably unoaked Chardonnay	125 mL
1 lb	skinless salmon fillets	500 g
1 tbsp	pickling spices	15 mL
2	shallots, thinly sliced	2

In a small saucepan, combine the vinegar, water, sugar and salt; bring to a boil. Remove from the heat and set aside to cool. Stir in the wine.

Cut the salmon into pieces about 1 × ¾ inch (2.5 × 2 cm). In a glass jar, layer one-third of the salmon pieces, one-third of the spices and one-third of the shallots. Repeat the layers twice more. Pour the vinegar mixture overtop to cover everything. Seal and refrigerate for 3 to 4 days before using.

To serve, remove the salmon pieces and shallots from the liquid, reserving the liquid (keep any unused salmon in the liquid for up to a week longer, refrigerated). *Makes 6 servings as salad and 12 servings as an appetizer on crackers.*

STILTON *and* PECAN SHORTBREAD

This lovely appetizer cookie, a big hit at my last New Year's party, is from *A Holiday Collection* (an ATCO Blue Flame Kitchen Cookbook, 2006). In 1930, the Blue Flame Kitchen service was established in Edmonton, Alberta, to help homemakers get the best results when using the "new cooking fuel," natural gas. Still going strong under the supervision of Barbara Barnes, the Kitchen is one of the last of its kind to be offered by a utility group in Canada. The ATCO Blue Flame Kitchen regularly puts out well-tested and innovative recipe collections to celebrate the food of Alberta and Canada.

1 cup	crumbled Stilton or other blue cheese	250 mL
½ cup	butter, softened	125 mL
¼ tsp	freshly ground pepper	1 mL
1 cup	all-purpose flour	250 mL
½ cup	finely chopped toasted pecans (see TIP on page 212)	125 mL

Using an electric mixer on medium speed, beat the cheese, butter and pepper together until almost blended with some pieces of cheese intact. Stir in the flour just until blended. Stir in the pecans. Shape the dough into 1-inch (2.5 cm) balls and place 2 inches (5 cm) apart on ungreased baking sheets. Using a fork dipped in flour, flatten each ball in a criss-cross pattern. Bake in the centre of a 350°F (180°C) oven until the edges are light golden, 15 to 20 minutes. Remove to racks to cool. Store in an airtight container in the refrigerator for up to 1 week or freeze for up to 1 month. *Makes about 30 cookies.*

SPICY SHRIMP *with* FRESH CORIANDER *and* LIME

I remember my older sister serving shrimp cocktails in special glass dishes, the bottom parts of which held ice to keep the seafood cold. Such sit-down appetizers were popular in the 1960s and 1970s. Perhaps you still have dishes like this at the back of the china cabinet? If so, just for fun, use them here to revive an old favourite with a new take on the shrimp. Otherwise, mound the shrimp on a platter and supply picks for a living room nibble before dinner.

1 lb	large raw shrimp, in their shells	500 g	1	jalapeño pepper, seeded and coarsely chopped	1
½ cup	lightly packed coriander leaves (no stems)	125 mL	1	clove garlic	1
1 tsp	grated lime zest	5 mL	1 tsp	ground cumin	5 mL
⅓ cup	fresh lime juice	75 mL	Pinch	each of salt, chili powder and dried oregano	Pinch
¼ cup	canola oil	50 mL	•	Fresh coriander sprigs	•

Peel and devein the shrimp, leaving the last segment of shell and the tails intact. Put the shrimp in a medium non-metallic bowl; set aside.

In a food processor, combine the coriander, lime zest, ¼ cup (50 mL) of the lime juice, 2 tbsp (25 mL) of the oil, the jalapeño pepper, garlic, cumin, salt, chili powder and oregano; process until finely minced. Pour over the shrimp, tossing to coat evenly. Cover and refrigerate for at least 1 hour or up to 3 hours.

Remove the shrimp from the marinade, shaking off the excess; pat dry. In a large heavy skillet over medium-high heat, heat the remaining 2 tbsp (25 mL) of oil until hot. Add the shrimp in a single layer and cook for 1 minute. Turn the shrimp; cook until firm and pink, about 30 seconds. Mound the shrimp on a serving platter. Sprinkle with the remaining lime juice; toss gently to coat. Serve warm or at room temperature, garnished with coriander sprigs. *Makes about 35 pieces.*

SPICY LAMB TURNOVERS *with* CURRIED YOGURT

Canadians have adopted savoury pies from all over the world: tourtière and quiche from France, shepherd's pie and Cornish pasties from Britain, spanakopita (spinach and cheese pie) from Greece. Here, Middle Eastern flavours enliven tiny turnovers. Cool yogurt sauce is a delicious accompaniment to these hot pastries. For best flavour, use a good-quality curry powder.

1 lb	boneless lamb shoulder	500 g	2 tsp	ground cumin	10 mL
2 tbsp	canola oil	25 mL	¼ tsp	salt	1 mL
2	green onions, chopped	2	Pinch	hot pepper flakes	Pinch
2	cloves garlic, minced	2	2	pkg (14 oz/397 g each)	2
1 tbsp	minced fresh ginger	15 mL		frozen puff pastry, thawed	
2 tbsp	blanched chopped almonds	25 mL	1	egg, beaten	1
¼ cup	fresh lemon juice	50 mL	•	Curried Yogurt (recipe follows)	•

Trim the fat from the lamb; cut into 1-inch (2.5 cm) cubes. In a food processor, process the lamb, 1 cup (250 mL) at a time, until finely ground.

In a skillet, heat the oil over medium heat. Sauté the onions, garlic and ginger until the onion is softened, about 3 minutes.

Add the lamb and almonds. Cook, stirring often and breaking the lamb up with a spoon, until the meat is no longer pink, 5 to 7 minutes. Pour off any fat. Stir in the lemon juice, cumin, salt and hot pepper flakes. Cook for 5 minutes, stirring often. Let cool in the refrigerator.

Working with a quarter of the pastry (half of one package) at a time, roll out each quarter into a 12- × 9-inch (30 × 23 cm) rectangle. Cut each rectangle into 12 even squares. Brush with egg. (Reserve any remaining egg in the refrigerator.) Place a generous 1 tsp (5 mL) of the lamb mixture in the centre of each square, making sure none gets on the edges. (Mounding it into a bit of a ball with your fingers helps.) Fold the pastry over to enclose the filling and form a triangle. Seal the edges by pressing all around with the floured tines of a fork. (The recipe can be prepared ahead to this point and refrigerated, covered, overnight. Or, freeze for up to 2 months sealed in freezer bags. Thaw in the refrigerator before baking.)

When ready to serve, arrange the turnovers on a baking sheet; brush with the reserved egg. Bake in the centre of a 400°F (200°C) oven until golden brown, 15 to 20 minutes. Serve hot with Curried Yogurt. *Makes 48 turnovers.*

GRILLED TOMATO *and* CHEESE QUESADILLAS

There is nothing like the taste of sun-warmed, vine-ripened tomatoes harvested during summer. They are teamed with Canadian Cheddar in this simple, flavourful interpretation of grilled cheese sandwiches.

CURRIED YOGURT

1 cup	plain yogurt	250 mL
3 tbsp	minced fresh coriander	45 mL
2 tsp	curry powder	10 mL
Pinch	salt	Pinch

1 cup	seeded, diced plum tomatoes	250 mL
2 tbsp	chopped fresh coriander or parsley	25 mL
1	jalapeño pepper, minced	1
1 tbsp	minced red or green onion	15 mL
1 tbsp	fresh lime juice	15 mL
•	Salt	•
4	flour tortillas (10-inch/25 cm)	4
1 cup	shredded extra-old Cheddar cheese	250 mL
•	Olive oil	•
•	Sour cream and chopped green onions	•

Line a sieve (preferably plastic or nylon) with cheesecloth; set over a bowl. Spoon the yogurt into the sieve; cover and let drain 1 hour in the refrigerator.

Spoon the yogurt into a serving bowl. Stir in the coriander, curry powder and salt. The sauce can be refrigerated, covered, for up to 1 day. *Makes about 1 cup (250 mL).*

In a bowl, combine the tomatoes, coriander, jalapeño, onion, lime juice and salt to taste. Arrange the tortillas on a work surface and spoon the tomato mixture over half of each tortilla. Sprinkle with the cheese. Fold the other half of the tortilla over the filling and press gently to seal. Brush lightly with oil and place on a greased grill over medium-high heat. Cook for about 4 minutes on each side or until browned and crisp. Cut each into 4 wedges and garnish with sour cream and green onion. *Makes 4 servings, 16 wedges.*

QUICK CHÈVRE *and* ROASTED PEPPER TARTS

Quebec is known for its chèvre. Other provinces, especially British Columbia, have some excellent producers too, and there is now a large Ontario company making good goat cheese. In fact, I even found some of the latter in an upscale food shop in Bermuda this year. These flavourful mouthfuls are a cinch to make and perfect to have on hand in the freezer for drop-in company.

12	slices bread (approx)	12	24	pieces bottled roasted	24
1 tbsp	olive oil (approx)	15 mL		red pepper (about	
4 oz	mild, unripened goat cheese	125 g		½ cup/125 mL)	
			½ tsp	crumbled dried rosemary	2 mL

Remove the crusts from the bread; roll each slice with a rolling pin to flatten it slightly. With a sharp cookie cutter, cut out 24 rounds from the bread slices slightly bigger than the tops of miniature tart cups; press the rounds firmly into the cups. Brush each lightly with some of the oil. Cut the cheese into 24 pieces; place a piece of cheese in each bread-lined tart cup. Top the cheese with a piece of pepper, a pinch of rosemary and a drizzle of oil. If you wish, place the tart pans in freezer bags; seal well. Freeze for up to 1 month.

Bake the fresh or frozen tarts in a 350°F (180°C) oven until the bread is golden brown and the cheese is hot, about 20 minutes. *Makes 24 tarts.*

JERK WINGS

The Caribbean has lured so many winter-weary Canadians to its warm sands for holidays that we've acquired a taste for some of its traditional dishes. "Jerk" is a Caribbean method of cooking where marinated chicken is smoked in a charcoal pit, but your oven will work just fine for this easy version. Serve it with beer as an appetizer, or accompany with rice and coleslaw for a family dinner. If you want to kick up the heat, add a pinch or two of dried hot pepper flakes to the marinade.

3¼ lb	chicken wings, tips removed	1.6 kg
1	onion, chopped	1
2	cloves garlic, chopped	2
1	Scotch bonnet pepper or 2 jalapeño peppers, chopped	1
¼ cup	orange juice	50 mL
2 tbsp	soy sauce	25 mL
2 tbsp	canola oil	25 mL
2 tbsp	white vinegar	25 mL
1½ tsp	ground allspice	7 mL
1½ tsp	dried thyme	7 mL
1½ tsp	salt	7 mL
1½ tsp	granulated sugar	7 mL
1 tsp	black pepper	5 mL
¼ tsp	ground cinnamon	1 mL
¼ tsp	ground nutmeg	1 mL
Dash	Tabasco sauce	Dash

Arrange the wings in a single layer in a shallow glass baking dish. In a food processor or blender, combine the remaining ingredients; process until fairly smooth. Pour the mixture over the wings, turning the wings to coat them well. Cover and refrigerate overnight.

Line a large baking sheet with foil; grease the foil. Arrange the wings on the sheet, reserving any marinade that doesn't cling to the wings. Bake, uncovered, in a 450°F (230°C) oven for 15 minutes. Turn the wings over; spoon the reserved marinade overtop. Bake until the wings are tender and no longer pink inside, another 15 to 20 minutes. *Makes 4 servings.*

CARAMELIZED ONION PIZZA *with* ANCHOVIES *and* BLACK OLIVES

Originating in Provence, where it's called *pissaladière*, this anchovy and onion tart makes a lovely appetizer and celebrates our good Canadian cooking onions that are available in abundance year-round.

2 tbsp	unsalted butter	25 mL
2 tbsp	olive oil	25 mL
3	onions, halved and thinly sliced	3
1½ tsp	dried thyme	7 mL
	Whole Wheat Pizza Dough (see page 46)	
•	Olive oil	•
1	can (1¾ oz/48 g) anchovy fillets	1
20	good-quality pitted black olives (approx)	20

In a large skillet, melt the butter in the oil over low heat. Stir in the onions and 1 tsp (5 mL) of the thyme. Cook, stirring often, until very soft but not browned, to caramelize, about 1 hour. Let cool.

Roll out the dough to a 12- × 10-inch (30 × 25 cm) rectangle. Brush lightly with oil. Arrange the onions on top. Cut the anchovy fillets lengthwise into 2 or 3 strips. Use the strips to make 9 crosses on top of the onions and place the olives attractively around these. Sprinkle with the remaining ½ tsp (2 mL) thyme and bake in a 425°F (220°C) oven until the crust is golden brown, about 25 minutes. Cut into squares to serve. *Makes 6 to 8 appetizer servings or 3 main-course servings.*

TIP: If anchovies are particularly salty, soak them in milk for 20 minutes before using.

ROASTED TOMATO *and* CHEESE TART

Serve this flavourful appetizer cut into squares with a sweet roasted local tomato half in each. Use whatever cheese you have on hand—Fontina, Gruyère, mozzarella, Cheddar, provolone—any good melting cheese.

½	pkg (14 oz/397 g) frozen puff pastry, thawed	½
1½ cups	grated cheese (about 6 oz/175 g)	375 mL
1 tbsp	chopped fresh rosemary (or 1 tsp/5 mL dried)	15 mL
½ tsp	black pepper	2 mL
16	pieces Slow-Roasted Tomatoes (see page 149)	16
1 tbsp	olive oil	15 mL
1	egg, beaten	1
¼ cup	freshly grated Parmesan cheese	50 mL

Roll out the pastry on a lightly floured surface to make an 11- × 11-inch (27.5 cm) square. Place on a baking sheet and fold in ½ inch (1 cm) all around the edge to make a border, pinching the edges together at the corners. Refrigerate for 30 minutes. With a fork, prick the pastry base all over and bake in a 400°F (200°C) oven for 20 minutes. Remove to a rack and let the pastry settle in the middle. If it's too puffy, you may have to gently push it down, but all will be well when you put the other ingredients on top.

Stir together the grated cheese, rosemary and pepper. Spread evenly over the pastry base. Place the tomatoes, cut side up, on top and drizzle all over with oil.

Brush the border with some of the beaten egg. Stir the Parmesan into the remaining egg and sprinkle over the tart; bake until the Parmesan is golden, 10 to 15 minutes. *Makes 4 servings.*

LEMON-PARSLEY HUMMUS

Hummus, in some form, is probably our most popular Middle Eastern treat. Serve this delicious and nutritious dip with pita triangles or raw vegetables; or spread it onto tortillas as a zesty base for a wrap with meat and cheese. Look for tahini in Middle Eastern grocery stores or health food stores.

1	can (19 oz/540 mL) chickpeas, drained and rinsed	1
2 cups	packed fresh parsley leaves	500 mL
2 tsp	grated lemon zest	10 mL
¾ cup	fresh lemon juice	175 mL
⅔ cup	tahini (sesame seed paste)	150 mL
2 tbsp	sesame oil	25 mL
1	clove garlic	1
1 tsp	salt	5 mL
1 tsp	ground cumin	5 mL
¼ tsp	cayenne	1 mL

Place all the ingredients in a food processor and process until smooth. Transfer to a bowl, cover and refrigerate until chilled or for up to 5 days. *Makes 3 cups (750 mL).*

GORGONZOLA FOCACCIA

Despite its name, this flatbread would be delicious made with a Canadian blue cheese like Bleu Ermite from Quebec. With its crisp onion topping and creamy filling, the focaccia makes a great appetizer with drinks or a delicious accompaniment to soup. Use my easy pizza dough recipe or cheat and buy ready-made pizza dough.

½	small red onion, thinly sliced	½		¾ cup	Gorgonzola cheese, at	175 mL
2 tbsp	red wine vinegar	25 mL			room temperature	
1 tbsp	granulated sugar	15 mL			(about 3 oz/75 g)	
•	Whole Wheat Pizza Dough	•		1 tbsp	butter, softened	15 mL
	(see page 46)			1 tsp	crumbled dried sage leaves	5 mL
•	Cornmeal	•		½ tsp	black pepper	2 mL
				2 tbsp	olive oil	25 mL

A range of cheese at the Trout Lake Farmers' Market in Vancouver

In a small bowl, combine the onion, vinegar and sugar; let stand for at least 30 minutes and no longer than 1 hour, stirring occasionally.

Punch down the dough and form it into a ball. Turn out onto a lightly floured surface and roll thinly to form a rectangle about 14 × 10 inches (35 × 25 cm), with the longer side closest to you.

Lightly sprinkle a baking sheet with cornmeal. Mash the cheese with the butter and half the sage. Spread over the right-hand half of the dough, leaving a 1-inch (2.5 cm) border at the edge. Brush the edge lightly with cold water and fold the other half over the filling, pressing the edges together to enclose the cheese mixture. Transfer to the prepared baking sheet. Make indentations all over the top with your fingertips. Drain the onions and scatter them, along with the remaining sage, overtop; sprinkle with pepper and drizzle with oil.

Sprinkle all over with 1 tsp (5 mL) cold water. Bake in the centre of a 425°F (220°C) oven until golden, 20 to 25 minutes. *Makes 4 servings.*

Jerusalem Artichokes

This knobby brown tuber that resembles green ginger root is, oddly enough, neither from Jerusalem nor an artichoke. One of our native vegetables, it was highly prized by the Huron First Nation, who introduced it to French explorers in the 17th century. Samuel de Champlain learned of it from the Algonquins and described it as "roots with the taste of artichokes." It was subsequently cultivated in France, where it was called "Canadian potatoes." A relative of the sunflower (*girasole* is Italian for "sunflower"), it was also called "girasole artichoke," a name that quickly morphed into Jerusalem artichoke after its introduction to England.

In the 19th century, Jerusalem artichokes were a popular garden vegetable, often lining fences at the back of perennial flower gardens. They spread with the abandon of a weed—very ironic in view of their scarcity now. You might find them in farmers' markets or pay a huge amount of money for them in specialty food shops as I have just done. However, I did want to include them here because they were such an important Canadian vegetable at the beginning of our country's settlement, and they are delicious, with a sweet, nutty taste and crisp texture, especially in the Jerusalem Artichoke and Wild Rice Pancakes (see facing page).

If you do find a reasonable source for Jerusalem artichokes, sometimes called sun chokes, or happen to discover these tall plants with small yellow flowers in your own garden, use them as you would potatoes. They are particularly good raw in salads or cooked in a stir-fry.

Like potatoes, artichokes turn dark upon peeling if exposed to air; to keep the flesh white, place in cold water to which you have added a small amount of lemon juice (acidulated water). This is not necessary, however, if you are using them right away.

WILD RICE PANCAKES *with* SOUR CREAM *and* CAVIAR

These quick-to-make, lacy little pancakes are delicious served warm, topped with sour cream and a dollop of luscious caviar, especially whitefish golden from Winnipeg.

1 cup	coarsely shredded peeled raw potato	250 mL
1 cup	cooked wild rice	250 mL
1	egg, beaten	1
1	green onion, thinly sliced	1
2 tbsp	all-purpose flour	25 mL
2 tbsp	canola oil (approx)	25 mL
½ tsp	salt	2 mL
½ tsp	pepper	2 mL
•	Sour cream	•
•	Caviar	•

Squeeze any moisture from the potato and combine the potato with the rice, egg, green onion, flour, half the oil, and the salt and pepper. Heat the remaining oil in a large skillet over medium heat. Cooking a few at a time, and using about 1 tbsp (15 mL) of the mixture for each pancake, place round mounds in the skillet and press to flatten. Cook until golden, about 2 minutes per side, adding a bit more oil if necessary. Serve with sour cream and caviar. *Makes about 16 pancakes.*

TIP: A scant ½ cup (125 mL) of raw rice will yield slightly less than 1½ cups (375 mL) of cooked rice. See page 171 for cooking instructions.

VARIATION:

JERUSALEM ARTICHOKE AND WILD RICE PANCAKES
Substitute 1 cup (250 mL) coarsely shredded peeled raw Jerusalem artichokes for the potato and proceed as for Wild Rice Pancakes. (About 6 ounces/175 g artichokes will yield around 1 cup/250 mL grated.)

QUICK BRANDIED CHICKEN LIVER PÂTÉ

Early settlers from the northwest of France brought their Old World dishes like pâtés to Quebec. They are now such countrywide favourites that supermarkets abound with inexpensive versions, but homemade pâté is still cheaper, more flavourful and takes only minutes to make.

¼ cup	butter	50 mL
1 lb	chicken livers, trimmed	500 g
1	clove garlic, crushed	1
1 tsp	crumbled dried sage	5 mL
½ tsp	dried thyme	2 mL
¼ cup	brandy	50 mL
½	pkg (8 oz/250 g) light cream cheese (½ cup/125 mL)	½
•	Salt and pepper	•
•	Sage leaves	•

In a large skillet, melt the butter over medium heat and reserve 2 tbsp (25 mL) in a small bowl. In the remainder, cook the livers, garlic, sage and thyme until the livers are browned but still slightly pink inside, about 5 minutes. Stir in the brandy; cook until almost evaporated, about 1 minute. Let cool.

Transfer to a food processor. Add the cheese and salt and pepper to taste. Purée until smooth. Spoon into a 2-cup (500 mL) serving dish or two 1-cup (250 mL) dishes. Place 1 or 2 sage leaves on top and pour the reserved butter over the top of the leaves and pâté. Refrigerate until firm, about 2 hours, and for up to 2 days. (Pâté also freezes well for up to 2 weeks if wrapped well in foil.) *Makes about 2 cups (500 mL).*

TOURTIÈRE TURNOVERS

The French-Canadian meat pie, traditionally served with the main course, has the new role here of a festive appetizer or cocktail bite. Serve the turnovers hot with the usual green tomato relish or fruity chili sauce to temper the richness of the pastry.

1	potato, peeled and quartered	1	¼ tsp	ground cinnamon	1 mL
1 lb	lean ground pork	500 g	¼ tsp	ground cloves	1 mL
1	onion, finely chopped	1	¼ cup	chopped fresh parsley	50 mL
1	stalk celery, with leaves, cut in 3	1	•	Salt and pepper	•
1	clove garlic, minced	1	2	pkg (14 oz/397 g each)	2
1 tsp	dried savory	5 mL		frozen puff pastry, thawed	
½ tsp	dried thyme	2 mL	1	egg, beaten	1

In a medium saucepan, cook the potato in boiling salted water until tender, 15 to 20 minutes. Remove with a slotted spoon, mash and set aside.

Bring ½ cup (125 mL) of the potato water to a boil. Add the pork, onion, celery, garlic, savory, thyme, cinnamon and cloves, breaking the pork up with a spoon. Bring to a simmer and cook uncovered, stirring occasionally, until the pork is no longer pink and the liquid has reduced by half, about 45 minutes.

Remove and discard the celery pieces. Stir in the potato, parsley, salt and pepper to taste and more of the other seasoning if desired. Let cool in the refrigerator.

Working with a quarter of the pastry (half of one package) at a time, roll out each quarter into a 12- × 9-inch (30 × 23 cm) rectangle. Cut each rectangle into 12 even squares. Brush each with egg. (Reserve any remaining egg in the refrigerator.) Place a heaping teaspoon (5 mL) of the pork mixture in the centre of each square, making sure none gets on the edges. (Mounding it into a bit of a ball with your fingers helps.) Fold the pastry over to enclose the filling and form a triangle. Seal the edges by pressing all around with the floured tines of a fork. (Turnovers can be prepared ahead to this point and refrigerated, covered, overnight. Or, freeze for up to 2 months sealed in freezer bags. Thaw in the refrigerator before baking.)

When ready to serve, arrange the turnovers on a baking sheet; brush with the reserved egg. Bake in the centre of a 400°F (200°C) oven until golden brown, about 20 minutes. Serve hot. *Makes 48 turnovers.*

Tourtière

Tourtière, a Quebec meat pie, dates back to that province's first settlers, who probably made it with wild game in the 1600s. Centuries of adaptation have resulted in almost as many recipes as cooks, but it is still traditionally served on Christmas Eve, not only in Quebec, but also in many other parts of the country, and it remains a quintessential Canadian dish.

There are a couple of theories about the pie's name. Many believe it comes from the "tourte" or passenger pigeon that was plentiful until the 20th century, when its extinction forced cooks to substitute pork or beef for the birds. Others trace its name to the French cooking utensil in which the pie was baked and suggest the early versions were made with game such as rabbit, venison, partridge or pheasants, depending on what the hunter could find.

WILD MUSHROOM *and* BACK BACON RISOTTO

Creamy risotto can serve as an appetizer, side dish or main course. Because it has Italian roots, prosciutto is often added at the end, but lean Canadian back bacon gives it a local twist. A large variety of dried wild mushrooms are usually available in the supermarket. Morels are particularly flavourful.

^ *Fresh morels*

4 cups	chicken stock	1 L	¼ tsp	black pepper	1 mL
1 oz	dried wild mushrooms	25 g	1 cup	arborio rice	250 mL
4 oz	back bacon	125 g	½ cup	dry white wine	125 mL
1 tbsp	butter	15 mL	1 cup	peas, fresh or frozen,	250 mL
1 tbsp	olive oil	15 mL		thawed	
1	onion, chopped	1	½ cup	freshly grated Asiago	125 mL
2	cloves garlic, minced	2		or Parmesan cheese	
1 tbsp	finely chopped fresh sage	15 mL			
	(or 1 tsp/5 mL dried, crumbled)				

In a medium saucepan, bring the stock to a boil. Add the dried mushrooms, remove from the heat, cover and let stand for 20 minutes.

Meanwhile, slice the bacon into thin julienne strips (¹/₈ inch/3 mm); set aside. (You should have about ²/₃ cup/150 mL.)

Remove the soaked mushrooms with a slotted spoon and set aside. Place the stock in the saucepan over low heat and bring to a simmer; keep warm.

In a large saucepan or deep skillet over medium heat, melt the butter in the oil. Add the onion, half the garlic, the sage and pepper; cook 3 minutes, stirring. Add the bacon and cook for 3 minutes, stirring. Add the reconstituted mushrooms; cook for 2 minutes. Add the rice and stir to coat it well; cook 1 minute.

Pour in ½ cup (125 mL) of the warm stock; cook, stirring constantly, until all the liquid is absorbed. Stir in the wine; cook, stirring constantly, until all the wine is absorbed. Continue to add the warm stock, ½ cup (125 mL) at a time, stirring constantly and waiting until the stock is absorbed before adding more, until the rice is creamy and just tender, about 20 minutes.

Stir in the peas, remaining garlic and cheese. Serve immediately. *Makes 3 servings as a main course and 6 to 8 servings as a starter.*

< *A clutch of partridges in Saskatchewan*

^ *The Naramata Bench wine region, with Penticton in the distance*

BRITISH COLUMBIA

WHEN SPANISH AND BRITISH EXPLORERS first appeared on the West Coast in the 1700s, they found well-established Native communities thriving on abundant seafood in a gentle climate. Food gathering and preparation traditions included fish traps, bentwood boxes for cooking and storage, drying techniques, harvesting of wild plants and plank cookery.

Since then, the cuisine of British Columbia has seen many different influences. Vancouver Island became a crown colony in 1849, and by the 1860s a genteel English outpost thrived on Vancouver Island. Today, Victoria holds fast to its British roots with traditional afternoon tea and pubs serving British ales.

The mainland became the colony of British Columbia in 1858 (both colonies joined Canada as a province in 1871) when the discovery of gold in the Cariboo brought thousands of fortune-seekers to the interior. As the gold rush slowed down, big ranches were established in the Cariboo and communities grew up along the Fraser and Thompson rivers, supplying produce for the growing coastal cities and Asian vegetables for the thousands of Chinese immigrants who laboured on the transcontinental railway in the last half of the 19th century.

Further inland, microclimates allowed the agricultural areas of the Okanagan and Similkameen valleys to flourish as fruit-growing regions, particularly ideal for tree fruits. Vineyards here now produce some of the best wine in the country, and the area is also known for its wealth of wild berries and mushrooms.

Along the coast, the Pacific gives forth its harvest: salmon (coho, chinook, pink, chum and sockeye), halibut, black cod, lingcod, tuna, rockfish, eulachon (long prized by First Nations for its oil), crab, oysters, scallops, shrimp and clams.

Vancouver Island and the Gulf Islands are steadily seeing an increase in farmers, growers, chefs and food activists who are working hard to establish the value of producing, preparing and consuming fresh local food. Today the cuisine of British Columbia blends this trend with food fashions from California and strong English, Chinese, First Nations, Japanese, Greek, Southeast Asian and Italian influences, all modified to suit the province's abundant fresh ingredients.

A PICNIC IN STANLEY PARK

Wine-Pickled Salmon
(page 5)
with Pumpernickel and Crème Fraîche

Caramelized Onion and Prosciutto Tart
(page 47)
Or
Summer Tossed Sushi Salad
(page 181)

Raspberry Nanaimo Bars
(page 236)
and Fresh Fruit

LEFT TO RIGHT: *Raspberry* >
Nanaimo Bars (page 236) and
Summer Tossed Sushi Salad (page 181)

SOUPS

HINT OF SPRING SOUP WITH CUMIN
CROUTONS ~ 25

ITALIAN ESCAROLE SOUP ~ 26

MONTEBELLO CURRIED BEET SOUP ~ 26

ROASTED ASPARAGUS SOUP ~ 27

HOMEMADE TOMATO SOUP WITH
BLUE CHEESE GARNISH ~ 28

SPLIT PEA SOUP WITH SMOKED
TURKEY AND SPINACH ~ 29

CHEDDAR APPLE SOUP ~ 31

ROASTED SWEET POTATO SOUP
WITH CARDAMOM CREAM ~ 31

PARSNIP AND PEAR SOUP WITH
FIVE-SPICE POWDER ~ 32

TOASTED GARLIC SOUP ~ 33

PUMPKIN BISQUE WITH CRANBERRY
OIL SWIRL ~ 33

BEAN SOUP WITH PARSLEY
AND BACON GARNISH ~ 34

CREAM OF WILD RICE AND
MUSHROOM SOUP ~ 35

HARVEST CORN CHOWDER ~ 36

HOT AND SOUR SOUP ~ 38

THAI TOM YUM SHRIMP SOUP ~ 39

FENNEL-ROASTED SEAFOOD CHOWDER ~ 41

HINT *of* SPRING SOUP *with* CUMIN CROUTONS

Gather together those wonderful greens of spring and early summer—asparagus, peas, green onions, lettuce and herbs—for a fresh-tasting soup. For best flavour, prepare it a day ahead and refrigerate in a tightly covered container.

¼ cup	butter	50 mL	3 cups	peas, fresh or frozen, thawed	750 mL
2	potatoes, peeled and diced	2	2 tbsp	chopped fresh parsley	25 mL
6	green onions, chopped	6	2 tbsp	chopped fresh chervil	25 mL
3 cups	shredded leaf or iceberg lettuce	750 mL	2 tbsp	chopped fresh basil	25 mL
			2 tbsp	chopped fresh mint	25 mL
6 cups	chicken broth	1.5 L	2 cups	light cream	500 mL
1 lb	asparagus, trimmed and chopped	500 g	Pinch	cayenne	Pinch
			•	Salt and pepper	•

CUMIN CROUTONS

2 tbsp	butter	25 mL	2 cups	diced French or Italian bread with crusts removed	500 mL
2 tsp	ground cumin	10 mL			

^ *Mint growing in the garden*

In a large saucepan, melt the butter over medium heat. Add the potatoes and green onions; cook and stir for 2 minutes. Add the lettuce; cook until wilted, about 2 minutes. Add the broth, asparagus and peas; bring to a boil over high heat. Reduce the heat to medium-low, cover and simmer until the potatoes and asparagus are tender, 5 to 10 minutes. Stir in the parsley, chervil, basil and mint.

In a blender purée the soup in batches until smooth. Return the soup to a clean saucepan. Stir in the cream and cayenne; season with salt and pepper to taste. (The soup can be prepared ahead to this point, covered and refrigerated for up to 1 day.)

To serve, reheat until piping hot but do not boil. Taste and adjust the seasoning. Ladle into heated bowls and sprinkle each with some Cumin Croutons.

CUMIN CROUTONS: In a large skillet, melt the butter with the cumin over medium heat. Add the bread; cook, stirring, until the croutons are golden brown and crisp, about 5 minutes. Remove to a plate lined with paper towel; let cool completely. (The croutons can be prepared ahead, cooled and stored in a tightly closed container in a cool, dry place for up to 1 day.) *Makes 10 servings.*

ITALIAN ESCAROLE SOUP

Every year, we grow a greater variety of greens in Canada, both sturdy cooking greens and lettuces. Escarole is lettuce with colour and body. It is often added just at the last minute to brothy summer soups to brighten the bowl. If its frilly green leaves are unavailable, you could substitute curly endive, which has finer and narrower leaves with a slightly more bitter flavour. This would make a perfect summer lunch with Gorgonzola Focaccia (see page 13).

8 cups	lightly packed coarsely chopped escarole	2 L
4 oz	prosciutto, in one piece	125 g
2 tbsp	olive oil	25 mL
2	onions, chopped	2
4	cloves garlic, minced	4
5 cups	chicken broth	1.25 L
½ tsp	pepper	2 mL
½ cup	stellini (star pasta) or other small soup noodles	125 mL
1 cup	fresh or frozen peas	250 mL
•	Freshly grated Parmesan cheese (optional)	•

Wash the escarole; drain. Place in a large heavy saucepan with just the water clinging to the leaves; cover and cook, stirring once, until wilted, 5 to 8 minutes. Drain; squeeze out the excess liquid. Chop finely and set aside.

Trim any fat from the prosciutto; chop finely. In the same saucepan, heat the oil over medium heat; cook the onions, garlic and prosciutto, stirring often, until the onions are softened, 5 to 10 minutes.

Stir in the broth, 1 cup (250 mL) of water and the pepper; bring to a boil. Add the pasta and escarole; reduce the heat to medium-low and simmer for 3 minutes.

Add the peas; cook until the peas and pasta are tender, 1 to 2 minutes. Ladle into warmed bowls and sprinkle with Parmesan (if using). *Makes 4 servings.*

MONTEBELLO CURRIED BEET SOUP

We all loved this pretty, but simple, soup that was part of a special dinner for food writers at Le Château Montebello overlooking the Ottawa River in Quebec. Curry powders differ, but try for just a hint of curry so it won't mask the wonderful flavour of the beets.

It is delicious hot or cold.

8	medium beets (1½ lb/750 g)	8
2	potatoes	2
2 tbsp	olive oil	25 mL
1	onion, chopped	1
2 tsp	curry powder or paste (approx)	10 mL
6 cups	chicken or vegetable broth	1.5 L
1 tbsp	liquid honey	15 mL
¼ tsp	salt	1 mL
¼ tsp	pepper	1 mL
•	Sour cream	•
•	Snipped fresh chives	•

Peel the beets and potatoes and cut into 1-inch (2.5 cm) cubes.

In a large saucepan, heat the oil over medium heat; cook the beets, potatoes, onion and curry powder, stirring often, until the onion is softened, about 10 minutes. Stir in the broth, honey, salt and pepper. Bring to a boil, reduce the heat to medium-low, cover and simmer until the vegetables are tender, about 25 minutes. Working in batches, transfer to a blender and purée until smooth. (The soup can be cooled, covered and refrigerated for up to 1 day.)

To serve, taste and adjust the seasoning if necessary. If serving it cold, ladle into chilled soup bowls, spoon a dollop of sour cream on top of each serving and sprinkle with chives. If serving it hot, return the soup to a clean saucepan, heat through until simmering and ladle into warmed bowls. Garnish with sour cream and chives. *Makes about 6 servings.*

ROASTED ASPARAGUS SOUP

Roasting lifts asparagus to a whole new flavour dimension in this delicate soup that is delicious hot or cold. A tiny bit of cream lends it richness, and if you wish to use the remainder of the container, it makes an interesting garnish. If not, snipped chives do the trick.

2 lb	asparagus	1 kg	1 cup	chopped parsnips	250 mL
2 tbsp	olive oil	25 mL	1 cup	chopped celery with leaves	250 mL
•	Salt and pepper	•	1/3 cup	whipping cream	75 mL
1/4 cup	butter	50 mL	1/4 tsp	grated nutmeg	1 mL
2 cups	chopped leeks (about 2, white and light green parts only)	500 mL	1/2 cup	whipping cream, lightly whipped and salted	125 mL
1/4 cup	all-purpose flour	50 mL	•	Thin slices of lemon and/or blanched asparagus tips	•
6 cups	chicken broth	1.5 L			

Trim the asparagus by breaking off any tough ends and wash well. Toss with the oil and spread in a single layer on a baking sheet or sheets; sprinkle with salt and pepper. Roast in a 500°F (260°C) oven until just tender but not browned (8 to 10 minutes). Set aside.

In a large saucepan, melt the butter; add the leeks and cook over low heat until softened, but not browned, about 5 minutes. Stir in the flour and cook for 2 minutes. Remove from the heat and gradually stir in the broth. Cook, stirring, over medium heat until slightly thickened, 2 to 3 minutes.

Add the parsnips and celery. Bring to a boil, stirring, over medium heat. Reduce the heat, cover and simmer for 20 minutes. Chop the roasted asparagus. Add to the saucepan and bring to a simmer; cook, uncovered, for 5 minutes.

Let cool slightly, then purée in a blender or food processor. (A blender results in a smoother soup. The soup may be prepared ahead to this point, covered and refrigerated for up to 1 day.)

If serving it hot, return the soup to a clean saucepan. Stir in the 1/3 cup (75 mL) cream and heat almost to a boil. Taste for seasoning and stir in salt, pepper and nutmeg. Serve in heated bowls, garnishing each with a spoonful of whipped cream and lemon slices and/or asparagus tips. (To blanch asparagus tips, add them to boiling water and cook, uncovered, until bright green, 3 to 5 minutes.) If serving it cold, refrigerate the purée until very cold. Stir in the cream and season just before ladling it into chilled bowls and garnishing as above. *Makes 6 to 8 servings.*

VARIATION:

CREAM OF FIDDLEHEAD SOUP

Substitute 1 lb (500 g) fresh fiddleheads or 2 packages (each 10 oz/300 g) frozen fiddleheads for the asparagus; cook them (see page 147) and add them to the soup instead of the roasted asparagus; proceed as above. Omit the olive oil.

HOMEMADE TOMATO SOUP *with* BLUE CHEESE GARNISH

Who doesn't love the comfort of a bowl of tomato soup and a grilled cheese sandwich? Here, I've added cheese to the soup itself for everyone to swirl in for an intriguing flavour. Use whatever blue cheese you happen to have on hand; Stilton, Gorgonzola or Canadian Bleu Ermite are all good choices. My mother made homemade tomato soup often with tomatoes from our garden, but it's even faster when you open a good-quality can of tomatoes.

2 tbsp	butter	25 mL	Pinch	cayenne		Pinch
1	onion, chopped	1	1	can (28 oz/796 mL) diced		1
1	stalk celery, chopped	1		tomatoes (undrained)		
2	cloves garlic, chopped	2	4 cups	chicken broth, preferably		1 L
1 tsp	smoked Spanish paprika*	5 mL		low-sodium		
½ tsp	dried oregano	2 mL	½ cup	crumbled blue cheese		125 mL
½ tsp	salt	2 mL	2 tbsp	cream cheese, softened		25 mL
½ tsp	pepper	2 mL				

In a large saucepan, melt the butter over medium heat; cook the onion and celery until softened, about 8 minutes, stirring often. Add the garlic and cook 1 minute. Remove the pan from the heat; stir in the paprika, oregano, salt, pepper and cayenne. Add the tomatoes and broth. Return to the heat and bring to a boil; reduce the heat, cover and simmer for 15 minutes. Cool slightly, then purée with an immersion blender or in batches in a regular blender. (The soup can be prepared to this point, cooled, covered and refrigerated.) Return to the saucepan and heat gently to serve. In a small bowl, stir together the blue cheese and cream cheese. Top each serving with a dollop of the mixture. *Makes 4 to 6 servings.*

* Available in specialty food shops.

TIP: If you have only whole canned tomatoes in the house, chop them with scissors right in the can or pan.

SPLIT PEA SOUP *with* SMOKED TURKEY *and* SPINACH

Since dried peas were easy to carry, they played an important part in the diet of voyageurs, who combined them with salt pork and water to make a hearty soup. These three ingredients alone would make a decent soup, but I have tarted things up with some bold flavours, lots of vegetables and lighter smoked turkey instead of pork.

2 cups	green split peas	500 mL	1 tsp	grated lemon zest	5 mL
2 tbsp	olive oil	25 mL	1 tsp	smoked paprika	5 mL
2	stalks celery, sliced	2	1	smoked turkey thigh or	1
2	jalapeño peppers,	2		drumstick	
	seeded and diced		5 cups	water	1.25 L
1	onion, chopped	1	4 cups	chicken broth	1 L
1	large potato, peeled and diced	1	¼ cup	fresh lemon juice	50 mL
1	carrot, diced	1	•	Salt and pepper	•
1	clove garlic, minced	1	2 cups	slivered fresh spinach	500 mL
2 tsp	ground cumin	10 mL			

Sort and rinse the peas; set aside. In a large saucepan over medium heat, heat the oil and cook the celery, jalapeños, onion, potato, carrot, garlic, half the cumin, lemon zest and paprika until the onion is softened, about 5 minutes. Add the turkey and peas. Stir in the water and broth, bring to a boil, reduce the heat, cover and simmer until the peas are tender, about 1½ hours.

Remove the turkey and cut any meat from the bone. Discard the bone and dice the meat. Return the meat to the soup with the lemon juice, remaining cumin, and salt and pepper to taste. (The soup can be made ahead, cooled, covered and refrigerated for 1 day or frozen for longer storage. Bring to a simmer and add additional broth or water if it's too thick.) Serve in warmed bowls, sprinkling each serving with lots of slivered spinach. *Makes 8 to 10 servings.*

∧   *Young pea plant (pea shoot) (top)*

Cheddar Apple Soup (facing page)

CHEDDAR APPLE SOUP

The contrast of sharp cheese and sweet apple is as delightful as the colour of this smooth, light soup—perfect for a fall starter.

¼ cup	unsalted butter	50 mL
2	small apples, peeled, cored and chopped	2
1	large leek, white and light green parts only, sliced	1
1	carrot, chopped	1
1	stalk celery, chopped	1
¼ cup	all-purpose flour	50 mL
2½ cups	chicken broth	625 mL
1½ cups	apple cider or juice	375 mL
1 tsp	curry powder	5 mL
1 tsp	ground cumin	5 mL
Pinch	hot pepper flakes	Pinch
8 oz	aged orange Cheddar, grated (about 2 cups/500 mL packed)	250 g
1 cup	freshly grated Parmesan cheese	250 mL
•	White pepper	•
•	Chopped fresh parsley or chives	•
•	Sour cream (optional)	•

In a large saucepan over medium heat, melt the butter. Add the apples, leek, carrot and celery; cook, stirring often, until softened, about 7 minutes. Add the flour and cook, stirring, for 2 to 3 minutes. Gradually stir in the broth, cider, curry powder, cumin and hot pepper flakes. Bring to a boil; reduce the heat to medium-low and simmer until the apples and vegetables are tender, 15 to 20 minutes. Cool slightly, then purée in batches in a blender, returning the purée to a clean pot. (The soup can be prepared to this point, cooled, covered and refrigerated for up to 1 day.) Return to a low simmer and gradually whisk in the cheeses. Simmer over low heat until the cheese has melted. (Do not boil.) Season with white pepper to taste. Serve in heated bowls, sprinkling each serving with parsley or chives and adding a dollop of sour cream (if using). *Makes 6 servings as a starter.*

ROASTED SWEET POTATO SOUP *with* CARDAMOM CREAM

Roasted sweet potatoes and slow-simmered leeks and carrot produce the rich, mellow flavour of this special soup.

4	sweet potatoes (about 3 lb/1.5 kg)	4
2 tbsp	butter	25 mL
2	leeks, white and light green parts only, thinly sliced	2
1	carrot, thinly sliced	1
5 cups	chicken broth	1.25 L
2 tsp	ground ginger	10 mL
½ tsp	salt	2 mL
¼ tsp	black pepper	1 mL
1 cup	light cream or milk (approx)	250 mL
1 cup	crème fraîche or sour cream	250 mL
½ tsp	ground cardamom	2 mL
•	Snipped chives or green onions	•

Pierce the potatoes in several spots, place on a baking sheet and roast in a 400°F (200°C) oven for about 50 minutes or until soft. Peel and cut into large chunks.

Meanwhile, in a large saucepan over low heat, melt the butter. Add the leeks and carrot; cook, stirring occasionally, for about 40 minutes or until softened and lightly browned. Stir in the broth, sweet potatoes, ginger, salt and pepper. Cover and simmer over medium heat for 20 minutes.

Transfer to a blender and purée until smooth. (The soup can be prepared to this point, cooled, covered and refrigerated up to 1 day or frozen for up to 2 months; thaw in the refrigerator overnight.)

Return the mixture to a clean saucepan. Stir in the cream, adding more if the soup is too thick; gently heat through but do not boil. Taste and adjust the seasoning if necessary.

Stir together the crème fraîche and cardamom; garnish each serving with a swirl of cardamom cream and a sprinkling of chives. *Makes 8 servings.*

PARSNIP *and* PEAR SOUP
with FIVE-SPICE POWDER

The sweetness of both parsnips and pears creates a pleasant surprise in this elegant soup that is just right to start a dinner party. A garnish of blue cheese marries well with the pears.

2 tbsp	unsalted butter	25 mL		5 cups	chicken broth	1.25 L
2	leeks, white and light green parts only, thinly sliced	2		1½ tsp	five-spice powder*	7 mL
				½ cup	whipping cream	125 mL
1 tsp	salt, preferably kosher	5 mL		•	Pepper	•
4	large parsnips, peeled and coarsely chopped (about 3 cups/750 mL)	4		½ cup	crumbled blue cheese	125 mL
				2 tbsp	snipped fresh chives or green onion tops	25 mL
2	large pears, peeled, cored and diced (about 2 cups/500 mL)	2				

^ *Chive flowers, which can be used as a garnish or in salads*

In a large saucepan over medium heat, melt the butter and cook the leeks until very soft, about 5 minutes. Add the salt and cook for 1 minute. Stir in the parsnips and pears; cook, stirring, for 3 minutes. Stir in the broth, bring to a simmer, cover and reduce the heat to low. Cook for 20 minutes. Stir in 1 tsp (5 mL) of the five-spice powder and simmer until the parsnips are very tender, about 5 more minutes. Cool slightly, then purée in a blender in batches and return to a clean saucepan. (The soup can be cooled, covered and refrigerated for up to 2 days.)

Return the soup to a simmer and stir in the cream. Season to taste with more salt, some pepper and the remaining ½ tsp (2 mL) five-spice powder.

In a small bowl, stir together the blue cheese and chives; garnish each serving with some of this mixture. *Makes 8 servings.*

* Five-spice powder, usually comprised of equal amounts of ground Szechwan peppercorns, cloves, cinnamon, fennel seeds and star anise, is now available in most supermarkets.

TOASTED GARLIC SOUP

In Canada, a combination of post-war Asian and Mediterranean immigration and jet travel brought garlic to our tables. Then, in the 1950s, the pungent pleasure of garlic bread and Caesar salad made it more mainstream. This simple adaptation of French onion soup celebrates the country's current love of the zesty little bulb.

2 tbsp	butter	25 mL
10	cloves garlic, minced	10
1 tbsp	all-purpose flour	15 mL
6 cups	beef broth	1.5 L
2 tbsp	chopped fresh parsley	25 mL
¼ tsp	pepper	1 mL
•	Salt to taste	•
4	eggs, beaten	4
6	slices baguette, toasted	6
1¼ cups	shredded Swiss cheese	300 mL
1¼ cups	shredded mozzarella cheese	300 mL

In a large saucepan, melt the butter over low heat. Add the garlic and flour; cook, stirring often, until lightly browned, 3 to 5 minutes. Stir in the broth, parsley and pepper. Bring to a boil over high heat, stirring constantly. Reduce the heat to low; simmer, covered, 20 minutes. Taste and add salt if necessary. (The soup can be prepared ahead to this point, cooled, covered and refrigerated for up to 1 day. Bring to a simmer before proceeding with the recipe.)

Slowly whisk the eggs into the soup. Heat gently, but do not boil or let the soup get too hot or the eggs will curdle. Place 6 warmed ovenproof soup bowls on a baking sheet. Ladle the soup into the bowls and place a slice of toast on each. Sprinkle the cheese evenly over the toast. Place under a hot broiler element and broil until the cheese melts, 1 to 2 minutes. Serve at once. *Makes 6 servings.*

PUMPKIN BISQUE *with* CRANBERRY OIL SWIRL

This smooth, full-flavoured soup is a perfect make-ahead first course for an autumn dinner party.

2 tbsp	butter	25 mL
2	leeks, white and light green parts only, thinly sliced	2
½ cup	diced carrot	125 mL
½ cup	diced parsnip	125 mL
5 cups	chicken broth	1.25 L
2½ cups	pumpkin purée (see page 206)	625 mL
1 tsp	dried thyme	5 mL
•	Salt and pepper	•
Pinch	hot pepper flakes	Pinch
½ cup	milk	125 mL
½ cup	cranberries, fresh or frozen, thawed	125 mL
¼ cup	olive oil	50 mL

In a large saucepan, melt the butter over low heat. Add the leeks, carrot and parsnip; cook until softened, about 10 minutes. Stir in the broth, pumpkin purée, thyme, ½ tsp (2 mL) salt, ¼ tsp (1 mL) pepper and hot pepper flakes. Bring to a boil, reduce the heat, cover and simmer until the vegetables are very soft, about 10 minutes.

Cool slightly, then purée in batches in a blender until smooth. (The soup can be cooled, covered and refrigerated for up to 1 day.) Return to a clean saucepan and stir in the milk; heat gently until hot but do not boil. Taste and adjust the seasoning.

Process the cranberries in a food processor or blender until very fine. Transfer to a bowl and stir in the oil to combine well. Cover and refrigerate overnight.

Press the cranberry mixture through a fine sieve set over a small bowl to extract the cranberry oil. Season with salt and pepper. (The cranberry oil can be made several days ahead, covered and refrigerated.) Whisk to combine well. Drizzle some cranberry oil over each bowl of soup to serve. *Makes about 8 servings.*

BEAN SOUP *with* PARSLEY *and* BACON GARNISH

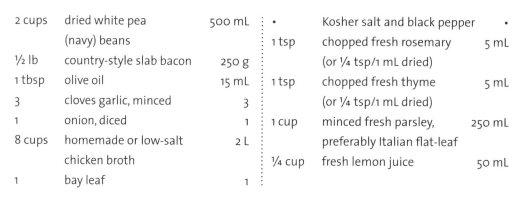

I remember the taste of dried bean soup from my childhood, and this version reproduces that flavour for me, with the fresh addition of lemon juice and parsley. However, if you want to skip the parsley mixture, stir the bacon into the soup to serve—still delicious.

^ *Oyama Sausage Co. at Granville Island Market, Vancouver, sells more than ten kinds of bacon*

2 cups	dried white pea (navy) beans	500 mL	•	Kosher salt and black pepper	•
½ lb	country-style slab bacon	250 g	1 tsp	chopped fresh rosemary (or ¼ tsp/1 mL dried)	5 mL
1 tbsp	olive oil	15 mL	1 tsp	chopped fresh thyme (or ¼ tsp/1 mL dried)	5 mL
3	cloves garlic, minced	3			
1	onion, diced	1	1 cup	minced fresh parsley, preferably Italian flat-leaf	250 mL
8 cups	homemade or low-salt chicken broth	2 L	¼ cup	fresh lemon juice	50 mL
1	bay leaf	1			

Sort the beans and rinse them. Place the beans in a large saucepan and add enough cold water to cover them by 4 inches (10 cm). Let soak overnight in the refrigerator.

Cut the bacon into ¾-inch (2 cm) slices, then into ¼-inch-wide (5 mm) strips. Drain the beans in a colander. In the same pan, cook the bacon over medium heat until well browned, about 12 minutes, stirring often. Drain on paper towels and set aside in the refrigerator if making the soup ahead. Discard the pan drippings.

Add the oil to the pan. Cook the garlic and onion until softened, about 5 minutes. Stir in the drained beans, broth and bay leaf. Bring to a boil, reduce the heat, partially cover and simmer until the beans are soft, 1 to 1½ hours. Discard the bay leaf. Using a slotted spoon, remove about 1 cup (250 mL) of the beans and place in a food processor with 1½ cups (375 mL) of the liquid. Purée until smooth and stir back into the soup. Stir in 1 tsp (5 mL) salt and ½ tsp (2 mL) pepper, the rosemary and thyme. Simmer for 5 minutes. Taste and add more salt if necessary. (The soup can be prepared to this point, cooled, covered and refrigerated for up to 1 day. Reheat gently to serve.)

In a bowl, toss together the parsley, lemon juice, ½ tsp (2 mL) salt and ¼ tsp (1 mL) pepper.

To serve, ladle the soup into warmed bowls and top each serving with a generous amount of the parsley mixture and some bacon strips. *Makes 6 servings.*

CREAM *of* WILD RICE *and* MUSHROOM SOUP

Many years ago, I had the pleasure of staying at elegant Minaki Lodge, which was nestled in the wilderness of northwestern Ontario. Unfortunately, the lodge has been destroyed by fire, but I still have the memory of a wonderful soup served there. It featured locally harvested wild rice, and I've added some wild mushrooms to the mix.

¼ cup	wild rice	50 mL		2 tbsp	all-purpose flour	25 mL
¾ cup	water	175 mL		2½ cups	chicken broth	625 mL
2 tbsp	butter	25 mL		1	bay leaf	1
4	slices lean side bacon, diced	4		1 cup	whipping cream	250 mL
1	small onion, chopped	1		•	Salt and white pepper	•
8 oz	wild mushrooms (cremini, shiitake, portobello or a mix), sliced	250 g				

Place the rice in a fine sieve and rinse well under cold running water. Bring the water to a boil in a small saucepan. Add the rice and return to a boil; cover, reduce the heat and simmer until the rice is just tender, 30 to 50 minutes.

Meanwhile, in a medium saucepan, melt the butter and add the bacon. Cook over medium heat, stirring often, until the bacon is almost crisp. Stir in the onion and cook over low heat, stirring often, until softened, about 5 minutes. Add the mushrooms and cook over medium heat until the liquid has evaporated, about 8 minutes. Stir in the flour and cook over low heat, stirring, for 2 minutes. Gradually stir in the broth and bring to a boil, stirring constantly. Add the bay leaf, reduce the heat, cover and cook for 10 minutes.

Remove the bay leaf and stir in the cooked rice with any moisture that might remain in the rice pan. Bring back to a boil.

Stir in the cream and season to taste with salt and white pepper. Bring just to the boil and serve immediately in heated soup bowls. *Makes 4 to 6 servings.*

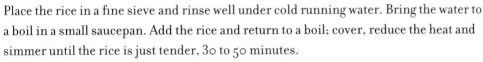

HARVEST CORN CHOWDER

The first recipe I ever had published in a cookbook was Corn Chowder. I was a teenager, and the recipe was included in one of the many community cookbooks of the fifties produced to aid schools, churches, hospitals and the like. This wee book was entitled *Duntroon and Glen Huron, Ont. Personal Recipes by Women's Auxiliary of Church of the Redeemer*, the little Anglican church for which my father acted as warden for many years and for whose women's auxiliary my mother was president at the time the cookbook was put together. My recipe developing skills have been honed since then, but the following corn chowder does bring back memories of that original recipe.

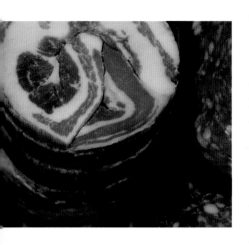

∧ *Pancetta*

4	slices pancetta* or side bacon, diced	4	1 tbsp	chopped fresh thyme (or 1 tsp/5 mL dried)	15 mL
1 tbsp	butter	15 mL	3 cups	corn kernels (approx 6 ears, or use frozen)	750 mL
2	stalks celery, diced	2	1	sweet red pepper, diced	1
1	onion, diced	1			
2 tbsp	all-purpose flour	25 mL	1 cup	whipping cream	250 mL
4 cups	chicken broth	1 L	2	cloves garlic, minced	2
1	large sweet potato, peeled and diced	1	•	Salt and pepper	•
			3	green onions, thinly sliced	3

In a large saucepan over medium-high heat, cook the pancetta until crisp. With a slotted spoon, remove to drain on paper towels; discard all but 2 tbsp (25 mL) of the drippings from the pan. (Refrigerate the pancetta if making the chowder ahead.)

In the same pan, melt the butter over medium heat; cook the celery and onion until very soft, about 10 minutes. Stir in the flour and cook 1 minute, stirring. Gradually stir in the broth, and bring to a boil. Add the sweet potato and thyme. Bring to a boil, reduce the heat, cover and simmer until the sweet potato is tender, about 20 minutes. Stir in the corn, red pepper, cream, garlic, and salt and pepper to taste. Simmer until the corn is tender, about 4 minutes. (The soup can be cooled, covered and refrigerated for up to 1 day. Bring to a simmer to continue.)

Stir in half the green onions; simmer for 5 minutes. Taste for seasoning. Garnish each serving with some of the remaining green onions and reserved pancetta. *Makes 6 servings.*

* Pancetta is unsmoked Italian bacon available at most supermarket deli counters.

HOT *and* SOUR SOUP

Popular in Chinese restaurants in Canada for well over two decades, this sensuous soup of contrasting textures and tastes remains a flavourful comfort food. Most ingredients are now available in many big supermarkets, but you may have to seek some out in Chinese grocery stores. I've updated it slightly with fresh mushrooms and lots of green onions.

8 oz	boneless lean pork	250 g	¼ cup	rice vinegar	50 mL
8 oz	fresh cremini or shiitake mushrooms	250 g	1 tbsp	Chinese hot chili sauce	15 mL
			¼ tsp	white pepper	1 mL
8 oz	fresh firm tofu	250 g	3 tbsp	cornstarch	45 mL
1	can (8 oz/227 mL) sliced bamboo shoot strips	1	3 tbsp	water	45 mL
			2	eggs, lightly beaten	2
8 cups	chicken broth	2 L	2 tsp	sesame oil	10 mL
¼ cup	soy sauce	50 mL	2	green onions, sliced	2
1 tbsp	shredded fresh ginger	15 mL			

Place the pork in the freezer just until firm, but not frozen, about 20 minutes. Slice as thinly as possible, then cut slices into narrow strips 1½ inches (4 cm) long. Set aside. If using shiitake mushrooms, remove the stems. Drain the tofu and bamboo shoots and rinse under cold water. Cut the mushrooms, tofu and bamboo shoots (if not already in strips) into strips the same size as the pork. Set aside.

In a large saucepan, combine the broth, soy sauce, ginger, mushrooms, bamboo shoots and pork. Bring to a boil over high heat; reduce the heat to low, cover and simmer for 3 minutes. Add the tofu, vinegar, chili sauce and pepper. Bring back to a boil. Whisk together the cornstarch and water; pour into the soup. Stir for a few seconds until the soup thickens, then slowly pour in the beaten eggs, stirring gently all the time. Remove from the heat. Taste for seasoning, adding more soy sauce, vinegar or chili sauce if desired. Ladle into a tureen or bowl. Stir in the sesame oil and sprinkle with green onions. Serve immediately. *Makes 4 to 6 servings.*

THAI TOM YUM SHRIMP SOUP

Canadians have fallen in love with the fragrant flavours of Thai cuisine, especially this delicious soup that is on every restaurant menu. Tom Yum Soup combines all the exotic tastes you associate with Thailand—lemon grass, chilies, galangal, kaffir lime leaves, fish sauce and fresh coriander. Traditionally a fiery soup, you can make it as hot as you like by the number of chilies you use. The cooking school that I attended in Thailand used 20 for this amount! (I used one or two for a magazine article.) Thai chefs usually leave all the seasoning ingredients in the soup, but then the diner has to pick out the pieces of galangal, chilies and lime leaves. I've strained mine out, but put the lemon grass pieces back in because they look attractive in the soup; just warn everyone to discard them.

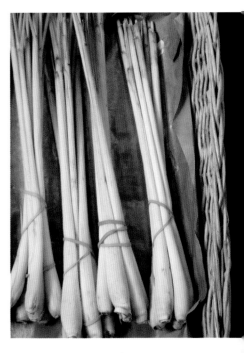

1 lb	medium shrimp, unpeeled	500 g	4 oz	shiitake mushrooms, stems discarded and caps sliced	125 g
2	stalks lemon grass	2			
5 cups	chicken broth	1.25 L	2	tomatoes, each cut into 8 wedges	2
12	thin slices peeled galangal	12			
6	small fresh green bird's eye (Thai) chilies, halved lengthwise	6	3 tbsp	fish sauce	45 mL
			3 tbsp	fresh lime juice	45 mL
6	kaffir lime leaves, torn	6	½ cup	chopped fresh coriander leaves	125 mL
4	cloves garlic, crushed	4			
3	shallots, sliced	3			

Peel and devein the shrimp, reserving the shells; set the shrimp aside in the refrigerator. Trim off and discard the top two-thirds of the lemon grass stalks; cut the remaining stalks diagonally into 1-inch (2.5 cm) pieces.

In a large saucepan, stir together the shrimp shells, lemon grass, broth, galangal, chilies and lime leaves. Bring to a boil over high heat. Reduce the heat to medium-low, cover and simmer for 20 minutes. Strain the broth, reserving the lemon grass pieces. Add the lemon grass back to the broth with the garlic and shallots; bring to a boil again. Add the mushrooms and tomatoes; bring back to a boil. Add the fish sauce. Reduce the heat to medium; simmer, uncovered, for 2 minutes.

Add the shrimp and cook for 1 minute. Remove from the heat and stir in the lime juice. Transfer to warmed soup bowls or a tureen and sprinkle with coriander. *Makes 4 to 6 servings.*

TIP: You can usually buy lemon grass in a supermarket, but you will probably have to go to an Asian grocery store for some ingredients. Or you can substitute other fresh hot chilies or dried chilies softened in water for the bird's eye chilies. You can use a ½-inch (1 cm) piece of fresh ginger, thinly sliced, for the galangal. Substitute 1 tsp (5 mL) grated lime zest for the kaffir lime leaves. If you like, use 1 can (14 oz/398 mL) straw mushrooms for the shiitake mushrooms.

∧ *Lemongrass (top)*

FENNEL-ROASTED SEAFOOD CHOWDER

Throughout the Maritimes, chowder recipes are numerous and are often well-guarded secrets. This one from Cape Breton, Nova Scotia, calls for poaching the seafood, but I love the bolder flavours roasting imparts in this contemporary version, which has just a hint of cream.

¼ cup	butter	50 mL		2 tsp	crushed fennel seeds	10 mL
3	potatoes, peeled and diced	3			or ground fennel	
2	stalks celery, diced	2		1 lb	clams, scrubbed	500 g
1	carrot, diced	1		1 lb	mussels, scrubbed and	500 g
1	onion, diced	1			debearded (see page 70)	
1	clove garlic, minced	1		½ lb	salmon fillet, cubed	250 g
¼ cup	all-purpose flour	50 mL		¼ cup	whipping cream	50 mL
6 cups	clam juice or fish stock	1.5 L		2 tbsp	chopped fresh basil	25 mL
2 tbsp	olive oil	25 mL		•	Salt and pepper	•

In a large saucepan, melt the butter over medium heat. Cook the potatoes, celery, carrot, onion and garlic until softened, stirring often, about 10 minutes. Stir in the flour and cook, stirring, for 2 minutes. Gradually stir in the clam juice; bring to a boil, stirring. Reduce the heat, cover and simmer until the vegetables are tender, about 10 minutes.

Meanwhile, stir together the oil and fennel in a large roasting pan. Add the clams and place in a 500°F (260°C) oven for 5 minutes. Stir in the mussels and roast for 5 minutes. Add the salmon and return to the oven until the clams and mussels open, about 5 more minutes. Discard any that do not open. Stir the contents of the roasting pan into the chowder. Stir in the cream and heat through, but do not boil. Stir in the basil and salt and pepper to taste. Serve immediately. *Makes 6 servings.*

BREADS & BRUNCHES

BRIE AND PROSCIUTTO BREAD
PUDDING ~ *43*

POACHED EGGS ON ASPARAGUS
WITH YOGURT HOLLANDAISE ~ *44*

CHORIZO AND SCRAMBLED EGG
BREAKFAST PIZZA ~ *46*

WHOLE WHEAT PIZZA DOUGH ~ *46*

CARAMELIZED ONION AND
PROSCIUTTO TART ~ *47*

SPICED PUMPKIN-DATE MUFFINS ~ *48*

BLUEBERRY AND WHITE CHOCOLATE

CRANBERRY STREUSEL
MUFFINS ~ *50*

APPLE BUTTER CINNAMON
ROLLS ~ *52*

APRICOT ALMOND
BREAD ~ *53*

CHEDDAR JALAPEÑO
CORNBREAD ~ *55*

LEMON ANISE LOAF ~ *56*

DRIED PEAR AND POPPY SEED
BREAD ~ *57*

SESAME WHEAT BISCUITS ~ *58*

IRISH SODA BREAD ~ *58*

THE PRAIRIES ~ *59*

BRIE *and* PROSCIUTTO BREAD PUDDING

Bread puddings were originally the product of frugal cooks who wanted to avoid wasting stale bread, but they have become so popular that they've taken on all sorts of delicious forms. One of these is a breakfast dish often called a strata, probably because it is usually layered bread, cheese, custard and other ingredients such as ham or sausage. The pudding was called "Wife Saver" in a number of the community cookbooks that popped up in the fifties because you had to make it the day before, thus saving "the wife" from having to cook in the early morning—a special treat for a day like Christmas. Whether you make this for Christmas brunch or overnight company through the year, you will discover why bread puddings have become a national treat. Try to find egg bread since it melds with the custard and melted cheese in an especially yummy way without even removing the crusts.

10 to 12	slices egg bread	10 to 12	3 cups	milk	750 mL
¼ cup	melted butter	50 mL	¼ cup	minced shallots	50 mL
4 oz	prosciutto, slivered	125 g	1 tbsp	Dijon mustard	15 mL
8 oz	Brie cheese, rind removed,	250 g	½ tsp	salt	2 mL
	cut into cubes		½ tsp	pepper	2 mL
1 cup	grated old Cheddar	250 mL	Dash	Tabasco sauce	Dash
	cheese		Dash	Worcestershire sauce	Dash
6	eggs	6	1 tsp	paprika	5 mL

Line a greased 13- × 9-inch (3 L) baking dish with half the bread, cutting it to fit. Brush with half the butter. Sprinkle with half the prosciutto and cheeses. Repeat the layers.

In a large bowl, whisk the eggs; whisk in the milk, shallots, mustard, salt, pepper, Tabasco sauce and Worcestershire sauce. Pour over the bread mixture, cover and refrigerate overnight.

Sprinkle with paprika and bake in the centre of a 350°F (180°C) oven until puffed and crisp on top, about 1 hour. Cut into squares to serve. *Makes 6 to 8 servings.*

∧ *At the Farmer's Market in Halifax*

POACHED EGGS *on* ASPARAGUS *with* YOGURT HOLLANDAISE

During asparagus season, my mother used to make asparagus on toast with sliced boiled eggs and white sauce, one of my favourite lunches as a youngster. I've turned that idea into a version of Eggs Benedict that is a winner for brunch or lunch. The low-fat hollandaise can fool anyone—even those who say they dislike yogurt. When asparagus is not in season you can, of course, substitute smoked salmon, peameal bacon or ham for the asparagus.

1 lb	asparagus	500 g	4	large slices focaccia or thick	4
2 tsp	olive oil	10 mL		French bread, toasted	
•	Salt and pepper	•	•	Yogurt Hollandaise	•
8	eggs	8		(recipe follows)	

Trim the asparagus by breaking off any tough ends and wash the spears well. Toss with oil and spread out in a single layer on a baking sheet; sprinkle with salt and pepper. Roast in a 500°F (260°C) oven until just tender but not browned, 8 to 10 minutes, turning once.

Pour enough boiling water into a large, shallow pan to come 3 inches (8 cm) up the side. Return to a boil, then reduce the heat to a gentle simmer. Break each egg into a small dish; gently slip each egg into the water. Cook until the whites are set but the yolks are still soft, about 3 minutes. Place the hot toast on 4 warm dinner plates, and top each with warm asparagus. Using a slotted spoon, patting the bottom to get rid of any moisture, gently transfer 2 eggs to top the asparagus on each serving and spoon on the Yogurt Hollandaise. *Makes 4 servings.*

YOGURT HOLLANDAISE

¾ cup	plain low-fat yogurt	175 mL	¼ tsp	salt	1 mL
2 tsp	fresh lemon juice	10 mL	¼ tsp	granulated sugar	1 mL
3	egg yolks	3	Pinch	black pepper	Pinch
½ tsp	Dijon mustard	2 mL	Dash	hot pepper sauce	Dash

In the top of a double boiler or heatproof bowl, whisk together the yogurt, lemon juice, egg yolks, mustard, salt, sugar, pepper and hot pepper sauce. Cook over simmering water, stirring constantly, until the sauce is thick enough to coat the back of a spoon, 6 to 8 minutes. (The sauce can be set aside at room temperature for up to 1 hour; reheat gently in double boiler.) *Makes 1 cup (250 mL).*

CHORIZO *and* SCRAMBLED EGG BREAKFAST PIZZA

This fun breakfast was inspired by the Breakfast Pizza at Melville Café in the University of Waterloo's School of Architecture building in Cambridge, Ontario. If you like, you can substitute breakfast or farmer's sausage for the chorizo; cook it right through and drain off extra fat after you sauté it.

•	Whole Wheat Pizza Dough for 12-inch (30 cm) crust (recipe follows)	•
1½ cups	grated Portuguese São Jorge cheese or extra old Cheddar cheese (or a mixture)	375 mL
1 cup	pizza sauce	250 mL
8 oz	chorizo sausage, diced	250 g
4	eggs	4
4	green onions, sliced	4
¼ tsp	pepper	1 mL

On a lightly floured surface, roll the dough into a 12-inch (30 cm) round and place on a greased pizza pan or heated pizza stone. Sprinkle with half the cheese and spread with the pizza sauce. Bake in the centre of a 425°F (220°C) oven for 15 minutes.

Meanwhile, in a large skillet over medium-high heat, cook the chorizo until crisp, about 5 minutes. In a medium bowl, whisk together the eggs, green onions and pepper. Add to the skillet and stir until softly set, about 1 minute. Spread over the partially baked pizza and sprinkle with the remaining cheese. Return to the oven for another 3 to 5 minutes, until browned and bubbly. *Makes 3 to 4 servings.*

WHOLE WHEAT PIZZA DOUGH

Italian immigrants brought pizza to Canada, and its popularity is unsurpassed by any other mainstream fast food. Just check the number of pizzerias in your local phone book! Homemade pizzas can be fun and more delicious, and they're a surprising breakfast treat.
I must admit that I often buy pizza dough at our local Italian supermarket, but this is almost as quick to make as driving across town to the store. It is easily doubled. Use all all-purpose flour if you don't have whole wheat flour on hand.

Pinch	granulated sugar	Pinch
⅔ cup	warm water	150 mL
1	envelope (8 g) active dry yeast	1
2 tbsp	canola oil	25 mL
1 cup	all-purpose flour (approx)	250 mL
½ cup	whole wheat flour	125 mL
½ tsp	salt	2 mL

In a small bowl, combine the sugar and water; sprinkle with the yeast and let stand in a warm place until bubbly and doubled in volume, about 5 minutes. Stir in the oil.

In a large bowl, mix together the flours and salt. Make a well in the centre and pour in the yeast mixture. With a fork, gradually blend together the flour and yeast mixtures to form the dough. With floured hands gather it into a ball.

Turn out onto a lightly floured surface; knead until elastic, about 5 minutes, adding just enough extra all-purpose flour to make a soft, slightly sticky dough. Place in a greased bowl, turning once to grease the ball all over. Cover the bowl with greased waxed paper and a tea towel. Let stand in a warm, draft-free place until tripled in size, 1½ to 3 hours.

Punch down the dough and form into a ball. Turn out onto a lightly floured surface and cover with the bowl; let stand for 10 minutes. Roll out and place on a pizza pan. *Makes one 12-inch (30 cm) crust.*

CARAMELIZED ONION *and* PROSCIUTTO TART

Quick to make and delicious, this savoury tart is lovely for a company brunch or easy to carry to a picnic site in its sturdy dish.

3	onions	3	1	sheet puff pastry		1
3 tbsp	unsalted butter	45 mL		(half a 16 oz/450 g pkg)*		
2	cloves garlic, minced	2	1½ cups	grated old Cheddar cheese,		375 mL
2 tsp	chopped fresh thyme	10 mL		preferably orange		
	(or ½ tsp/2 mL dried)		4 oz	prosciutto, coarsely chopped		125 g
1 tsp	granulated sugar	5 mL	2	eggs		2
¼ tsp	black pepper	1 mL	¼ cup	crème fraîche or sour cream		50 mL
			½ tsp	paprika		2 mL

Cut the onions in half lengthwise, then thinly slice them crosswise. Melt the butter in a large skillet over medium heat. Add the onions, garlic, thyme, sugar and pepper. Reduce the heat to medium-low and cook, stirring often, until golden but not brown, 25 to 30 minutes. Cool.

Carefully ease the sheet of puff pastry into an 8-inch (2 L) glass baking dish. Prick the bottom several times with a fork. Scatter the onion mixture over the pastry, sprinkle with 1 cup (250 mL) of the cheese, then the prosciutto. Whisk the eggs and crème fraîche together until smooth and pour over the top. Sprinkle on the remaining ½ cup (125 mL) of cheese and the paprika. Bake in the centre of a 400°F (200°C) oven until the pastry is golden brown, about 35 minutes. Transfer to a rack to cool for 10 to 15 minutes before cutting into squares to serve. If making ahead, cool and refrigerate; bring to room temperature before serving. *Makes 6 servings.*

* If a 16 oz (450 g) package is unavailable, use half a 14 oz (397 g) package and roll out to a square 10 × 10 inches (25 × 25 cm).

SPICED PUMPKIN-DATE MUFFINS

The combination of pumpkin and dates makes these easy muffins moist and good keepers.

1	egg	1
½ cup	milk	125 mL
½ cup	pumpkin purée (see page 206)	125 mL
½ cup	granulated sugar	125 mL
¼ cup	canola oil	50 mL
1 tbsp	grated orange zest	15 mL
1½ cups	all-purpose flour	375 mL
2 tsp	baking powder	10 mL
½ tsp	baking soda	2 mL
½ tsp	salt	2 mL
½ tsp	ground cinnamon	2 mL
½ tsp	grated nutmeg	2 mL
½ cup	finely chopped dates	125 mL
•	Decorating sugar crystals or granulated sugar	•

In a small bowl, beat the egg. Stir in the milk, pumpkin purée, sugar, oil and orange zest; blend thoroughly.

In a large bowl, sift or stir together the flour, baking powder, baking soda, salt, cinnamon and nutmeg. Add the dates and stir to coat with the flour. Add the pumpkin mixture; mix with a spoon just until the dry ingredients are moistened. Spoon into greased or paper-lined muffin tins, filling each cup three-quarters full. Sprinkle each top with about ¼ tsp (1 mL) sugar. Bake in the centre of a 400°F (200°C) oven until lightly browned and a tester comes out clean, 20 to 25 minutes. *Makes 10 to 12 muffins.*

BLUEBERRY *and* WHITE CHOCOLATE MUFFINS *with* SUGAR SPRINKLE

Blueberries and white chocolate are happy companions and make these muffins special, so if you have a container of coarse sugar crystals tucked away in the pantry, this is the time to use it. If not, these are still probably the best muffins you are likely to taste.

¼ cup	butter, softened	50 mL
⅔ cup	granulated sugar	150 mL
1	egg	1
1 tsp	vanilla	5 mL
1¾ cups	all-purpose flour	425 mL
2 tsp	baking powder	10 mL
Pinch	salt	Pinch
⅔ cup	milk	150 mL
1½ cups	blueberries	375 mL
⅔ cup	white chocolate chips	150 mL
1 tbsp	sugar crystals (optional)	15 mL

In a large bowl, cream the butter with the sugar until fluffy; beat in the egg, then the vanilla.

Sift or stir together the flour, baking powder and salt. Add to the butter mixture alternately with the milk, making three additions of dry ingredients and two of milk, stirring just enough to combine. Do not overmix. Gently stir in the blueberries and chocolate chips. Using an ice cream scoop, spoon into 12 greased or paper-lined muffin cups. Sprinkle each with some of the coarse sugar, if using. Bake in the centre of a 375°F (190°C) oven until golden and firm to the touch, about 25 minutes. *Makes 12 muffins.*

Blueberry and White Chocolate Muffins
with Sugar Sprinkle (facing page)

CRANBERRY STREUSEL MUFFINS

These lovely muffins, chock full of zesty red berries, will tempt even the sleepiest taste buds in the morning. They would be a great treat to serve European visitors who have neither muffins nor cranberries on their usual menu.

STREUSEL TOPPING

2 tbsp	all-purpose flour	25 mL	¼ tsp	ground cinnamon	1 mL
2 tbsp	granulated sugar	25 mL	2 tbsp	butter	25 mL

MUFFINS

2 cups	fresh cranberries, coarsely chopped	500 mL	1 tsp	vanilla	5 mL
			2 cups	all-purpose flour	500 mL
½ cup	icing sugar	125 mL	2 tsp	baking powder	10 mL
¼ cup	butter, softened	50 mL	Pinch	salt	Pinch
¼ cup	granulated sugar	50 mL	½ cup	milk	125 mL
1	egg	1			

STREUSEL TOPPING: In a small bowl, combine the flour, sugar and cinnamon. Cut in the butter until the mixture is crumbly; set aside.

MUFFINS: In a medium bowl, combine the cranberries and icing sugar; set aside. In a large bowl, cream the butter and sugar until fluffy. Beat in the egg and vanilla. In a separate bowl, combine the flour, baking powder and salt. Add the dry ingredients to the creamed mixture alternately with the milk, making three additions of dry ingredients and two of milk, stirring just until combined; do not overmix. Gently stir in the sugared cranberries.

Spoon the batter into 12 small or 9 medium greased or paper-lined muffin cups. Sprinkle evenly with the streusel topping. Bake in the centre of a 375°F (190°C) oven until the tops are firm to the touch and a tester inserted in a centre comes out clean, 25 to 30 minutes. Let cool in the pan for 5 minutes, then turn out and cool completely on a rack. *Makes 12 small or 9 medium muffins.*

Bread-Making

The wheat that settlers brought with them flourished in our soil, especially in the Prairies where mills soon sprang up, but many early settlers had to rely on grinding their own grain into flour. The bread that resulted, often without leavening and sometimes baked over open fires, could be indigestible "dough cakes." The best of these was bannock, a simple type of scone made with flour, salt and a bit of fat. As baking powder became available, it was added to bannock and to biscuits, scones and oatcakes.

Settlers used various types of leavening. Those who lived on farms often grew hops to make a kind of leavening called barm, augmented sometimes by adding boiled potatoes and a little salt. In towns, many preferred brewers' or distillers' yeast, but these did not give uniform results. Prospectors during the gold rush carried yeast "sourdough" starters for breads as part of their supplies. Sometimes individual grocers prepared yeasts for sale, but soon there were nationally known brands. Eventually, too, commercially made bread became so accessible that some gave up making their own bread because of uncertain results in wood stoves. In the 1930s, sliced white bread was met with great enthusiasm, but the following decades brought much better commercial bread. Now there are many nutritious whole grain breads available, and artisan breads, made to appear homemade, are very popular.

In the late 1990s, there was a revival of homemade bread with the invasion of the bread machine. Many men took to baking bread with this modern device. Right now, bread machines seem to be put up on the shelf, but you could use one for making the Whole Wheat Pizza Dough (page 46) or dough for the Apple Butter Cinnamon Rolls (page 52).

Photo taken at Montreal's famous Fairmount Bagel Bakery

APPLE BUTTER CINNAMON ROLLS

Chelsea buns and cinnamon rolls have long been favourite breakfast fare. My kids used to love gooey Chelsea buns filled with candied fruit and nuts as a treat on Christmas morning. In these easy-to-make rolls, I've cut way down on the sugar. They are still appealing, especially to those who don't like overly sweet breads or who should limit sugar. Look for pure apple butter at farmers' markets or in the produce section of most supermarkets.

Halifax, Nova Scotia

3 tbsp	granulated sugar	45 mL	2½ to	all-purpose flour	625 to 750 mL
¼ cup	lukewarm water	50 mL	3 cups		
1	envelope (8 g) active	1	¼ tsp	baking soda	1 mL
	dry yeast		1	egg, beaten	1
½ cup	well-shaken buttermilk	125 mL	2 tbsp	butter, softened	25 mL
¼ cup	shortening	50 mL	¾ cup	apple butter	175 mL
½ tsp	salt	2 mL	2 tsp	ground cinnamon	10 mL
			½ cup	chopped walnuts	125 mL

GLAZE

½ cup	icing sugar	125 mL	1 tsp	vanilla	5 mL
1 tbsp	milk (approx)	15 mL			

Dissolve 1 tbsp (15 mL) of the granulated sugar in the water. Sprinkle the yeast on the water and let stand 5 minutes.

In a large bowl, stir together the buttermilk, shortening, salt and remaining sugar. Stir in 1 cup (250 mL) of the flour. Stir the yeast mixture briskly and add to the bowl. Stir in the baking soda and egg until well combined. Mix in enough of the remaining flour to produce a smooth dough. Turn out onto a lightly floured surface and knead until very smooth and elastic, about 5 minutes. Place in a greased bowl, turning the dough to grease all sides, cover and let rise in a warm place until doubled, about 45 minutes. (A heating pad turned to low makes a good surface for this.)

Roll the dough into a 14- × 10-inch (35 × 25 cm) rectangle. Spread with the soft butter, leaving a ½-inch (1 cm) border. Stir together the apple butter and cinnamon; spread overtop, leaving a 1-inch (2.5 cm) border at the top of the long side. Sprinkle with the nuts. Roll up from the bottom of the long side into a tight roll, pushing in the apple butter gently as you roll. With a sharp knife, cut the roll into 10 equal pieces and place the pieces, cut side down, in a greased 9-inch (2.5 L) springform pan. Cover and let rise until doubled, about 45 minutes. Meanwhile, stir together the icing sugar, milk and vanilla, adding more milk if necessary to make a glaze that is thick but pourable.

Bake the buns in the centre of a 375°F (190°C) oven until golden brown, 25 to 30 minutes. Set the pan on a rack and let cool 5 minutes. Remove the outer ring and set the rolls on a plate. Drizzle the top with glaze. Serve warm or at room temperature. *Makes 10 buns, 6 to 8 servings.*

APRICOT ALMOND BREAD

Quick breads or tea breads, sophisticated versions of Canada's earliest quick bread, bannock, were great favourites in the 1920s, when they were often made with dates, raisins and other dried fruits as they became available. They were thinly sliced and buttered, appearing with tea, in lunch boxes and on bazaar bake tables. These loaves are still popular because they're so quick and easy to make. Start with this simple batter, succulent apricots and the ever-favourite almond flavour for the first tea bread; then make a few substitutions to create the Cranberry Walnut Loaf and Tangerine Date Loaf variations. They are all sure to be popular as lovely treats to have on hand for afternoon tea or a leisurely breakfast.

½ cup	butter, softened	125 mL	½ tsp	salt	2 mL
¾ cup	granulated sugar	175 mL	¾ cup	milk	175 mL
2	eggs	2	1 cup	chopped dried apricots	250 mL
½ tsp	almond extract	2 mL	¾ cup	slivered almonds,	175 mL
½ tsp	vanilla	2 mL		chopped and toasted	
2 cups	all-purpose flour	500 mL		(see TIP on page 217)	
2 tsp	baking powder	10 mL			

GLAZE

| ¼ cup | icing sugar | 50 mL | 1 tbsp | water | 15 mL |
| 1 tbsp | almond liqueur* | 15 mL | | | |

Line a 9- × 5-inch (2 L) loaf pan with parchment paper.

In a large bowl, cream the butter, then beat in the sugar until fluffy. Beat in the eggs, one at a time. Stir in the almond extract and vanilla.

In a separate bowl, stir together the flour, baking powder and salt. Stir into the butter mixture alternately with the milk, making 3 additions of dry ingredients and 2 of milk. Fold in the apricots and almonds.

Spoon into the prepared pan and bake in the centre of a 350°F (180°C) oven until a cake tester inserted in the centre comes out clean, about 1 hour and 10 minutes. Let cool in the pan on a rack for 5 minutes.

For the glaze, stir together the icing sugar, almond liqueur and water. Slowly pour over the bread and let sit 10 minutes longer. Remove the loaf from the pan, carefully peel off the paper and cool completely on the rack. Wrap well in plastic wrap and store for 24 hours before slicing. (The loaf will keep at room temperature for up to 3 days. Or wrap foil over the plastic wrap and store in the freezer for up to 2 weeks.) *Makes 1 loaf.*

* If you prefer, use 2 tbsp (25 mL) water and ½ tsp (2 mL) almond extract instead of 1 tbsp (15 mL) each almond liqueur and water.

(continued on page 55)

TOP TO BOTTOM: *Apricot Almond Bread (page 53). Cranberry Walnut Loaf (variation on facing page)*

CHEDDAR JALAPEÑO CORNBREAD

Settlers learned about using cornmeal for bread from First Nations people. This easy cornbread is the perfect accompaniment to chili, stews or barbecued ribs.

1 cup	cornmeal	250 mL
1 cup	shredded old Cheddar cheese	250 mL
¾ cup	all-purpose flour	175 mL
1 tbsp	granulated sugar	15 mL
1 tbsp	baking powder	15 mL
½ tsp	salt	2 mL
2 tbsp	minced jalapeño pepper (about 2)	25 mL
1 cup	milk	250 mL
⅓ cup	canola oil	75 mL
2	eggs, beaten	2

In a large bowl, combine the cornmeal, cheese, flour, sugar, baking powder and salt. Stir in the jalapeño pepper.

Combine the milk, oil and eggs; beat lightly. Add to the dry ingredients and stir with a fork just until blended. Pour the batter into a greased 8-inch (2 L) square cake pan. Bake in the centre of a 400°F (200°C) oven until it's risen and golden and a tester inserted in the middle comes out clean, about 30 minutes. Cool on a rack and cut into squares to serve warm or at room temperature. *Makes 16 squares.*

APRICOT ALMOND BREAD (continued)

VARIATIONS:

CRANBERRY WALNUT LOAF

Substitute 2 tsp (10 mL) grated lemon zest and ¼ tsp (1 mL) cinnamon for the almond extract, chopped raw cranberries for the apricots and toasted chopped walnuts for the almonds. For the glaze, use 2 tbsp (25 mL) fresh lemon juice as the liquid.

TANGERINE DATE LOAF

Substitute 4 tsp (20 mL) grated tangerine zest for the almond extract, chopped dates for the apricots and toasted chopped pecans for the almonds. Substitute 1 tsp (5 mL) baking soda for half the baking powder (i.e., use 1 tsp/5 mL of each) and tangerine juice for the milk. For the glaze, use 2 tbsp (25 mL) tangerine juice as the liquid and add 1 tbsp (15 mL) grated tangerine zest.

LEMON ANISE LOAF

Moist and lemony, with a subtle licorice flavour, this lovely bread just calls out for a cup of tea.

½ cup	butter, softened	125 mL	1½ tsp	aniseed, crushed	7 mL
1 cup	granulated sugar	250 mL	1 tsp	baking powder	5 mL
2	eggs	2	1 tsp	baking soda	5 mL
1 tbsp	grated lemon zest	15 mL	½ tsp	salt	2 mL
1 tsp	vanilla	5 mL	1 cup	milk	250 mL
2¼ cups	all-purpose flour	550 mL			

GLAZE

3 tbsp	fresh lemon juice	45 mL	2 tbsp	water	25 mL
3 tbsp	granulated sugar	45 mL			

Line a 9- × 5-inch (2 L) loaf pan with parchment paper.

In a large bowl, cream the butter, then beat in the sugar until fluffy. Beat in the eggs, one at a time. Stir in the lemon zest and vanilla.

In a separate bowl, stir together the flour, aniseed, baking powder, baking soda and salt. Stir into the butter mixture alternately with the milk, making 3 additions of dry ingredients and 2 of milk. Spoon into the prepared pan and bake in the centre of a 350°F (180°C) oven until a cake tester inserted in the centre comes out clean, about 1 hour. Cool in the pan on a rack for 10 minutes, then remove from the pan, carefully remove the paper and set the loaf on the rack over waxed paper.

GLAZE: In a small saucepan, stir together the lemon juice, sugar and water. Bring to a boil, and then boil gently until slightly thickened, about 5 minutes.

Poke holes in the top and sides of the hot loaf with a cake tester. Brush the lemon syrup over the top and sides of the loaf, using all the syrup. Cool completely on the rack. Wrap in plastic wrap and store 24 hours before slicing. (The loaf will keep at room temperature for up to 3 days. Or wrap in heavy foil and freeze for up to 2 weeks.) *Makes 1 loaf.*

DRIED PEAR *and* POPPY SEED BREAD

The textures of pear and poppy seed make an intriguing combination in this delightful loaf.

1½ cups	diced dried pears	375 mL	1 tsp	baking soda	5 mL
½ cup	pear nectar	125 mL	½ tsp	baking powder	2 mL
½ cup	butter, softened	125 mL	½ tsp	salt	2 mL
½ cup	packed brown sugar	125 mL	½ tsp	ground cardamom	2 mL
2	eggs	2	3 tbsp	poppy seeds	45 mL
¼ cup	liquid honey	50 mL	⅔ cup	plain low-fat yogurt	150 mL
2¼ cups	all-purpose flour	550 mL			

TOPPING

1 tbsp	liquid honey	15 mL	2 tsp	poppy seeds	10 mL

Line a 9- × 5-inch (2 L) loaf pan with parchment paper.

Combine the pears and pear nectar in a small bowl and microwave at High for 2 minutes. Stir well and set aside to cool. (Or bring to a boil in a small saucepan and set aside to cool.)

In a large bowl, cream the butter, then beat in the brown sugar until fluffy. Beat in the eggs, one at a time. Stir in the honey and the pear mixture.

In a separate bowl, stir together the flour, baking soda, baking powder, salt and cardamom. Stir in the poppy seeds. Stir into the butter mixture alternately with the yogurt, making 3 additions of dry ingredients and 2 of yogurt. Spoon into the prepared pan and bake in the centre of a 350°F (180°C) oven until a cake tester inserted in the centre comes out clean, about 1 hour and 10 minutes. Let cool in the pan on a rack for 5 minutes.

TOPPING: Brush the loaf with honey and sprinkle with poppy seeds.

Let the loaf cool for 10 minutes longer, then remove it from the pan; carefully remove the paper and cool completely. Wrap in plastic wrap and store for at least 24 hours before slicing. (The loaf will keep at room temperature for up to 3 days. Or wrap in foil and freeze for up to 2 weeks.) *Makes 1 loaf.*

SESAME WHEAT BISCUITS

In the early part of the 20th century, students in home economics classes across the country were taught to make baking powder or tea biscuits with a light touch. They remained popular with busy housewives who needed a quick bread substitute, and were often made with cream. Now, we are all seeking out more nutritious baked goods. Whole wheat flour adds both nutrients and flavour to these fluffy biscuits, and using buttermilk cuts down on the fat. Enjoy them warm with butter and jam—the perfect accompaniment to a leisurely breakfast, and a taste of the past.

1 cup	whole wheat flour	250 mL
1 cup	all-purpose flour	250 mL
¼ cup	sesame seeds	50 mL
1 tbsp	granulated sugar	15 mL
1 tbsp	baking powder	15 mL
½ tsp	baking soda	2 mL
½ tsp	salt	2 mL
⅓ cup	cold shortening or butter, in bits	75 mL
1	egg, beaten	1
⅔ cup	well-shaken buttermilk	150 mL

In a large bowl, stir together the whole wheat and all-purpose flour, sesame seeds, sugar, baking powder, baking soda and salt. Cut in the shortening until the mixture is like coarse crumbs. Combine the egg and buttermilk, then stir into the flour mixture with a fork until the dough follows the fork around the bowl. Turn out onto a floured surface (the mixture will be sticky at first); knead gently 20 times. Roll to ¾-inch (2 cm) thickness. Cut into 3-inch (8 cm) circles and place on an ungreased baking sheet. Bake in the centre of a 450°F (230°C) oven until golden brown and firm, about 12 minutes. *Makes 9 biscuits.*

IRISH SODA BREAD

This light version of that wonderful bread brought to our shores with Irish settlers would be a great accompaniment to Chipotle Maple Baked Beans (see page 101).

1½ cups	all-purpose flour	375 mL
1½ cups	whole wheat flour	375 mL
1 tbsp	granulated sugar	15 mL
1½ tsp	baking powder	7 mL
½ tsp	baking soda	2 mL
½ tsp	salt	2 mL
2 tbsp	butter	25 mL
1⅓ cups	well-shaken buttermilk	325 mL

In a large bowl, whisk together the all-purpose and whole wheat flour, sugar, baking powder, baking soda and salt. Cut in the butter until crumbly. Add the butter-milk all at once; stir with a fork just until combined.

On a lightly floured surface and with floured hands, press the dough into a ball and knead lightly 10 times. Place on a lightly greased baking sheet and gently pat into a round loaf, about 2 inches (5 cm) high. With a sharp knife, cut a ½-inch-deep (1 cm) cross on top. Bake in the centre of a 375°F (190°C) oven until a tester inserted in the centre comes out clean, about 35 to 45 minutes. Cool on a rack and slice into wedges to serve. *Makes 1 loaf or 8 wedges.*

THE PRAIRIES

THE FIRST GLIMPSE I EVER HAD of the Prairies was from a train window as I travelled across the country. I fell asleep to the endless rocks, trees and lakes of Northern Ontario and woke up to the endless Prairie sky. Since then, I've seen my most glorious sunrise and the most stars I've ever witnessed at one time in the blackness of that same sky.

Flying across the Prairies, however, it's the huge patchwork quilt of fields below that catches your attention. Enormous blocks of golden wheat are interspersed with smaller blocks of blue flax and bright yellow canola blooms. Oats and barley are other important crops, but it's wheat that dominates the landscape. The wheat belt runs through all three Prairie provinces—Manitoba, Saskatchewan and Alberta. First planted in the last half of the 19th century, wheat was the gold of the West and one of the foundations of Canada's economy. It's also one of the reasons Canadians have a long tradition of baking as flour mills gradually appeared across the Prairies.

Canola has become increasingly important since research has proven the nutritious significance of the oil. From canola comes another important Prairie delicacy: high-quality honey. Both canola and buckwheat honey are produced in all three provinces. Although mustard is not made here, seed grown on the Prairies is the raw material used to produce the famous Dijon condiment.

Ironically, Prairie history did not include agriculture. First Nations dominating the area lived primarily on buffalo, which they dried and mixed with fat and berries, usually saskatoon berries. The pemmican was a welcome addition to the diet of the first explorers, French and Scottish fur traders of the Hudson's Bay Company and the North West Company, as well as early settlers. The 1847 Christmas dinner at Fort Edmonton (recorded by artist Paul Kane) showed the great dependence on buffalo: "boiled buffalo hump and

Bales of hay and a view of the Rockies near Pincher Creek in Alberta

calf, dried moose nose, white fish, buffalo tongue, beavers' tails, roast wild goose, potatoes, turnips and bread, but no pies or dessert." Overhunting led to the demise of the huge buffalo herds, but beef took its place and remains an important aspect of the economy, particularly in Alberta.

Lord Selkirk, who brought a group of displaced Scottish crofters to the Red River Valley in 1812, is credited with the first European settlement, but the true opening up of the West came after immigration promotions set up in 1896 by the Minister of the Interior. Development of the railway brought a sea of immigrants and Eastern Canadians who moved onto homesteads, and towns sprang up.

Until the 1950s, British settlers dominated Prairie cuisine with their roast beef, Yorkshire pudding, cakes (often named after British royalty) and tearooms. Where other immigrants settled, they also held onto their home country's culinary traditions: the French, particularly around Winnipeg; the Mennonites on the Manitoba plains; Hutterites in Alberta; Icelanders at Gimli; Scandinavian farmers from the Dakotas and American ranchers in the foothills of southern Alberta. From the time they began arriving at the end of the 19th century, however, Ukrainians, with their traditional perogies, cabbage rolls and specialty breads, have constituted a strong thread in Prairie cooking. This was quite an influence since there were 500,000 Ukrainians in Canada by 1957.

Eventually immigrants from other countries began to leave their culinary mark. Winnipeg attracted a large Filipino population, and flavours from the West Indies and the Middle East have made their way into the food scene in Winnipeg, Edmonton, Saskatoon and Calgary. Chefs in upscale restaurants combine new ideas with local products, but family recipes reflecting both the region's ingredients and its cultural heritage remain important.

A PRAIRIE BRUNCH

Brie and Prosciutto Bread Pudding
(page 43)

Mixed Green Salad
with Mustard Vinaigrette
(page 168)

Tea-Infused Winter Fruits with
Prune Brandy Cream
(page 222)

Apricot Coffee Cake with
Butterscotch Walnut Filling
(page 200)

< *Old-style Prairie grain elevator*
in Saskatchewan

FISH & SEAFOOD

OVEN-ROASTED HALIBUT WITH
CAPER-HERB VINAIGRETTE ~ *63*

EAST COAST LOBSTER ROLLS ~ *63*

CORN-CRUSTED ROAST SALMON ~ *64*

GLAZED HOT AND SWEET SALMON
WITH BOK CHOY ~ *64*

QUICK SEAFOOD STEW ~ *67*

SEAFOOD POT PIE ~ *68*

GRILLED ARCTIC CHAR WITH
ORANGE-ONION SALSA ~ *69*

MUSSELS IN COCONUT BROTH ~ *70*

PICKEREL BLT ~ *73*

OYSTER STEW ~ *73*

THE NORTH ~ *75*
A MIDNIGHT SUN SUPPER ~ *75*

OVEN-ROASTED HALIBUT *with* CAPER-HERB VINAIGRETTE

Halibut is found on both coasts and is delicious when cooked properly—that is, not overcooked. Here it is quickly roasted on its own in a fast oven according to the Canadian rule of 10 minutes per inch (2.5 cm) thickness of fish, then it is dressed with a piquant vinaigrette that would be excellent with any firm-fleshed fish.

4	thick halibut fillets or steaks (about 6 oz/175 g each)	4
•	Olive oil	•
•	Sea salt and pepper	•
¼ cup	olive oil	50 mL
1 tsp	grated lemon zest	5 mL
2 tbsp	fresh lemon juice	25 mL
2	cloves garlic, minced	2
2 tbsp	minced fresh parsley, preferably Italian flat-leaf	25 mL
1 tsp	fresh thyme leaves (or ¼ tsp/ 1 mL dried)	5 mL
1 tsp	capers, rinsed	5 mL
•	Lemon slices (optional)	•

Brush the fish with olive oil. Place on a large foil-lined rimmed baking sheet. Sprinkle with salt and pepper and roast in a 450°F (230°C) oven until the centre turns opaque, about 10 minutes.

Meanwhile, in a small bowl, stir together the ¼ cup (50 mL) oil, zest, juice, garlic, parsley, thyme and capers. Transfer the fish to a warm platter and spoon the vinaigrette on top. Garnish with lemon slices if desired. Serve hot, warm or at room temperature. *Makes 4 servings.*

EAST COAST LOBSTER ROLLS

The Atlantic provinces are blessed with some of the best seafood in the world, and these sandwiches help celebrate the good quality of East Coast lobster.

2 cups	cubed (½-inch/1 cm) cooked lobster meat	500 mL
1 cup	mayonnaise (preferably homemade)	250 mL
¼ cup	finely chopped celery	50 mL
2 tsp	finely chopped green onion or chives	10 mL
2 tsp	fresh lemon juice	10 mL
•	Salt and pepper	•
8	large crusty rolls, halved and buttered	8
•	Lettuce	•

In a small bowl, combine the lobster, mayonnaise, celery, green onion, lemon juice, and salt and pepper to taste.

Line half of each roll with lettuce. Scoop the lobster mixture on top. Cover with the remaining halves. *Makes 8 servings.*

CORN-CRUSTED ROAST SALMON

A crisp cornmeal topping ensures that the salmon stays moist during roasting. Accompany with Garlic Potato Wedges (page 145) and Maple Cabbage Slaw (page 168) for an easy and casual "fish and chip" supper.

⅓ cup	cornmeal	75 mL
2 tbsp	all-purpose flour	25 mL
½ tsp	salt	2 mL
¼ tsp	black pepper	1 mL
¼ tsp	cayenne	1 mL
2 tbsp	plain yogurt	25 mL
2 tbsp	milk	25 mL
1 tbsp	fresh lime juice	15 mL
4	skinless salmon fillets	4
	(1½ lb/750 g total weight)	
•	Lime wedges	•

Stir together the cornmeal, flour, salt, pepper and cayenne in a shallow dish. In a separate shallow dish, whisk the yogurt, milk and lime juice together until smooth. Dip each salmon fillet in the yogurt mixture to coat it well, then dip in the cornmeal mixture, turning the fillet to coat it thinly on both sides. Lay the fillets on a lightly oiled baking sheet. (The salmon can be covered and refrigerated for up to 4 hours; let it stand at room temperature for 30 minutes before cooking.)

Roast in a 450°F (230°C) oven for 8 to 10 minutes, turning once, until the fish starts to flake with a fork but the centre is still moist. Serve with lime wedges to squeeze over the fish. *Makes 4 servings.*

GLAZED HOT *and* SWEET SALMON *with* BOK CHOY

This flavourful combination makes a quick and easy meal that is delightful for both family and company. Serve it with steamed jasmine rice.

¼ cup	sweet chili sauce*	50 mL
2 tbsp	slivered fresh ginger	25 mL
2 tbsp	soy sauce	25 mL
2 tbsp	oyster sauce	25 mL
1	small red chili, finely chopped	1
4	salmon fillets (6 oz/175 g each)	4
8	heads baby bok choy	8

In a glass measure, combine the chili sauce, ginger, soy sauce, oyster sauce and chili; remove 3 tbsp (45 mL) to a glass dish. Place the salmon in the dish and coat the fillets with the mixture. Set aside for 30 minutes.

Remove the salmon with any marinade that clings to the fillets. Place, skin side down, on a parchment-lined rimmed baking sheet. Bake in a 450°F (230°C) oven until the fish flakes easily when tested with a fork, about 10 minutes.

Meanwhile, slice the bok choy in half lengthwise and steam until tender but still bright green and crisp, about 2 to 3 minutes. Heat the remaining marinade in the microwave for 30 seconds and drizzle over the bok choy and salmon. *Makes 4 servings.*

* Sweet chili sauce is a Thai sweet-sour sauce used for barbecues and dipping; it is available in supermarkets.

Glazed Hot and Sweet Salmon
with Bok Choy (facing page)

QUICK SEAFOOD STEW

Perfect for casual entertaining, this bright, fresh stew takes five minutes to finish after making the tomato base ahead. Just add good bread and a crisp green salad to the menu. Feel free to vary the fish and seafood with whatever is available and good in the market.

2 tbsp	olive oil	25 mL	¼ tsp	black pepper	1 mL
1	Spanish onion, chopped	1	¼ tsp	hot pepper flakes	1 mL
4	cloves garlic, minced	4	¼ tsp	saffron threads, crumbled	1 mL
1	sweet red pepper, diced	1	2	bay leaves	2
1	can (28 oz/796 mL) diced	1	1 lb	haddock or cod fillets	500 g
	tomatoes (undrained)		1 lb	mussels	500 g
1 cup	clam juice	250 mL	8 oz	large shrimp, peeled	250 g
1 cup	dry white wine	250 mL		and deveined (12 to 16)	
½ tsp	dried thyme	2 mL	¼ cup	chopped fresh parsley	50 mL
½ tsp	salt	2 mL	2 tbsp	chopped green onion	25 mL

In a large heavy saucepan, heat the oil over medium heat. Cook the onion, garlic and red pepper until softened, about 5 minutes. Stir in the tomatoes, clam juice, wine, thyme, salt, black pepper, hot pepper flakes, saffron and bay leaves. Bring to a boil; reduce the heat and simmer uncovered, stirring occasionally, until thickened slightly, 12 to 15 minutes. Remove the bay leaves. (The recipe can be made ahead, covered and refrigerated for up to 2 days. Bring to a simmer before proceeding.)

Cut the fish into bite-sized pieces. Scrub the mussels under cold running water, removing any beards and discarding any mussels that don't close when tapped. Add with the fish to the tomato mixture, cover and cook over medium-low heat for 3 minutes. Add the shrimp, but do not stir; baste all the seafood with the tomato mixture. Cover and cook until the shrimp are pink, the mussels are open and the fish flakes with a fork, about 2 more minutes. Discard any mussels that do not open. Serve immediately, sprinkled with parsley and green onion. *Makes 4 to 6 servings.*

SEAFOOD POT PIE

This is an elegant pie, rich in seafood and with a flaky pastry. For a delicious meal, serve it with a crisp spinach and walnut salad dressed with a lemon vinaigrette.

¼ cup	butter	50 mL	Pinch	cayenne pepper	Pinch
1	small onion, chopped	1	2 tbsp	chopped fresh dill	25 mL
1 cup	sliced mushrooms	250 mL	1 lb	each cooked flaked salmon,	500 g
¼ cup	all-purpose flour	50 mL		crab and shrimp	
1 tsp	dried tarragon	5 mL	½ cup	sour cream	125 mL
1 cup	clam juice	250 mL	1 cup	shredded Swiss cheese	250 mL
⅔ cup	light cream or milk	150 mL	•	Flaky Pastry (recipe follows)	•
2 tsp	Dijon mustard	10 mL	1	egg	1
¼ tsp	each salt and black pepper	1 mL	1 tbsp	milk	15 mL

FLAKY PASTRY

1 cup	all-purpose flour	250 mL	2 oz	cold cream cheese, cubed	50 g
Pinch	salt	Pinch	2 tbsp	sour cream	25 mL
¼ cup	cold butter, cubed	50 mL	2 tbsp	ice water	25 mL

In a large skillet, melt the butter over medium heat; add the onion and mushrooms and cook for 7 minutes. Stir in the flour and tarragon; cook, stirring, for 1 minute. Whisk in the clam juice and cream; cook, stirring constantly, until thickened. Stir in the mustard, salt, pepper and cayenne. Remove from the heat and stir in the dill; transfer to a bowl, cover with plastic wrap and refrigerate until cool.

Gently stir the salmon, crab, shrimp and sour cream into the cooled mushroom mixture. Spread in a greased 8-cup (2 L) round or 11- × 7-inch (2 L) rectangular glass baking dish. Sprinkle the Swiss cheese overtop. (The filling can be covered and refrigerated for up to 1 day.) Roll out the pastry to a 9-inch (23 cm) circle or a 12- × 8-inch (30 × 20 cm) rectangle. Place over the filling and crimp the edges.

Beat the egg with the milk; brush over the pastry. Cut steam vents. If desired, make decorative cut-outs from the pastry scraps; arrange on top and brush with the glaze. Bake in a 425°F (220°C) oven for 15 minutes. Reduce the heat to 375°F (190°C); bake until the pastry is golden brown and the filling is steaming, 30 to 40 minutes longer. Let stand for 5 to 10 minutes before serving. *Makes 8 servings.*

FLAKY PASTRY: In a food processor, blend the flour with the salt; pulse in the butter and cream cheese until crumbly. Add the sour cream and ice water; pulse briefly until combined. (Do not overprocess.) Gather the pastry together and transfer it to a lightly floured surface. Knead gently a few times just to form it into a ball. Press into a disc; wrap in plastic wrap and refrigerate until chilled, about 30 minutes. (The pastry can be refrigerated for up to 1 day or frozen for up to 2 months.) *Makes enough for an 8- or 9-inch (20 or 23 cm) pie.*

GRILLED ARCTIC CHAR *with* ORANGE-ONION SALSA

Arctic char is very popular in the North and gaining fans in the South, where it is perfect barbecue fare because of its firm, mild flesh. If Arctic char is unavailable, substitute salmon for this easy recipe of slow-grilled fish and a fresh-tasting sauce.

1 lb	Arctic char fillet (with skin)	500 g	¼ cup	chopped fresh coriander or parsley	50 mL
1	medium orange	1			
2 tbsp	canola oil	25 mL	½	medium red onion, chopped	½
¼ cup	fresh lime juice	50 mL	1	clove garlic, minced	1
•	Salt and black pepper	•	½ tsp	ground cumin	2 mL
¼ tsp	cayenne	1 mL	¼ cup	coarsely chopped black olives	50 mL

Place the fish in a shallow glass dish. With a zester or coarse grater, remove the outer zest from the orange. (You should have about 2 tbsp/25 mL.) Whisk together half the zest, the oil, half the lime juice, a pinch of pepper and half the cayenne. Pour over the fish and turn to coat well, leaving it skin side up. Cover and marinate for 30 minutes at room temperature or up to 2 hours in the refrigerator.

Meanwhile, make the salsa. Remove the remaining white part of the rind from the orange and, holding the orange over a dish to catch any juice, cut it into segments with a sharp knife, cutting between the membrane and the flesh. Cut each segment in two, place in the dish and stir in the remaining lime juice, salt and pepper to taste, the remaining cayenne, fresh coriander, onion, garlic, cumin and olives. The salsa can be prepared, covered and refrigerated for up to 2 hours.

Discarding the marinade, place the fillet, skin side down, on a greased grill over low heat; close the lid and cook until the fish is opaque and flakes easily when tested with a fork, about 20 to 30 minutes. Insert a spatula between the skin and the fish, removing the fish and leaving the skin on the grill. (When the grill cools, it will come off easily.) Serve accompanied by the salsa. *Makes 2 to 3 servings.*

∧ *Inuvik, Northwest Territories (bottom)*

MUSSELS *in* COCONUT BROTH

Moules marinière, mussels steamed with white wine, is a wonderfully simple classic dish we've adopted from the French. I remember particularly enjoying a fine Belgian version topped with frites at Henry Burger's in Hull, Quebec. For a change of pace, try this Thai twist—particularly good as a starter for an Asian menu. You will find everything in a large supermarket, but if you are shopping in an Asian market, you can substitute eight torn kaffir lime leaves for the lime zest.

^ *Toasting summer with champagne near Niagara-on-the-Lake*

2	stalks lemon grass	2	1 cup	chicken stock	250 mL
1	small fresh chili pepper, seeded and chopped	1	1	can (14 oz/398 mL) light coconut milk	1
1	clove garlic, chopped	1	4 lb	mussels, scrubbed and debearded	2 kg
1 tbsp	chopped fresh ginger	15 mL			
1	strip (2 inch/5 cm) lime zest	1	½ cup	chopped fresh coriander	125 mL
1 cup	bottled clam juice	250 mL	•	Lime wedges	•

Trim off the tops and ends of the lemon grass, removing the outer layers, then chop coarsely. Combine the lemon grass, chili, garlic, ginger and lime zest in a food processor (preferably a mini chopper) and whiz to a coarse paste.

In a large saucepan, combine the clam juice, chicken stock, coconut milk and lemon grass paste; bring to a boil, reduce the heat and simmer for 5 minutes. Add the mussels, cover and cook, shaking the pan over the heat occasionally, until all the mussels have opened, 3 to 5 minutes. Discard any that don't open. Serve sprinkled with coriander and accompanied by lime wedges. *Makes 4 main-course servings or 6 to 8 starters.*

NOTE: When you buy fresh mussels, remove them from the plastic bag and refrigerate in a bowl draped with damp paper towel, or wrap them in damp newspaper. Cultured mussels will often gape open, but they should close when tapped or rinsed under cold water. Just before cooking, scrub and remove any beards, discarding mussels that do not close when tapped.

Pickerel BLT *(facing page)*

PICKEREL BLT

Fish gains a new dimension of flavour on the barbecue. Cooked skin side down, it holds its shape for this fun take on an old favourite sandwich. Pickerel has firm, flaky white flesh and lovely flavour, but you can use any firm-fleshed fish here.

½ cup	mayonnaise	125 mL
2	cloves garlic, minced	2
1 tbsp	paprika, preferably smoked	15 mL
½ tsp	black pepper	2 mL
Pinch	cayenne pepper	Pinch
1 lb	pickerel fillets with skin	500 g
8	slices sturdy white bread or 4 crusty rolls	8
2	tomatoes, sliced	2
•	Salt and pepper	•
8	slices crisply cooked side bacon	8
4	leaves lettuce (leaf or Boston)	4

In a small bowl, stir together the mayonnaise, garlic, paprika, black pepper and cayenne. Remove two-thirds of the mixture to another bowl and set aside. Spread the remainder on the flesh side of the fish.

Place the fish, skin side down, on a greased grill over medium heat. Close the lid and cook until the fish is opaque and flakes easily with a fork, about 16 minutes.

Meanwhile, toast the bread and spread one side of each slice thinly with the reserved mayonnaise mixture. Top 4 slices with tomato and sprinkle them with salt and pepper. Place 2 strips of bacon on each. Insert a spatula between the skin and the fish, removing the fish and leaving the skin on the grill. (When the grill cools it will come off easily.) Place one-quarter of the fish on each sandwich; top with lettuce. Top with the remaining toast slices and serve immediately. *Makes 4 servings.*

OYSTER STEW

Oysters have a long history as holiday food in Canada. Even in Ontario, midway between two oceans, barrels of fresh oysters were brought from the coast in the 19th century. Our family has continued this tradition by serving oysters on the half shell on Christmas Eve each year, and we also enjoy this hearty stew at some point over the Christmas season. It would make a great après-ski dish with rolls and a green salad.

½ cup	unsalted butter	125 mL
1 cup	finely chopped celery	250 mL
1 cup	leeks, white and light green parts only, thinly sliced	250 mL
1 cup	finely grated carrots	250 mL
1	onion, finely chopped	1
½ cup	whole wheat or all-purpose flour	125 mL
2 cups	light cream	500 mL
2 cups	milk	500 mL
2 cups	shucked oysters with liquor (about 30 oysters)	500 mL
1 cup	minced clams with liquor	250 mL
•	Pepper	•
•	Fresh coriander or parsley sprigs	•

In a large saucepan, melt half the butter; stir in the celery, leeks, carrots and onion. Cover tightly and cook over low heat for 30 minutes, stirring occasionally.

Meanwhile, in a separate saucepan, heat the remaining butter over medium heat; whisk in the flour and cook, stirring, for 2 or 3 minutes. Do not brown. Remove from the heat and gradually whisk in the cream and milk. Return to the heat and cook until smooth and thickened, whisking constantly. Stir the sauce into the vegetable mixture. Add the oysters and clams with their liquor; cook, uncovered, over low heat until the oysters just start to curl, about 5 minutes. Season with pepper to taste; garnish each serving with coriander or parsley. *Makes about 8 servings.*

THE NORTH

THIS VAST EXPANSE OF LAND called the North includes Yukon, Northwest Territories and Nunavut. It encompasses one-third of Canada's land mass and is sparsely populated. Aboriginal peoples make up most of this population, with the Inuit living on the coast and the Arctic Archipelago.

For generations, Native peoples were self-sufficient, following the cycle of the seasons and herds of caribou, always moving camp to new hunting and gathering grounds. That lifestyle started to change when the first European fur traders and whalers introduced their goods and the ways of the outside world. Many Inuit moved into permanent settlements and began to live on foods very different from their traditional diet. In remote areas, caribou, muskox, moose, seal, fish and wild birds remained staples, but a mixed diet of these foods and imported white bread, sugar, canned and packaged foods became common.

The communities of Dawson and Whitehorse were settled during the gold rush at the end of the 19th century. Whitehorse and Yellowknife became territorial capitals in the middle of the 20th century, and a large number of outsiders began arriving to work in government and business.

Food remains a difficult commodity to procure since provisions shipped in from the South are expensive, and fruits and vegetables aren't easy to grow here. But the land, as it has always done, still provides. There's a huge range of wild animals: muskox and hare in the High Arctic islands, caribou and ptarmigan in the barrens and woodlands, moose in the lowlands. An incredible variety of birds, including wild geese, partridge and pheasant, are either traditionally dried or frozen for winter eating. With many little lakes, two large freshwater lakes (Great Slave and Great Bear) and endless miles of coastline, there is an abundance of both freshwater and saltwater species: lake trout, pickerel, pike, jackfish, whitefish, Arctic char, clams, baby shrimp, seal and whale.

Of necessity, cuisine in the North is a blend of ancient tradition and modern taste, using whatever ingredients, homegrown or imported, fresh or preserved, are available. But whatever is served is offered with a spirit of true Canadian hospitality.

A MIDNIGHT SUN SUPPER

Wild Rice Pancakes with Sour Cream
and (Whitefish) Caviar
(page 15)

Grilled Arctic Char with
Orange-Onion Salsa
(page 69)

Wild Rice and Cranberry Salad
(page 172)

Cheddar Jalapeño Cornbread
(page 55)

(Wild) Blueberry Bread Pudding
with Whisky Sauce
(page 216)

POULTRY

ROAST CHICKEN WITH
GARLIC ~ 77

CURRIED CHICKEN POT PIE
WITH PHYLLO CRUST ~ 78

NEW WORLD COQ
AU VIN ~ 79

GREEN CURRY CHICKEN ~ 80

GREEK GRILLED CHICKEN ~ 81

MOROCCAN CHICKEN STEW WITH
SAFFRON DUMPLINGS ~ 82

CHICKEN PIRI PIRI ~ 84

CHICKEN TORTILLA WRAPS ~ 84

ROAST PHEASANT WITH
HONEY-FIG SAUCE ~ 85

CHINESE-STYLE ROAST DUCK ~ 86

CITRUS-GLAZED ROAST GOOSE ~ 89

WILD MUSHROOM AND LEEK
STUFFING ~ 90

ROAST TURKEY WITH WILD RICE
AND SAUSAGE STUFFING ~ 91

ROAST CHICKEN *with* GARLIC

Sometimes, I roast unpeeled cloves of garlic with chicken, then squeeze the soft pulp into the gravy. This time, I'm suggesting a garlicky mixture to be massaged under the skin for a succulent, moist roast. If you butterfly the chicken, it cooks more evenly and faster, but you can also roast the chicken whole; just allow more time.

1	roasting chicken	1	½ tsp	sea salt	2 mL
	(4 to 5 lb/2 to 2.5 kg)		½ tsp	pepper	2 mL
½	lemon	½	1 cup	chicken stock	250 mL
1 tbsp	soft butter	15 mL	1 tbsp	soy sauce	15 mL
2 tsp	Dijon mustard	10 mL	1 tbsp	cornstarch	15 mL
3	cloves garlic, minced	3			

If you wish to butterfly the chicken, cut out the backbone. Set the chicken breast side down and use sturdy kitchen shears. Cut down along both sides of the backbone, staying as close as possible to the bone. Open up the chicken like a book; flip over on its back and flatten with your hands. Rinse and pat dry. Rub all over with the lemon half and place skin side up.

In a small bowl, stir together the butter, mustard, garlic, salt and pepper. With your fingers, carefully loosen the skin from the breast and thighs. Rub most of the butter mixture evenly under the skin and rub the remainder on the outside of the drumsticks. (The chicken can be prepared, covered and refrigerated for up to 8 hours. Bring to room temperature before roasting.)

Place the chicken, skin side up, on a rack in a shallow roasting pan and roast in a 400°F (200°C) oven until an instant-read thermometer inserted into the thickest part of the thigh registers 185°F (85°C), about 1 hour and 15 minutes. Transfer to a warm platter, tent with foil and let rest for 10 to 15 minutes before carving, to allow the juices to settle into the meat.

Skim any fat from the pan drippings. Place the roasting pan over high heat; stir in the stock and soy sauce. Bring to a boil. Dissolve the cornstarch in 1 tbsp (15 mL) cold water. Slowly stir into the pan and cook, stirring, until thickened. Season to taste with salt and pepper; serve in a warm gravy boat alongside the chicken. *Makes 6 servings.*

CURRIED CHICKEN POT PIE
with PHYLLO CRUST

A crisp, light phyllo crust lifts this delicious pot pie into make-ahead company fare.

1 tbsp	canola oil	15 mL	1 lb	butternut squash or sweet	500 g
2 tbsp	curry paste (mild Madras)	25 mL		potatoes, diced (½-inch	
1	large leek, white and light	1		/1 cm) (about 3 cups/750 mL)	
	green parts only, thinly sliced		1	sweet red pepper, diced	1
	(about 1½ cups/375 mL)		6 cups	diced cooked chicken or turkey	1.5 L
1	can (14 oz/398 mL) light	1	4 tsp	cornstarch	20 mL
	coconut milk		4 tsp	fresh lime juice	20 mL
1 cup	chicken stock	250 mL	1 cup	fresh or frozen green peas	250 mL
			6	sheets phyllo pastry	6
			3 tbsp	melted butter	45 mL

In a large saucepan over medium-low heat, heat the oil; stir in the curry paste and leek. Cook, stirring, until the leek is softened, about 5 minutes. Stir in the coconut milk, stock, squash and red pepper. Bring to a boil, stirring up any bits from the bottom of the pan. Cover, reduce the heat and simmer until the squash is tender, about 10 minutes. Stir in the chicken, bring back to a simmer and cook for 5 minutes.

In a small bowl, stir together the cornstarch and lime juice; add a little of the cooking liquid, then stir the mixture back into the pan. Cook, stirring, for 2 minutes. Remove from the heat and let cool slightly. Stir in the peas. Pour into an ungreased 13- × 9-inch (3 L) baking dish. Refrigerate until cold.

Place the sheets of phyllo pastry between 2 sheets of waxed paper; cover with a damp tea towel to prevent them from drying out. Place 1 of the sheets over the chicken mixture, folding under the excess pastry around the edges to fit inside the dish. Lightly brush the pastry with butter. Repeat with the remaining sheets and butter, making sure to brush the top sheet. (The recipe can be prepared to this point, covered and refrigerated for up to 12 hours. Remove from the refrigerator 30 minutes before cooking.)

Bake in a 375°F (190°C) oven until the pastry is golden and the filling bubbly, 25 to 30 minutes. *Makes 4 to 6 servings.*

NEW WORLD COQ *au* VIN

In the 1960s, we were all enamoured with trying our hand at fancy French dishes when we cooked for company. Coq au Vin was one of the first "grown-up" recipes many of us learned to make and it's still a great favourite. I've streamlined the method but left the flavour. Rather than a French Burgundy, Beaujolais or Côtes du Rhône red, try a Canadian white such as Chardonnay or Sauvignon Blanc.

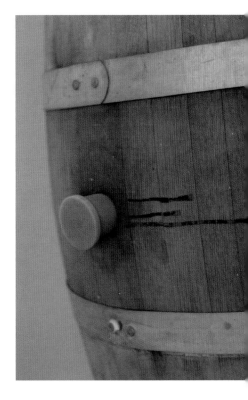

1 tbsp	butter	15 mL	•	All-purpose flour	•
1 tbsp	olive oil	15 mL	1½ cups	white wine	375 mL
12	peeled pearl or	12	1¼ cups	chicken stock	300 mL
	silver skin onions		2	cloves garlic, minced	2
8 oz	pancetta,* diced	250 g	4	sprigs fresh thyme	4
8 oz	small cremini mushrooms	250 g		(or 1 tsp/5 mL dried)	
8	bone-in chicken thighs	8	1 tbsp	tomato paste	15 mL
	with skin		½ cup	chopped fresh parsley	125 mL
•	Salt and pepper	•			

∧   *Wine barrel*

In a large ovenproof skillet, melt the butter in the oil over medium heat. Cook the onions and pancetta until golden, about 5 minutes. With a slotted spoon, remove to a plate and set aside. Add the mushrooms to the skillet and cook until softened, about 3 minutes. Remove with a slotted spoon to the plate with the onions. Increase the heat to medium-high.

   Sprinkle the thighs with salt and pepper, then coat with the flour. Add half the chicken to the skillet, skin side down, and cook, turning once, until browned, 12 to 14 minutes. Transfer to a plate and repeat with the remaining chicken. Pour off any fat from the skillet and add the wine. Bring to a boil, stirring up any brown bits from the bottom of the pan; boil gently for 5 minutes. Stir in the stock, garlic, thyme and tomato paste; bring to a boil, stirring. Return the chicken to the pan and nestle the onions, mushrooms and pancetta around it. Bring to a simmer and place, uncovered, in a 350°F (180°C) oven; cook until the chicken is no longer pink inside, 45 minutes. (The chicken can be cooled, covered and refrigerated for up to 1 day. Reheat in a 350°F (180°C) oven, uncovered, until hot through-out, 30 to 40 minutes.) Sprinkle with parsley to serve. *Makes 4 servings.*

* Pancetta is unsmoked Italian bacon available at most supermarket deli counters.

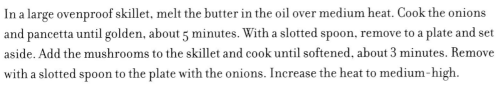

GREEN CURRY CHICKEN

In the Canadian love affair with all Thai food, this is probably the most popular chicken dish. Green curry paste is available in the Asian section of most large supermarkets. It can be quite fiery, so add the amount that suits your own taste.

¾ lb	boneless skinless chicken breasts	375 g	2 tbsp	fish sauce	25 mL
			1 tbsp	packed brown sugar	15 mL
1	can (14 oz/398 mL) coconut milk	1	1 tsp	grated lime zest or 3 torn	5 mL
1 tbsp	green curry paste (or more to taste)	15 mL		kaffir lime leaves (stems removed)	
¾ lb	small purple Asian egg-plants, trimmed and cut into ½-inch (1 cm) pieces	375 g	•	Salt and pepper	•
			2	large chilies, 1 green and 1 red, thickly sliced on the diagonal	2
1 cup	lightly packed fresh basil leaves	250 mL		(optional)	

Thinly slice the chicken across the grain and set aside.

Being sure not to shake the coconut milk can, open it and pour off and reserve the thin liquid from the top. Spoon out ⅔ cup (150 mL) of the thick milk. Combine the remainder of the milk in the can with the reserved thin milk and set aside.

In a non-stick wok or very large skillet over medium-high heat, fry the ⅔ cup (150 mL) thick milk, stirring constantly, until the oil begins to separate out, about 5 to 8 minutes. Add the curry paste and stir-fry until fragrant, 1 to 2 minutes. Add the eggplant; stir-fry for 2 minutes. Add the chicken; stir-fry for 1 minute. Stir in the remaining coconut milk; bring to a boil. Reduce the heat to medium-low; simmer uncovered, stirring often, until the eggplant is slightly soft and the chicken is no longer pink inside, about 4 minutes.

Stir in half the basil, the fish sauce, sugar and lime zest. Taste and add salt and pepper if necessary. Spoon into a warm serving dish; garnish with the chilies and remaining basil leaves. Serve immediately. *Makes 4 servings.*

GREEK GRILLED CHICKEN

One of the most popular salads in Canadian restaurants is lemony Greek salad with its feta and olives, and I've used these familiar flavours in this easy barbecued chicken recipe. A simple marinade and a fresh tomato salad to tuck into the pitas with the grilled chicken all bring Greek sunshine to your table. Slice a cucumber to add to the pitas if you like.

¼ cup	fresh lemon juice	50 mL	1 tsp	grated lemon zest	5 mL
3 tbsp	olive oil	45 mL	¾ cup	feta cheese, crumbled	175 mL
1 tbsp	chopped fresh oregano	15 mL	¼ cup	black olives, coarsely	50 mL
	(or 1 tsp/5 mL dried)			chopped (about 12)	
4	skinless boneless chicken	4	¼ cup	chopped fresh parsley	50 mL
	breast halves		•	Salt and pepper	•
4	small tomatoes, sliced	4	4	pita breads, halved	4

In a glass dish just big enough to hold the chicken in a single layer, combine 3 tbsp (45 mL) of the lemon juice, 2 tbsp (25 mL) of the oil and the oregano. Add the chicken and turn to coat well. Cover and marinate for 1 hour (or up to 4 hours in the refrigerator).

In a shallow bowl, arrange the tomato slices and drizzle with the remaining lemon juice and oil; sprinkle with the lemon zest, feta cheese, olives, parsley, and salt and pepper to taste. Set aside at room temperature for up to 2 hours.

Place the chicken on a greased grill over medium heat and sprinkle with salt and pepper. Cook until no longer pink inside, about 8 to 12 minutes, turning once. Wrap the pita breads in foil and place on the side of the grill to heat through during the last few minutes. Open the pitas up to form pockets. Cut the chicken into thin slices and tuck into the pita pockets; tuck the tomato salad alongside and serve immediately. *Makes 4 servings.*

MOROCCAN CHICKEN STEW *with* SAFFRON DUMPLINGS

One of my husband, Kent's, all-time favourite suppers is what he calls Chicken and Dumplings—chicken braised with herbs, potatoes, carrots, parsnips and onions, then topped with fluffy dumplings. When I switched to Middle Eastern flavours in this version, he was still pretty happy. Be sure to use a pot large enough to allow 3 inches (8 cm) of space for the dumplings to rise.

4	whole chicken legs	4	4	carrots, quartered	4
2 tbsp	all-purpose flour	25 mL	2	onions, quartered	2
2 tsp	ground cumin	10 mL	2½ cups	chicken broth	625 mL
1 tsp	ground ginger	5 mL	1 tbsp	liquid honey	15 mL
¼ tsp	ground cinnamon	1 mL	½ cup	dried apricots	125 mL
¼ tsp	cayenne	1 mL	1 cup	fresh or frozen peas	250 mL
2 tbsp	olive oil	25 mL			

SAFFRON DUMPLINGS

2 cups	sifted cake and pastry flour (approx)	500 mL	¼ tsp	saffron, crumbled	1 mL
			2 tbsp	shortening	25 mL
4 tsp	baking powder	20 mL	⅔ cup	milk (approx)	150 mL
½ tsp	salt	2 mL			

Separate the drumsticks from the thighs and wipe the chicken with paper towels.

In a sturdy plastic bag, combine the flour, cumin, ginger, cinnamon and cayenne. Shake the chicken in the bag, in batches, to coat all the pieces with the flour mixture.

In a large saucepan, heat half the oil over medium heat. Add the chicken in batches and brown on all sides, adding more oil as needed; remove the browned pieces to a warm bowl.

Add the carrots and onions to the pan; cook for 5 minutes, stirring often. Stir in the broth; bring to a boil, scraping up any brown bits from the bottom of the pan.

Return the chicken and any juices to the pan; stir in the honey and apricots. Return to a boil; reduce the heat to very low, cover and simmer until the chicken is tender and no longer pink inside, about 40 to 45 minutes. Stir in the peas. Taste and adjust the seasoning if necessary.

SAFFRON DUMPLINGS: Meanwhile, stir or sift together the flour, baking powder, salt and saffron in a large bowl. Cut in the shortening until the mixture is the consistency of oatmeal. Stir in the milk, adding a few more drops if necessary to make a sticky dough.

Evenly dust a large plate with flour. With a tablespoon, cut out dumplings and drop onto the floured plate. Quickly drop the dumplings onto the gently simmering stew, spacing them evenly. Cover the pan tightly and simmer, without lifting the lid, for 15 minutes. Serve immediately. *Makes 4 servings.*

CHICKEN PIRI PIRI

In Cambridge, Ontario, where I live, there is a large Portuguese population, happily resulting in a number of good Portuguese grocery stores that are my source for chorizo, Portuguese cheeses, hot piri piri sauce and breads. Talking to the proprietors of these shops inspired me to travel to Portugal. On one of our trips there, our apartment was within walking distance of a lovely little neighbourhood restaurant that made delicious grilled Piri Piri Chicken. If you can find piri piri sauce and want a fierier version, substitute it for the hot pepper flakes.

2	cloves garlic, minced	2
1	bay leaf, finely crushed	1
2 tsp	paprika	10 mL
1 tsp	hot pepper flakes	5 mL
1 tsp	coarse sea or kosher salt	5 mL
¼ tsp	black pepper	1 mL
¼ cup	dry white wine	50 mL
2 tbsp	olive oil	25 mL
4	chicken legs (thighs and drumsticks attached)	4

If you have a mini chopper, combine the garlic, bay leaf, paprika, hot pepper flakes, salt and pepper in it and process into a paste. If not, chop the garlic and bay leaf as fine as possible and combine with the other ingredients in a small bowl. Stir in the wine and olive oil. Place the chicken in a sturdy plastic bag and pour in the marinade. Close tightly and squeeze to coat the chicken well. Place in a bowl in the refrigerator for at least 4 hours and up to 24 hours, turning occasionally.

Let stand at room temperature for 30 minutes. Reserving the marinade, place the chicken, skin side down, on a greased grill over medium heat; close the lid and cook for 10 minutes. Turn the chicken and brush with the marinade; discard any remaining marinade. Cook the chicken until the juices run clear, about 35 to 40 minutes longer, watching the temperature carefully. *Makes 4 servings.*

CHICKEN TORTILLA WRAPS

My son and daughter-in-law get constant requests for these juicy wraps from their cottage friends. If you wish, form them into round patties and serve on lightly toasted hamburger buns with guacamole and sliced tomato. Start the meal with thick corn chowder (see page 36) and pass pieces of melon for dessert.

1	egg	1
¼ cup	dry breadcrumbs	50 mL
2 tbsp	grated red onion	25 mL
2 tbsp	fresh lime juice	25 mL
2 tsp	chili powder	10 mL
¾ tsp	salt	4 mL
1 lb	lean ground chicken	500 g
•	Canola oil	•
4	flour tortillas (10 inches/25 cm)	4
1	avocado, sliced	1
•	Shredded lettuce	•
•	Tomato salsa	•
•	Sour cream	•

In a bowl, beat the egg; stir in the breadcrumbs, onion, lime juice, chili powder and salt. Gently mix in the chicken and lightly shape into 4 long ovals about 2 inches (5 cm) wide and ¾ inch (2 cm) thick. (The recipe can be made ahead to this point. Cover and refrigerate up to 1 hour.)

Brush both sides of the burgers with oil. Place on an oiled barbecue grill over medium heat and cook, turning once, until the centres are no longer pink, 5 to 6 minutes per side.

Meanwhile, stack the tortillas and wrap in foil. Place on the side of the grill to warm.

Place a burger in the centre of each warm tortilla. Set out avocado, lettuce, salsa and sour cream in individual bowls. Everyone can add his or her own toppings and roll up the tortilla to enclose the burger and toppings. *Makes 4 burgers or wraps.*

ROAST PHEASANT *with* HONEY-FIG SAUCE

Hunting wild birds has long been a tradition across the country. Hunters in the Prairies might return with duck and prairie chicken; for Newfoundlanders and northerners, it could be partridge, ptarmigan, turrs and wild geese; in Ontario, wild grouse, ducks and pheasant. If fresh figs are unavailable, substitute dried figs, stemmed and quartered.

1	pheasant (about 2 lb/1 kg)	1	3 tbsp	liquid honey	45 mL
12	small shallots or pearl onions	12	1 tbsp	fresh lemon juice	15 mL
¼ cup	butter	50 mL	•	Bouquet garni*	•
•	Salt and pepper	•	4	fresh figs, stemmed	4
1 cup	dry white wine	250 mL		and quartered	
1 tbsp	brandy	15 mL	2 tbsp	all-purpose flour	25 mL
¼ cup	chopped dried figs	50 mL	1 cup	chicken stock	250 mL

^ *Fresh figs (top)*

^ *Honey (bottom)*

Remove any giblets from the pheasant, reserving them for another use, such as stock.

Pat the pheasant dry inside and out with paper towels. Place 2 shallots in the cavity and truss the pheasant by tying the legs together and the wings to the sides.

In a large skillet, melt half the butter over medium-high heat. Add the pheasant and cook, turning it until it's browned on all sides, 6 to 8 minutes. Place the pheasant breast side up on a rack in a shallow roasting pan. Sprinkle with salt and pepper and drizzle with any butter remaining in the skillet. Roast, uncovered, in a 400°F (200°C) oven, basting occasionally with pan juices, until a meat thermometer inserted in the thigh registers 185°F (85°C) and the juices run clear when a thigh is pierced with a skewer, 45 to 55 minutes.

Meanwhile, melt the remaining butter in the same skillet over medium heat. Add the remaining 10 shallots and cook, stirring, until golden, 5 minutes. Stir in the wine and brandy and bring to a boil, scraping up any brown bits from the bottom of the skillet. Stir in the dried figs, honey, lemon juice and bouquet garni; reduce the heat to medium-low. Cover and cook until the shallots are just tender when pierced with a knife, about 10 minutes. Add the fresh figs and simmer for 2 minutes. (The shallots and sauce can be prepared 1 day ahead, covered and refrigerated. Bring to a simmer before basting the pheasant.) Five minutes before the pheasant is cooked, baste with some of the juices from the skillet.

Remove the pheasant to a warm platter. With a slotted spoon, arrange the shallots and fig quarters around it, tent loosely with foil and let stand in a warm place while you finish the sauce.

* Make a bouquet garni by enclosing 3 sprigs of fresh parsley, 3 sprigs of fresh thyme (or 1 tsp/5 mL dried) and 2 bay leaves inside two stalks of celery and tie well with string.

(continued on next page)

ROAST PHEASANT *with* HONEY-FIG
 SAUCE *(continued)*

Place the roasting pan over a burner and stir the flour into the drippings. Cook, stirring, over medium heat for 2 minutes. Gradually stir in the stock and the contents of the skillet; cook, stirring, until thickened and bubbly, 3 to 5 minutes. Discard the bouquet garni and season to taste with salt and pepper. Carve the pheasant and serve with the sauce. *Makes 4 servings.*

CHINESE-STYLE ROAST DUCK

Instead of steaming the duck first, I've roasted it in a low oven with Asian seasonings, then raised the heat to crisp and brown it for an easy interpretation of Chinese-style duck. Serve with Wasabi Mashed Potatoes (page 142) and Sautéed Sugar Snaps (page 148).

1	duck (about 4 lb/2 kg)	1
1¼ tsp	five-spice powder*	6 mL
4	slices fresh ginger	4
2	cloves garlic, slightly crushed	2
4 tsp	soy sauce	20 mL
2 tsp	rice vinegar	10 mL

Rinse the duck and pat it dry with paper towels. Using a needle, prick the skin all over on an angle, being careful not to prick the meat. Rub ¼ tsp (1 mL) of the five-spice powder inside the duck and place the ginger and garlic in the cavity. Rub the remaining five-spice powder all over the outside of the duck. Combine the soy sauce and vinegar; brush all over the outside and place the duck on a rack in a shallow roasting pan. Roast, uncovered, in a 275°F (140°C) oven for 3 hours. Increase the temperature to 400°F (200°C) and roast until the skin is crisp and brown, 30 to 40 minutes longer. *Makes 4 servings.*

* Five-spice powder, usually comprised of equal amounts of ground Szechwan peppercorns, cloves, cinnamon, fennel seeds and star anise, is now available in most supermarkets.

Chinese-Style Roast Duck (facing page)

CITRUS-GLAZED ROAST GOOSE

Geese were useful additions to pioneer farms. Their down provided warm quilts for cold winter nights; their feathers and wings made excellent dusters; their eggs were worth four hens' eggs; and they provided a beautiful Christmas dinner long before people raised and ate turkey. If cooked with care, a roast goose can be grease free; the citrus in this burnished beauty cuts the richness as well. The Wild Mushroom and Leek Stuffing (page 90), heated alongside in a greased baking dish, would be delicious with the goose.

1	goose (10 to 11 lb/4.5 to 5 kg)	1	2 tbsp	orange liqueur	25 mL
½	lemon	½	1 tsp	soy sauce	5 mL
•	Salt and pepper	•	½ tsp	ground ginger	2 mL
1	orange, sliced	1	1 cup	orange juice	250 mL
4 cups	boiling water	1 L	1 tbsp	cornstarch	15 mL
½ cup	Seville orange marmalade	125 mL			

Remove any loose fat from the goose. Remove and reserve the giblets, neck and wing tips for making stock, if desired. Wipe the goose inside and out with a damp cloth and dry thoroughly. If desired, remove the wishbone for easier carving.

Rub the lemon half all over the goose inside and out, squeezing the juice as you do so. Sprinkle the cavities lightly with salt and pepper; place the orange slices in the cavities. Fasten the neck skin to the body with a skewer; skewer or sew the body cavity closed. With kitchen string, tie the legs together; tie the wings and legs close to the body. With a needle, prick the skin all over, being careful not to pierce the meat, to allow fat to escape during roasting. Place the goose, breast side down, on a rack in a large shallow roasting pan. Pour 2 cups (500 mL) of the boiling water over the goose. Roast, uncovered, in a 400°F (200°C) oven for 30 minutes.

Reduce the heat to 325°F (160°C); roast for 1 hour longer. Pour off and discard the liquid in the pan. Turn the goose over; prick again with the needle and pour the remaining 2 cups (500 mL) boiling water overtop. Roast for 1 hour longer. Prick the goose again. Pour off and discard the drippings in the pan. Roast for 1 hour longer.

Mix together the marmalade, liqueur, soy sauce and ginger; brush over the goose. Return to the oven and roast until the juices run clear when a thigh is pierced and a meat thermometer registers 190°F (90°C), 30 to 60 minutes longer (that is, 4 to 4½ hours in total). Transfer the goose to a cutting board, cover loosely with foil and let stand for 15 minutes before carving.

Meanwhile, skim all the fat from the pan; pour in the orange juice and bring to a boil, scraping up any brown bits from the bottom and mashing them. Dissolve the cornstarch in ¼ cup (50 mL) cold water; stir into the pan. Cook, whisking constantly, until slightly thickened. Season with salt and pepper to taste. Serve in a warm gravy boat alongside the goose. *Makes 8 servings.*

WILD MUSHROOM *and* LEEK STUFFING

Wild mushrooms and dried cranberries add lots of flavour to a fairly traditional stuffing.

∧   *French baguettes*

12 cups	cubed (1-inch/2.5 cm) Italian or French bread	3 L	1½ cups	chicken or turkey stock	375 mL
2 tbsp	olive oil	25 mL	¾ cup	dried cranberries	175 mL
•	Salt and pepper	•	¼ cup	chopped fresh parsley	50 mL
¼ cup	butter	50 mL	2 tbsp	chopped fresh sage (or 2 tsp/10 mL crumbled dried)	25 mL
3	leeks, white and light green parts only, cleaned and chopped	3	2 tbsp	chopped fresh thyme (or 2 tsp/10 mL crumbled dried)	25 mL
2	stalks celery, chopped	2			
1 lb	mixed wild mushrooms (cremini, shiitake, portobello), coarsely chopped	500 g			

Toss the bread cubes with the oil and spread out on a large rimmed baking sheet. Sprinkle with salt and pepper. Bake in a 375°F (190°C) oven until golden, about 20 minutes. Let cool.

In a large skillet, melt half the butter over medium-low heat. Add the leeks and celery; cook until softened, about 10 minutes, stirring often. Spoon into a large bowl. In the same skillet, melt the remaining butter over medium-high heat. Add the mushrooms, sprinkle with salt and pepper and cook until the liquid evaporates, about 8 minutes. Stir into the leek mixture. Stir in the bread cubes, stock, cranberries, parsley, sage and thyme. Season with salt and pepper to taste. *Makes 12 cups (3 L) stuffing, enough for a 16 to 20 lb (7.2 to 9 kg) turkey.*

ROAST TURKEY *with* WILD RICE
and SAUSAGE STUFFING

If your turkey is not big enough to accommodate all the stuffing, heat the extra in a greased casserole dish covered with foil alongside the turkey for the last 40 minutes of cooking. Drizzle with turkey drippings for extra flavour and moisture.

STUFFING

1 cup	wild rice	250 mL	2 cups	chopped celery	500 mL
2½ cups	chicken stock	625 mL	½ tsp	dried thyme	2 mL
1 lb	bulk sausage meat	500 g	½ tsp	crumbled dried sage	2 mL
2 tbsp	butter	25 mL	Pinch	granulated sugar	Pinch
2	onions, chopped	2	•	Salt and pepper	•
2	apples, peeled and diced	2			

TURKEY

1	turkey (12 to 16 lb/5.5 to 7.2 kg)	1	•	Salt and pepper	•
1/2	lemon	1/2	•	Canola oil	•

GRAVY

2½ cups	chicken or turkey stock	625 mL	2 tbsp	cornstarch	25 mL

STUFFING: Put the rice in a fine sieve and rinse under cold water. Combine the rice and stock in a medium saucepan. Bring to a boil, reduce the heat, partially cover and simmer until the rice is tender, 45 to 55 minutes. Drain in a sieve if necessary.

Meanwhile, in a large skillet over medium heat, cook the sausage meat, breaking it up with a spoon, until it is no longer pink, 10 to 15 minutes. With a slotted spoon, transfer to a large bowl.

Drain off any fat from the skillet and melt the butter over medium heat. Cook the onions and apples until soft, about 5 minutes. Add the celery, cover and cook for 5 minutes. Add to the sausage with the cooked rice, thyme, sage, sugar, and salt and pepper to taste. (The stuffing can be cooled, covered and refrigerated for up to 1 day. Bring to room temperature before using.)

TURKEY: Remove the giblets and neck from the turkey and reserve for stock, if desired. Pat the turkey dry inside and out. Rub the lemon half all over the turkey, inside and out, squeezing the juice as you do so. Sprinkle the inside of the turkey with salt and pepper.

Loosely stuff the neck and body cavities with stuffing, placing any extra in a casserole (see above). Skewer the cavities shut. Tie the legs together or tuck them under the band of skin; tuck the wings under the back. Place, breast side up, on a rack in a roasting pan.

(continued on next page)

ROAST TURKEY *with* WILD RICE *and* SAUSAGE STUFFING *(continued)*

Brush all over with oil and sprinkle with salt and pepper. Tent the turkey with foil, tucking in the sides but leaving the ends open. Roast in a 325°F (160°C) oven for 3 hours, basting occasionally (use canola oil until there are enough drippings). Remove the foil and roast until a meat thermometer inserted into the thickest part of the thigh registers 185°F (85°C), 45 to 60 minutes for the smaller turkey and 1 to 1½ hours longer for the bigger one. Transfer to a carving board and tent with foil; let stand for 20 or 30 minutes before carving. Remove the stuffing to a serving dish.

GRAVY: Remove any excess fat from the drippings left in the roasting pan. Place over medium heat and add the stock. Bring to a boil, stirring up any brown bits from the bottom. Dissolve the cornstarch in 2 tbsp (25 mL) cold water and add to the pan. Cook, stirring, until smooth and thickened, about 5 minutes. Season with salt and pepper to taste and serve in a warm gravy boat with turkey and stuffing. *Makes 8 to 16 servings (depending on the size of the turkey).*

PORK

SLOW-ROASTED PORK SHOULDER WITH
SPICED APPLE RELISH ~ 95

APPLE THYME GRILLED PORK CHOPS ~ 97

FRESH PINEAPPLE SWEET AND SOUR PORK ~ 97

MAPLE-GLAZED GRILLED PEAMEAL BACON ~ 98

CHIPOTLE MAPLE BAKED BEANS ~ 101

STICKY-CRISP BARBECUED RIBS ~ 101

Pork

The first permanent settlers of Upper Canada relied greatly on pork, relieved by fish and game when possible, since there was no feed for keeping cattle and sheep. The hams and shoulders were usually smoked (I remember my grandmother smoking these in a barrel over corncobs, but often maple sticks provided the smudge). The rest was preserved in strong brine as salt pork. In some places, a butchering bee was held and everything, even sausage making, was finished in one day.

I still think of pork as true Canadian meat and often serve it to international guests. It is certainly one of my favourites for dinner parties.

Sadly, the pigs bred for supermarkets are lean and homogeneous breeds that lack flavour and moisture. However, a few of the rare heritage breeds that have more fat to make the meat flavourful and moist are coming back. A couple of these heritage breeds are Berkshire and Tamworth.

Because of the higher fat content, it is harder to overcook heritage pork, unlike the leaner kind. For maximum tenderness of any type of pork, lean cuts like pork tenderloin and loin chops should be just slightly pink when served. For larger, tougher cuts like the shoulder, slow, long cooking is the key.

The other thing to avoid in supermarket pork is the word "seasoned," which means it has been injected with a brine containing salt and sodium phosphate. It's meant to ensure longer shelf life and to retain moisture even if it is overcooked, but the meat is less flavourful than unseasoned, and you are actually paying for water.

SLOW-ROASTED PORK SHOULDER
with SPICED APPLE RELISH

A pork roast is one of my favourite dinner party dishes. Slow-cooking this inexpensive cut renders the meat moist and absolutely delicious, especially when served with scalloped potatoes and creamy coleslaw. Leftovers make great sandwiches on country-style bread or ciabatta rolls.

8 lb	bone-in pork shoulder with skin	3.5 kg	½ tsp	pepper	2 mL
			¼ cup	fresh lemon juice	50 mL
6	cloves garlic, minced	6	2 tbsp	olive oil	25 mL
2 tbsp	fennel seeds	25 mL	1½ cups	apple cider	375 mL
½ tsp	hot pepper flakes	2 mL	•	Spiced Apple Relish	•
1 tsp	sea salt	5 mL		(recipe follows)	

Score the shoulder skin all over by slicing deeply about ½ inch (1 cm) apart. Make 1-inch-deep (2.5 cm) slits all over the meat side. In a mini chopper or by hand, chop the garlic, fennel seeds, hot pepper flakes, salt and pepper until coarsely ground. Rub all over the roast, pushing the mixture into the slices on the skin and slits in the meat. Cover with plastic wrap, set on a platter and marinate overnight in the refrigerator. Bring to room temperature for 30 minutes before roasting.

Place the pork, skin side up, on a rack in a shallow roasting pan. Roast, uncovered, in a 450°F (230°C) oven for 20 minutes. Pour half the lemon juice and the oil overtop and pour half the cider into the pan. Reduce the heat to 300°F (150°C) and roast for 2 hours. Baste with the remaining lemon juice and cider; roast for another 2½ hours. Transfer to a cutting board and let rest, covered with foil, for 20 minutes before carving. (Cut off bits of the crackle, or skin, as treats to serve on the meat platter.) Serve with Spiced Apple Relish. *Makes 8 servings with leftovers.*

SPICED APPLE RELISH

4	apples, peeled and diced	4	1	cinnamon stick (3 inches/8 cm)	1
3 tbsp	brown sugar	45 mL			
1 tbsp	fresh lemon juice	15 mL	Pinch	each of ground cloves and nutmeg	Pinch
½ tsp	hot pepper flakes	2 mL			
			¼ cup	apple cider	50 mL

Combine all the ingredients in an 8-inch (2 L) square baking dish, cover with foil and bake for 1 hour in a 300°F (150°C) oven. Remove the cinnamon stick and serve the relish warm. *Makes about 2 cups (500 mL).*

Apple Thyme Grilled
Pork Chops (facing page)

APPLE THYME GRILLED PORK CHOPS

Any fruit cooked on the barbecue is delicious, and grilled apple quarters make a juicy accompaniment for these easy pork chops.

4	pork loin chops (about ¾ inch/ 2 cm thick)	4
¼ cup	apple juice	50 mL
¼ cup	fresh lemon juice	50 mL
1 tbsp	cider vinegar	15 mL
1 tbsp	canola oil	15 mL
½ tsp	dried thyme	2 mL
2	apples, peeled and quartered	2
2 tbsp	liquid honey	25 mL

Trim the excess fat from the chops; arrange in a shallow dish.

Stir the apple juice, lemon juice, vinegar, oil and thyme together; pour over the chops, turning to coat. Cover and marinate in the refrigerator for at least 2 hours or up to 4 hours. Let stand at room temperature for 30 minutes.

Reserving the marinade in a small saucepan, place the chops on a greased grill over medium heat; cook, turning once, for 10 minutes or until still slightly pink inside.

Meanwhile, boil the marinade for 3 minutes. Dip the apples into the marinade and place on the grill. Stir the honey into the marinade; brush generously over the chops and apples. Cook, turning the apples often, for about 5 minutes longer or just until the pork is no longer pink inside and the apples are tender. *Makes 4 servings.*

FRESH PINEAPPLE SWEET *and* SOUR PORK

After the completion of the Canadian Pacific Railway in 1885, many Chinese people opened restaurants, originally in British Columbia, but eventually throughout the country. This simple dish was probably one of the first adapted to Canadian tastes and remains a favourite. Since we get such lovely fresh pineapples now, I've used fresh instead of the canned pineapple I used to use. Lean pork tenderloin makes it a quick dish that is delicious on hot steamed rice, a perfect mid-week family meal.

1 lb	pork tenderloin	500 g
4 tsp	cornstarch	20 mL
⅓ cup	rice vinegar	75 mL
3 tbsp	granulated sugar	45 mL
2 tbsp	ketchup	25 mL
2 tbsp	soy sauce	25 mL
3 tbsp	peanut or canola oil	45 mL
3	green onions, sliced	3
1	onion, cubed	1
1	sweet red pepper, cubed	1
1	clove garlic, minced	1
1 tbsp	minced fresh ginger	15 mL
2 cups	fresh pineapple cubes	500 mL

Cut the pork into ½-inch (1 cm) slices and cut the slices in two. Toss with the cornstarch and set aside. Whisk together the vinegar, sugar, ketchup and soy sauce until the sugar is dissolved; set aside.

In a large wok or skillet, heat the oil over high heat. Working in batches, stir-fry the pork until crisp and browned, removing each batch to a plate lined with paper towels.

Add 2 of the green onions, onion, red pepper, garlic and ginger to the wok; stir-fry for 2 minutes, adding more oil if necessary. Add the vinegar mixture and cook, stirring, until thick and bubbly. Add the pineapple, browned pork and remaining green onion. Stir to combine well and heat through. *Makes 4 servings.*

MAPLE-GLAZED GRILLED PEAMEAL BACON

Canadian back bacon (often coated with cornmeal and referred to as peameal bacon) is famous in other countries for its leanness and good flavour. It is good sliced and fried, and I often slow-roast a whole piece of it in the oven. However, if you do it on the barbecue as I have done here, you may never want to cook it any other way!

¼ cup	maple syrup	50 mL	1	centre-cut peameal bacon	1
2 tbsp	Dijon mustard	25 mL		roast (about 3 lb/1.5 kg)	
2 tsp	all-purpose flour	10 mL	•	Fresh parsley sprigs	•
½ tsp	black pepper	2 mL			

In a glass measure, whisk together the maple syrup, mustard, flour and pepper. Microwave on the High setting (100%) for 1 minute, until thickened; set aside. Or combine the maple syrup, mustard, flour and pepper in a small saucepan and cook over medium heat until thickened, about 5 minutes.

Preheat a gas barbecue to high. When hot, switch off one burner (if your barbecue has two burners) or the two outside burners on a three-burner grill; reduce the heat of the remaining burner to medium.

Rinse the bacon; pat it dry with paper towels. Put the bacon on the greased grill over the unlit burner; brush the top and sides with half the maple syrup mixture. Close the lid and cook for 30 minutes, checking often and adjusting the heat to maintain the grill temperature at about 350°F (180°C). (If your barbecue doesn't have a thermometer, set an oven thermometer on the top rack of the grill.)

Turn the bacon over and brush with the remaining glaze. Cook until a meat thermometer inserted in the centre of the roast registers 130°F (55°C), 35 to 45 minutes.

Remove the bacon to a cutting board. Tent loosely with foil; let stand for 10 minutes. Cut crosswise into thin slices; arrange on a heated platter and garnish with parsley sprigs. *Makes 6 to 8 servings.*

Maple-Glazed Grilled Peameal Bacon (facing page)
served with Chipotle Maple Baked Beans (page 101)

Dried Beans

Had it not been for dried beans and peas, many of our early settlers would have starved during the long Canadian winters. Native people, who were already growing beans, corn and squash ("the three sisters"), introduced beans to French settlers, who quickly made them a staple part of their diet. Then, and for years after, these low-cost vegetables were a crucial source of nutrition in an age before refrigeration and year-round fresh produce. In various parts of the country, especially the Maritimes, they even became a Saturday night tradition—baked beans with brown bread.

Navy beans are part of that group of legumes (seed pods that split on two sides when ripe, widely known as "pulses") that includes soybeans, chickpeas, kidney beans, peas and lentils. Rich in complex carbohydrates, they are an excellent source of plant protein, a good source of fibre and low in fat.

Of the 25 varieties of dried beans and lentils grown and used here, the white pea bean or navy bean is the most popular. Ontario's second-largest bean crop is the yellow-eye bean, a Maritimer's favourite with molasses. Soybeans are also widely grown in Ontario while lentils are grown mainly in the Prairies, with Saskatchewan leading the other provinces.

CHIPOTLE MAPLE BAKED BEANS

I usually start the fall season off with a big dish of baked beans for Halloween night. In this new version, the touch of heat and smokiness of chipotle complement the sweetness of maple syrup, and the very best accompaniment is creamy coleslaw. For a treat, I place strips of pork belly (side pork) in a single layer in a baking dish to roast alongside for the last two hours, until all the fat has been rendered out and the meat is very crisp.

3 cups	dried white pea (navy) beans	750 mL
4 oz	salt pork, diced	125 g
1	can (28 oz/796 mL) tomatoes, preferably crushed	1
1	Spanish onion, chopped	1
1 cup	maple syrup	250 mL
1 tbsp	chipotle chili pepper*	15 mL
½ tsp	salt	2 mL

Rinse the beans, discarding any blemished ones. In a large pot, cover the beans with about 12 cups (3 L) cold water; cover and refrigerate overnight.

Drain the beans, cover again with cold water and bring to a boil; reduce the heat and simmer, covered, until tender, for 30 to 40 minutes.

Reserving the cooking water, drain the beans and transfer to a 16-cup (4 L) casserole or bean pot. Stir in the salt pork, tomatoes and onion. Stir the maple syrup, chipotle chili pepper, salt and 1 cup (250 mL) of the cooking water together and pour over the bean mixture; stir well to combine. Cover and bake in a 300°F (150°C) oven for 3 hours, stirring once or twice. Uncover and bake until thickened, about another hour. *Makes 8 servings.*

* A powdered spice found in the spice aisle of the supermarket.

STICKY-CRISP BARBECUED RIBS

Ribs are an established part of the Canadian barbecue tradition. Oven-roast and marinate these delicious ribs the day before your party. They just need a quick grilling to heat them through and brown them. If you have smoked paprika on hand, you might like the added smokiness.

6 lb	meaty pork spareribs	2.7 kg
¾ cup	all-purpose flour	175 mL
1 tbsp	paprika, preferably smoked	15 mL
1	clove garlic, minced	1
¼ tsp	pepper	1 mL
¾ cup	chili sauce	175 mL
¾ cup	ketchup	175 mL
¼ cup	apple jelly	50 mL
2 tbsp	cider vinegar	25 mL
1 tbsp	Worcestershire sauce	15 mL
1 tsp	chili powder	5 mL

Trim any fat from the ribs. In a large plastic bag, combine the flour, paprika, garlic and pepper. Add the ribs (cut the racks in half if they're too big for the bag) and shake well to coat. Arrange, meaty side up, in a single layer in a shallow roasting pan or pans. Roast in a 325°F (160°C) oven until tender, about 1¼ hours.

In a saucepan, combine the chili sauce, ketchup, jelly, vinegar, Worcestershire sauce and chili powder. Bring to a boil, reduce the heat and simmer for 2 minutes; let cool. Pour the sauce over the ribs in the pan (or use a large plastic bag), turning the ribs to coat them well. Cover and marinate in the refrigerator for at least 4 hours or up to 24 hours.

Let stand at room temperature for 30 minutes before grilling. Reserving any sauce, place the ribs (meaty side up) on a greased grill over medium-high heat. Cook, brushing with sauce occasionally and turning once, until crisp and browned, about 15 minutes. Cut into serving pieces and serve immediately. *Makes 8 servings.*

BEEF & VEAL

PEPPERED ROAST TENDERLOIN
WITH RED WINE SAUCE ~ 103

MUSTARD-HERB ROAST BEEF ~ 105

SPICY DARK AND DELICIOUS
BEEF CHILI ~ 106

BEEF AND TOMATO CURRY ~ 107

OVEN-BRAISED SHORT RIBS
WITH CHINESE GREENS ~ 108

SIMPLE BEEF STEW WITH ORANGE-
WALNUT GREMOLATA ~ 109

BRAISED BEEF WITH CARAMELIZED
ROOT VEGETABLES ~ 110

CAESAR BURGERS ~ 112

GAME FILET WITH WILD
MUSHROOMS ~ 113

BRAISED VEAL SHANKS WITH
WILD MUSHROOMS AND
POTATOES ~ 115

TWO-CHEESE VEAL LOAF ~ 116

PAN-SEARED VEAL CHOPS WITH
BALSAMIC GLAZE ~ 116

PEPPERED ROAST TENDERLOIN
with RED WINE SAUCE

This beef tenderloin is simple but sophisticated company fare, and especially easy because you can make the sauce ahead of time.

1	beef tenderloin (3 lb/1.5 kg)	1	1 tbsp	Dijon mustard	15 mL
•	Salt and pepper	•	1 tbsp	anchovy paste	15 mL
2 tbsp	olive oil	25 mL	1 tsp	dried thyme	5 mL
4	cloves garlic	4	•	Red Wine Sauce	•
1 tbsp	black peppercorns	15 mL		(recipe follows)	

∧ *Vineyard near*
Niagara-on-the-Lake

With a sharp knife, remove any silverskin from the beef and sprinkle the roast with salt and pepper. Heat a heavy shallow roasting pan over 2 burners on high heat. Add 1 tbsp (15 mL) of the oil and place the tenderloin in the pan. Sear until well browned on all sides, 8 to 10 minutes. Remove the tenderloin to a platter.

Meanwhile, combine the garlic, peppercorns, mustard, anchovy paste and thyme in a small food processor and process until it forms a paste. (Alternatively, mince garlic by hand. Place the peppercorns in a sturdy plastic bag and crush with a heavy skillet. Stir together with the mustard, anchovy paste and thyme.) Stir in the remaining oil. Spread the peppercorn mixture over the tenderloin, place on a rack in the roasting pan and roast in a 450°F (230°C) oven until a meat thermometer registers 140°F (60°C), 30 to 40 minutes, depending on the thickness of the roast. The meat should be quite pink inside for the best texture and flavour. Remove to a carving board, tent with foil and let rest for 10 minutes before carving. Slice thinly and serve with the Red Wine Sauce. *Makes 10 to 12 servings.*

RED WINE SAUCE

3 tbsp	butter	45 mL	1 tbsp	chopped fresh thyme	15 mL
2	small onions, coarsely chopped	2		(or 1 tsp/5 mL dried)	
1	stalk celery, coarsely chopped	1	2	bay leaves	2
1	carrot, coarsely chopped	1	¼ cup	all-purpose flour	50 mL
¾ cup	dry red heavy-bodied wine	175 mL	4 cups	beef stock	1 L
4	cloves garlic, minced	4	•	Salt and pepper	•

In a large deep skillet over medium heat, melt the butter. Add the onions, celery and carrot; cook until browned, 8 to 10 minutes, stirring often. Stir in the wine, garlic, thyme and bay leaves; bring to a boil and boil until reduced by half. Stir in the flour and cook, stirring, for 1 minute. Stir in ½ cup (125 mL) of the stock, then bring to a boil, scraping up any

(continued on next page)

PEPPERED ROAST TENDERLOIN *with* RED WINE SAUCE *(continued)*

browned bits from the bottom of the skillet. Gradually stir in the remaining stock; bring to a boil, stirring constantly. Cook, stirring often, until thickened, 5 to 8 minutes. Season to taste with salt and pepper. Strain through a fine sieve, pressing down on the solids. (The sauce can be cooled, covered and refrigerated for up to 1 day.) Reheat to serve. If you wish thicker sauce, let it simmer for a few minutes, stirring often. *Makes about 4 cups (1L).*

VARIATION:

DELUXE ROASTED BEEF TENDERLOIN

I normally never put the same recipe in two books, but this version that appeared in *A Year in My Kitchen* and in *Canadian Living* publications has become a classic. I made it for the wedding suppers for both our children and usually serve it for my Canada Day birthday party. Use a 4 lb (2 kg) tenderloin; prepare it by removing the silverskin as above, but omit the searing. Marinate the beef overnight in a mixture of ½ cup (125 mL) Worcestershire sauce, 2 tbsp (25 mL) each Scotch whisky and brown sugar, 1 tsp (5 mL) pepper, 2 minced cloves garlic and 1 piece (1 inch/2.5 cm) fresh ginger, thinly sliced. Remove from the marinade, shaking off any excess. Place on a foil-lined baking sheet and rub all over with 2 tbsp (25 mL) coarse salt. Roast in a 500°F (260°C) oven for 10 minutes. Turn over and roast until a meat thermometer registers 140°F (60°C), 10 to 15 minutes longer. (The beef can be cooled, wrapped in foil and refrigerated for up to 2 days.) Serve at room temperature with Pink Peppercorn–Mustard Sauce (page 160).

MUSTARD-HERB ROAST BEEF

Marinating a less expensive oven roast and roasting at a low temperature yields meat almost as tender as any premium oven roast. Instead of the inside round roast, you could choose an outside round, eye of round, sirloin tip or a rump roast for equally good flavour. For best results, only roast these cuts of beef to rare or medium-rare.

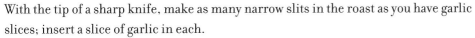

1	inside round beef roast (about 4 lb/1.8 kg)	1	⅓ cup	dry sherry	75 mL
3	cloves garlic, thinly sliced lengthwise	3	⅓ cup	soy sauce	75 mL
			¼ cup	canola oil	50 mL
			2 cups	beef stock	500 mL
1 tbsp	dry mustard	15 mL	1 tbsp	cornstarch	15 mL
1 tbsp	dried thyme	15 mL			

With the tip of a sharp knife, make as many narrow slits in the roast as you have garlic slices; insert a slice of garlic in each.

In a small bowl, stir together the mustard and thyme; rub the mixture all over the beef and put it in a sturdy plastic bag set in a bowl. In a small glass measure, stir together the sherry, soy sauce and oil. Pour over the beef; seal the bag and turn to coat well. Refrigerate for at least 24 hours or up to 36 hours, turning the bag occasionally.

Remove the beef from the bag; discard the marinade. Put the meat on a rack in a small shallow roasting pan; pour 2 cups (500 mL) water into the pan. Roast, uncovered, in a 500°F (260°C) oven for 30 minutes. Reduce the oven temperature to 275°F (140°C) and roast the beef until a meat thermometer registers 140°F (60°C), 1¼ to 1¾ hours longer. Transfer to a cutting board and tent loosely with foil; let stand for 30 minutes.

Add the stock to the roasting pan; bring to a boil over medium-high heat, stirring to scrape up any brown bits from the bottom of the pan. In a small bowl, stir together the cornstarch and 2 tbsp (25 mL) cold water until smooth; stir into the stock. Cook, stirring constantly, until thickened, about 1 minute. If you prefer thicker gravy, let it boil, stirring occasionally, until it's reduced and thickened slightly. Pour into a heated pitcher. Cut the beef into thin slices and serve with the gravy. *Makes 8 servings.*

SPICY DARK *and* DELICIOUS BEEF CHILI

Chili, con carne or without, has been a favourite for many years because it is easy, delicious and so flexible in its ingredient demand. If you like, pass sour cream, grated Cheddar and chopped green onions for all to garnish their own servings. Crusty bread, cornbread or rice and a green salad are welcome accompaniments.

^ *Jalapeño peppers*

1 lb	round steak	500 g	12 oz	small button mushrooms	375 g
2 tbsp	canola oil	25 mL	4	cloves garlic, minced	4
1 tbsp	unsweetened cocoa powder	15 mL	2	jalapeño peppers, seeded and chopped	2
1 tbsp	all-purpose flour	15 mL	2	stalks celery, diced	2
1 tbsp	chili powder	15 mL	1	sweet green pepper, diced	1
1 tbsp	ground cumin	15 mL	2	dried ancho chilies, minced	2
1 tbsp	paprika	15 mL		or ground, or 1 tsp (5 mL)	
1 tsp	dried oregano	5 mL		ancho chili powder (optional)	
1 tsp	granulated sugar	5 mL	1	can (28 oz/796 mL) diced	1
1 tsp	salt	5 mL		tomatoes (undrained)	
1 tsp	ground coriander	5 mL	1	can (6 oz/170 g) tomato paste	1
½ tsp	hot pepper flakes	2 mL	2	cans (19 oz/540 mL each) dark	2
2	onions, chopped	2		red kidney beans (undrained)	

Cut the beef into ½-inch (1 cm) chunks. In a large saucepan over medium-high heat, heat half the oil. Brown the beef in batches, about 3 minutes a batch, transferring each batch with a slotted spoon to paper towels.

Meanwhile, stir together the cocoa powder, flour, chili powder, cumin, paprika, oregano, sugar, salt, ground coriander and hot pepper flakes. Set aside.

Add the remaining 1 tbsp (15 mL) oil to the pan and lower the heat to medium. Cook the onions for 3 minutes. Stir in the mushrooms, garlic, jalapeño peppers, celery, green pepper and spice mixture. Cook, stirring, for 2 minutes. Stir in 2 cups (500 mL) of water; bring to a boil, stirring up any brown bits from the bottom. Stir in the browned beef, ancho chilies (if using), tomatoes and tomato paste; bring to a boil, reduce the heat, cover and simmer for 45 minutes, stirring occasionally. Stir in the kidney beans; simmer for 10 minutes. *Makes 6 servings.*

BEEF *and* TOMATO CURRY

Multiculturalism brought new flavours from many parts of the world during the 1970s. It was in this decade that my next-door neighbour taught me to make curries with spices her father sent to her from Bombay. Today, instead of dried chilies I use fresh ones, choosing from the vast array of hot peppers in all our markets. Look for smallish red and green chilies, but Thai bird's eye or Scotch bonnets might be a bit too hot for most. Serve with basmati rice, chutney and a refreshing cucumber salad or Cucumber Raita (page 160).

2 lb	lean stewing beef	1 kg	½ tsp	salt	2 mL
3	cloves garlic, minced	3	½ tsp	ground cardamom	2 mL
2 tbsp	minced fresh ginger	25 mL	2 tbsp	canola oil	25 mL
2	fresh green chilies, finely chopped	2	2	onions, chopped	2
			1 tsp	ground cloves	5 mL
2	fresh red chilies, finely chopped	2	1 tsp	ground cinnamon	5 mL
1½ tsp	ground turmeric	7 mL	1	can (19 oz/540 mL) diced tomatoes (undrained)	1
1½ tsp	ground cumin	7 mL	•	Fresh coriander leaves for garnish (optional)	•
1½ tsp	ground coriander	7 mL			

^ *Neon sign at Granville Island, Vancouver*

Trim the excess fat from the beef and cut the meat into 1-inch (2.5 cm) cubes; set aside. In a mini chopper or small bowl, combine the garlic, ginger, chilies, turmeric, cumin, coriander, salt and cardamom; set aside.

In a large saucepan, heat the oil over medium heat; add the onions and cook for 7 minutes. Reduce the heat to medium-low and stir in the garlic mixture; cook, stirring, for 3 minutes. Add the beef and stir to coat it well with the spices and onion mixture. Stir in the cloves, cinnamon, tomatoes and their juice. Bring to a boil, stirring to scrape up any brown bits from the bottom. Reduce the heat to low; cover and simmer until the beef is very tender, about 1½ hours. (The curry can be cooled, covered and refrigerated for up to 2 days. Reheat gently, stirring often. It's even better when made a day ahead.) Garnish with fresh coriander, if desired. *Makes 6 to 8 servings.*

OVEN-BRAISED SHORT RIBS
with CHINESE GREENS

One of my favourite ways to cook beef short ribs is oven braising as a classic stew with tomatoes, onions and carrots. Although this one is also slow-cooked in the oven, it is fragrant with star anise and fresh ginger. It should be made one day and served the next, since it is much easier to remove all the fat after it has hardened. Serve with steamed rice to soak up all the wonderful sauce.

1½ cups	low-sodium chicken broth	375 mL	1	onion, halved and sliced	1
½ cup	low-sodium soy sauce	125 mL	8	whole star anise	8
½ cup	sake or dry sherry	125 mL	1 tbsp	granulated sugar	15 mL
½ cup	water	125 mL	3 lb	beef short braising ribs	1.5 kg
8	cloves garlic, peeled	8	12	baby bok choy, halved	12
1	piece fresh ginger	1		lengthwise	
	(1½ inches/4 cm), sliced		2 tbsp	cornstarch	25 mL

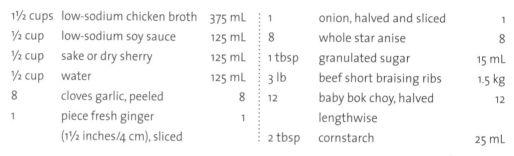

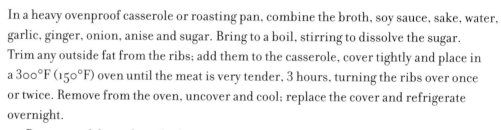

^ *Baby bok choy*

In a heavy ovenproof casserole or roasting pan, combine the broth, soy sauce, sake, water, garlic, ginger, onion, anise and sugar. Bring to a boil, stirring to dissolve the sugar. Trim any outside fat from the ribs; add them to the casserole, cover tightly and place in a 300°F (150°F) oven until the meat is very tender, 3 hours, turning the ribs over once or twice. Remove from the oven, uncover and cool; replace the cover and refrigerate overnight.

Remove and discard any fat from the top of the casserole. Let sit at room temperature for 30 minutes. Reheat, covered, in a 350°F (180°C) oven until hot throughout, about 30 minutes.

Steam the bok choy over boiling water until tender, about 3 minutes. With a slotted spoon, remove the meat to a heated serving dish. Arrange the bok choy alongside, cover and keep warm. Remove any bones, slices of ginger and star anise from the sauce. Bring to a boil on top of the stove. Dissolve the cornstarch in 2 tbsp (25 mL) cold water; add to the sauce and stir until thickened and smooth. Drizzle over the ribs and boy choy to serve, passing the remaining sauce in a warm gravy boat. *Makes 4 servings.*

SIMPLE BEEF STEW *with* ORANGE-WALNUT GREMOLATA

Often when I prepare beef stew, I cook strips of orange peel along with the meat. Here, I've sprinkled grated orange zest in a bit of a gremolata over the finished stew. Browning the beef in a hot oven is easier and faster than doing it in batches on top of the stove. This method dramatically cuts down on the fat as well.

2½ lb	stewing beef	1.25 kg	3	cloves garlic, halved	3
¼ cup	all-purpose flour	50 mL	3	shallots, thinly sliced	3
•	Salt and pepper	•	2 tbsp	Dijon mustard	25 mL
2 cups	beef stock	500 mL	½ tsp	crushed dried rosemary	2 mL
¼ cup	tomato paste	50 mL	½ tsp	crushed dried thyme	2 mL
½ lb	small mushrooms	250 g	1 cup	dry red wine	250 mL
½ lb	baby carrots	250 g	•	Gremolata (recipe follows)	•

∧ *Jean Talon Market, Montreal*

If the meat is not cubed, cut it into 1½-inch (4 cm) cubes. In a sturdy plastic bag, toss the beef with the flour, ½ tsp (2 mL) salt and ¼ tsp (1 mL) pepper. Spread the beef cubes out in a large greased shallow roasting pan; roast in a 500°F (260°C) oven until lightly browned, 10 to 15 minutes, stirring once.

Meanwhile, in a large flameproof casserole or Dutch oven, combine the stock, tomato paste, mushrooms, carrots, garlic, shallots, mustard, rosemary and thyme; bring to a boil. Stir in the browned beef.

Stir the wine into the browning pan; bring to a boil, scraping up any brown bits from the bottom of the pan. Stir the liquid into the meat mixture; cover and bake in a 300°F (150°C) oven until the beef is fork-tender, about 3 hours. (The stew can be prepared up to 2 days ahead. Cool uncovered; cover and refrigerate. Bring to room temperature for 30 minutes. Gently reheat on top of the stove or place in a 350°F/180°C oven until hot throughout, 30 to 40 minutes.) Sprinkle some gremolata over each serving of stew.
Makes 6 servings.

GREMOLATA

½ cup	coarsely chopped fresh parsley	125 mL	1	clove garlic, minced	1
			1 cup	walnut halves, toasted	250 mL
2 tbsp	coarsely grated orange zest	25 mL			

In a small bowl, stir together the parsley, orange zest and garlic; stir in the walnuts. (The gremolata, without the walnuts, can be covered and refrigerated for up to 1 day. Add the nuts just before serving.)

BRAISED BEEF *with* CARAMELIZED ROOT VEGETABLES

When I make a pot roast, I usually just plunk all the vegetables into the pot for the last hour of cooking, but for this recipe I couldn't resist roasting them separately in the oven while the beef browns because they gain so much flavour that way. Then I just reheat them at the end in the braising liquid or gravy. The beef itself improves in flavour if you want to roast it ahead too; strain the gravy and let the beef cool in it, add the caramelized vegetables, cover and refrigerate for up to 2 days. Reheat the whole thing, covered, in a 350°F (180°C) oven for 30 minutes. Turn any leftovers into a beef pie by dicing the meat and vegetables, stirring in any gravy and topping with biscuits or a puff pastry crust.

1	boneless cross rib or blade beef roast (4 lb/1.8 kg)	1		3 tbsp	olive oil	45 mL
				1	onion, chopped	1
⅓ cup	all-purpose flour	75 mL		1	stalk celery, chopped	1
•	Salt and pepper	•		8	cloves garlic, peeled and smashed	8
3	carrots	3				
2	parsnips, in 1-inch (2.5 cm) chunks	2		2 cups	full-bodied red wine	500 mL
				2 cups	beef stock	500 mL
2	sweet potatoes, in 1-inch (2.5 cm) chunks	2		2 tbsp	tomato paste	25 mL
				2 tsp	herbes de Provence*	10 mL
1	celery root, peeled, in 1-inch (2.5 cm) chunks	1		1 tsp	dried rosemary	5 mL
				1	bay leaf	1

Place the roast on a plate and sprinkle with flour, turning the meat over to coat it well. Reserve the remaining flour. Place the roast on a rack in a shallow pan and sprinkle with salt and pepper. Set aside while the oven preheats to 450°F (230°C).

Chop one of the carrots and set aside; cut the other two into 1-inch (2.5 cm) chunks. Arrange the carrot chunks, parsnips, sweet potatoes and celery root in a single layer on a parchment-lined rimmed baking sheet. Toss with 1 tbsp (15 mL) of the oil and sprinkle with salt and pepper. Place both the roast and vegetables in the heated oven and roast for 20 minutes, turning the vegetables once. Transfer the vegetables to a medium saucepan and refrigerate when cool. Reduce the oven temperature to 325°F (160°C).

* Herbes de Provence varies in ingredients and proportions but can include thyme, savory, rosemary, marjoram, sage, lavender, bay leaves, basil and fennel seeds. If unavailable, substitute 1 tsp (5 mL) dried thyme and ½ tsp (2 mL) each dried basil and marjoram or savory.

(continued on page 112)

CAESAR BURGERS

BRAISED BEEF *with* CARAMELIZED ROOT VEGETABLES *(continued)*

Even if you're a "no anchovies on my pizza" kind of person, don't leave the anchovy paste out here, as it mellows wonderfully with the other Caesar flavours—garlic, lemon and Worcestershire.

Meanwhile, heat the remaining oil in a large Dutch oven or ovenproof casserole over medium heat; add the reserved chopped carrot, onion, celery and garlic. Sprinkle with salt and pepper; cook for 8 minutes until the vegetables are beginning to brown, stirring often. Stir in any reserved flour and cook, stirring, for 2 minutes. Add the wine and bring to a boil, scraping up any bits from the bottom; boil for 2 minutes. Stir in the stock, tomato paste, half the herbes de Provence, rosemary and bay leaf. Add the beef and any drippings. Cover tightly and place in the oven for 2½ hours, turning the meat once.

1	egg	1
¼ cup	freshly grated Parmesan cheese	50 mL
2 tbsp	fresh lemon juice	25 mL
1 tbsp	anchovy paste	15 mL
1 tbsp	Worcestershire sauce	15 mL
¼ tsp	black pepper	1 mL
1¼ lb	ground beef	625 g
2 tbsp	olive oil	25 mL
1	clove garlic, minced	1
4	kaiser rolls, halved	4
4	leaves romaine lettuce	4

Remove the beef to a heated platter and tent with foil. Strain the braising liquid into the saucepan containing the vegetables, pressing on any solids, and stir in the remaining 1 tsp (5 mL) herbes de Provence. Place over medium heat until the vegetables are hot and the liquid is bubbly, about 10 minutes, stirring often. Meanwhile, slice the meat across the grain into ½-inch-thick (1 cm) slices. Arrange on a platter with the vegetables alongside. Drizzle the meat with the gravy and pass the rest in a warm gravy boat. *Makes 6 to 8 servings.*

In a bowl, beat the egg; mix in half the cheese, the lemon juice, anchovy paste, Worcestershire sauce and pepper until well blended. Gently mix in the beef. Shape into four ¾-inch-thick (2 cm) patties.

Place on a greased grill over medium-high heat; cook, turning once, until the meat is no longer pink inside, 10 to 12 minutes.

Meanwhile, combine the oil and garlic; brush over the cut side of the rolls. Place on the grill and toast. Place the patties on the rolls; sprinkle with the remaining cheese and top with the romaine. *Makes 4 servings.*

GAME FILET *with* WILD MUSHROOMS

When several of Pam Collacott's students who hunt wanted to know how to cook the game they had in their freezers, she came up with this delicious recipe at her Trillium Cooking School near Ottawa, Ontario. The author of several cookbooks, Pam is also a food stylist and appears regularly on CTV. Her work with the Nutrition Education Committee of the Breakfast for Learning Foundation recently took her to Yellowknife, where she enjoyed a great variety of game—bison, caribou, muskox, partridge and pheasant. If game is unavailable, you can prepare this recipe with a tender cut of beef such as tenderloin, strip loin, rib eye or top sirloin.

2 tbsp	canola oil	25 mL	1 cup	undiluted canned	250 mL
12	caribou or goose breast	12		beef broth	
	medallions (2 oz/50 g each)		¼ cup	medium dry sherry	50 mL
¼ cup	butter	50 mL		or Madeira	
1 tbsp	all-purpose flour	15 mL	¼ cup	brandy or cognac	50 mL
¾ cup	minced shallots	175 mL	•	Salt and pepper	•
1 tsp	juniper berries,	5 mL	¼ cup	wild mushrooms, sliced	50 mL
	slightly crushed		1	tart apple, peeled and diced	1
1 tsp	chopped fresh rosemary	5 mL	•	Fresh parsley and rosemary	•
	(or ½ tsp/2 mL dried)			sprigs for garnish	
1	clove garlic, minced	1			

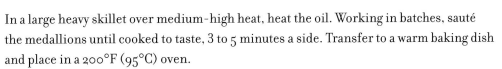

In a large heavy skillet over medium-high heat, heat the oil. Working in batches, sauté the medallions until cooked to taste, 3 to 5 minutes a side. Transfer to a warm baking dish and place in a 200°F (95°C) oven.

Mix together 1 tbsp (15 mL) of the butter and the flour; set aside.

In the skillet in which the medallions were cooked, melt 1 tbsp (15 mL) of the butter over medium heat. Cook ¼ cup (50 mL) of the shallots, the juniper berries, rosemary and garlic for 2 minutes, stirring. Stir in the broth, sherry and brandy; bring to a boil. Gradually whisk in the flour mixture and cook until thickened, stirring. Season to taste with salt and pepper.

Meanwhile, in another skillet over medium heat, melt the remaining butter. Stir in the remaining ½ cup (125 mL) shallots, the mushrooms and diced apple. Cook, stirring often, until the apples and vegetables are tender, about 7 minutes. Season to taste with salt and pepper.

To serve, spoon the mushroom mixture onto a warm platter. Top with the medallions and drizzle with some of the sauce. Garnish the platter with parsley and rosemary sprigs and pass the extra sauce in a warm gravy boat. *Makes 6 servings.*

∧ *Bison (top)*

∧ *Mask in Yellowknife (bottom)*

BRAISED VEAL SHANKS *with* WILD MUSHROOMS *and* POTATOES

Succulent, oven-braised veal teams well with crusty bread or polenta. Toss arugula with a simple vinaigrette to go alongside.

¼ cup	olive oil (approx)	50 mL	4	potatoes, cut into 1-inch (2.5 cm) cubes	4
2	onions, chopped	2	6	veal shanks (about 3 lb/1.5 kg)	6
4	carrots, cut into 1-inch (2.5 cm) pieces	4	¼ cup	all-purpose flour	50 mL
1 tbsp	chopped fresh thyme (or 1 tsp/5 mL dried)	15 mL	•	Salt and pepper	•
1 tbsp	chopped fresh rosemary (or 1 tsp/5 mL dried)	15 mL	1 cup	dry red wine, preferably Pinot Noir	250 mL
2	bay leaves	2	2 cups	beef stock	500 mL
1 lb	wild mushrooms (cremini, portobello and/or shiitake), trimmed if necessary and thickly sliced	500 g	12	cloves garlic, peeled	12
			1 cup	peas, fresh or frozen, thawed	250 mL
			⅓ cup	chopped fresh parsley, preferably Italian flat-leaf	75 mL
			1 tbsp	grated lemon zest	15 mL

In a large Dutch oven over medium heat, heat 2 tbsp (25 mL) of the oil. Add the onions, carrots, thyme, rosemary and bay leaves; cook for 10 minutes, stirring often. Add the mushrooms and potatoes; cook for 4 minutes, stirring occasionally. With a slotted spoon, remove the vegetables to a large bowl.

Coat the shanks with flour, shaking off the excess. Heat 1 tbsp (15 mL) of the remaining oil in the same pot over high heat. Brown the shanks well, in batches, sprinkling lightly with salt and pepper and adding more oil as necessary. Add the browned shanks to the bowl containing the vegetables.

Sprinkle any remaining flour into the pot and cook, stirring, for 1 minute. Gradually stir in the wine and bring to a boil, scraping up any brown bits from the bottom. Stir in the stock and the whole garlic cloves; return to a boil.

Return the veal, browned vegetables and any juices to the pot. Bring back to a boil, cover and cook in a 350°F (180°C) oven until the veal is very tender, about 1 hour and 45 minutes. Discard the bay leaves. (The shanks can be cooled, covered and refrigerated for up to 1 day. Bring to room temperature for 30 minutes. Reheat on top of the stove over medium-low heat or in a 350°F/180°C oven, stirring occasionally, until hot, 30 to 35 minutes.)

Just before serving, add the peas and heat through. Taste and adjust the seasoning. Combine the parsley and lemon zest in a small bowl. Serve the veal and vegetables with some sauce spooned overtop and sprinkled with the parsley mixture. *Makes 6 servings.*

∧ *Wild mushrooms: portobello, shiitake and oyster (top)*

∧ *Potato field (bottom)*

115

TWO-CHEESE VEAL LOAF

For decades, meat loaf has been a traditional family supper and blue plate special in diners across the country. Because it is easily extended to feed many mouths, some associate it with Depression cooking or boarding school, but it has recently taken on many delicious forms using anything from ground chicken, pork or beef to a combination of meats. This loaf with its wonderful Italian flavours uses lean veal as a base. I always pop potatoes into the oven to bake alongside.

1	egg	1
1	small onion, finely chopped	1
½ cup	dry breadcrumbs	125 mL
⅓ cup	milk	75 mL
⅓ cup	freshly grated Parmesan cheese	75 mL
¼ cup	chopped (oil-packed) sun-dried tomatoes	50 mL
2 tbsp	tomato paste	25 mL
1 tbsp	slivered fresh basil	15 mL
¾ tsp	salt	4 mL
¼ tsp	pepper	1 mL
1 lb	lean ground veal	500 g
1 cup	diced provolone cheese	250 mL
2 oz	pancetta, thinly sliced	50 g

In a large bowl, beat the egg slightly. Stir in the onion, breadcrumbs, milk, Parmesan, tomatoes, paste, basil, salt and pepper. Break up the veal and add. With moistened hands, gently mix everything together.

Press one-third of the meat mixture evenly into a greased 9- × 5-inch (2 L) loaf pan; sprinkle half of the provolone cheese overtop. Press another third of the meat mixture on top; sprinkle with the remaining cheese. Cover with the remaining meat mixture and top with slices of pancetta. If possible, cover and refrigerate the loaf for 1 hour and up to 24 hours so the flavours develop and the loaf firms.

Bake in a 350°F (180°C) oven until well browned and a meat thermometer registers 170°F (77°C), about 1 hour. Let sit for 5 minutes. Drain off any fat and slice to serve. *Makes 4 servings.*

PAN-SEARED VEAL CHOPS *with* BALSAMIC GLAZE

This is just the type of quick dish I love doing for our weekday supper. Mashed potatoes and steamed broccoli are the only accompaniments you need.

2	veal loin chops, about ¾ inch (2 cm) thick	2
•	Salt and pepper	•
2 tbsp	olive oil	25 mL
1	clove garlic, minced	1
1 tbsp	minced fresh rosemary	15 mL
¼ cup	balsamic vinegar	50 mL
2 tbsp	water	25 mL
1 tsp	brown sugar	5 mL

Sprinkle the chops with salt and pepper. In a small bowl, mix together 1 tsp (5 mL) of the oil, the garlic and rosemary. Spread over both sides of the chops.

Heat the remaining oil in a heavy skillet over medium-high. Add the chops and cook to the desired doneness, about 7 minutes a side for medium-rare, turning once. Transfer to a heated platter and place in a warm oven.

Pour the balsamic vinegar and water into the skillet and bring to a boil, scraping up any brown bits from the bottom. Stir in the brown sugar and cook until syrupy, about 1 or 2 minutes. Drizzle on the chops to serve. *Makes 2 servings.*

"Finest Quality MEATS"

LAMB
LOIN CHOPS
15.99 LB. 35.20 KG

LAMB

LAMB SHANKS BRAISED
WITH FIGS AND ROOT
VEGETABLES ~ 119

MINT-CHILI LAMB RACKS ~ 120

LEMON-ROSEMARY
GRILLED LAMB ~ 120

LAMB KOFTAS WITH TOMATO
YOGURT SAUCE ~ 122

ONTARIO ~ 123
A MIDSUMMER GRILL ~ 125

Lamb

Although many of our early settlers came from Britain, where fields were dotted with sheep, lamb hasn't been part of our Canadian heritage. Upper Canada farmers first raised pigs that were relatively easy to feed, then cows as soon as they had cleared enough land on which to grow their feed. As they moved west onto the Prairies, wild game was abundant, and more cattle were raised to graze easily on open land.

However, since sheep adapt well to all climates and feed, lamb is the staple meat in many parts of the world, especially the Middle East, North Africa and the Mediterranean basin. With immigration from some of these areas, lamb became more popular, and its consumption, particularly in Ontario, has increased greatly over the last few years.

Sheep farm in Nova Scotia

LAMB SHANKS BRAISED *with* FIGS *and* ROOT VEGETABLES

Lamb shanks are just right for long, slow cooking to make them melt-in-your-mouth delicious. This Middle Eastern stew highlights our own homey root vegetables. Serve over couscous tossed with coriander.

4	lamb shanks (about 2½ lb/ 1.2 kg total)	4	½ cup	drained, chopped canned tomatoes	125 mL
•	Salt and black pepper	•	1	pkg (8 oz/250 g) dried figs (about 2 cups/500 mL)	1
⅓ cup	all-purpose flour	75 mL	2 tbsp	butter	25 mL
2 tbsp	olive oil	25 mL	1 tbsp	packed brown sugar	15 mL
3	cloves garlic, minced	3	2	onions, cut into 1-inch (2.5 cm) cubes	2
2 tsp	paprika	10 mL	2	carrots, cut into 1-inch (2.5 cm) cubes	2
2 tsp	dried basil	10 mL			
1 tsp	dried thyme	5 mL	2	parsnips, cut into 1-inch (2.5 cm) cubes	2
1 tsp	ground cumin	5 mL			
1 tsp	ground coriander	5 mL	2	summer turnips, cut into 1-inch (2.5 cm) cubes	2
1 cup	dry red wine	250 mL			
2½ cups	chicken stock	625 mL			

∧ *Dried figs*

Dry the lamb shanks well, then sprinkle with salt and pepper and coat with flour. Heat half the oil in a large Dutch oven over medium-high heat. Working in batches, brown the shanks all over, removing them to a plate as they brown and adding more oil to the pan as necessary.

Add any remaining flour to the pan, along with the garlic, paprika, basil, thyme, cumin and coriander; cook over medium heat, stirring, for 1 minute. Stir in the wine; bring to a boil, scraping up any brown bits from the bottom of the pan. Stir in 1½ cups (375 mL) of the stock and the tomatoes. Return the shanks to the pan, along with any juices that have accumulated on the plate.

With scissors, cut the stems from the figs and quarter them. Add them to the pan and bring to a boil. Cover and cook in a 350°F (180°C) oven until the lamb is very tender, about 2 hours, stirring occasionally.

Meanwhile, in a deep skillet or shallow flameproof casserole, melt the butter and sugar over medium heat. Add the onions, carrots, parsnips and turnips, stirring to coat them with the butter mixture. Sprinkle with salt and pepper to taste; stir in the remaining 1 cup (250 mL) stock and bring to a boil. Bake, uncovered, alongside the pan containing the lamb shanks, until the vegetables are tender, about 45 minutes, stirring occasionally. Stir the vegetables into the cooked shanks. (The dish can be cooled, covered and refrigerated for up to 1 day. Reheat on top of the stove over medium-low heat until hot, about 35 minutes, stirring occasionally.) *Makes 4 servings.*

MINT-CHILI LAMB RACKS

Mint jelly has long been a favourite accompaniment for lamb, but forget that bright green condiment and enjoy an easy, fresh, sweet and sour mint sauce with this elegant cut of meat.

2	lamb racks (7 to 8 ribs each)	2
1/3 cup	finely chopped fresh mint	75 mL
1/4 cup	sweet chili sauce*	50 mL
2 tbsp	rice vinegar	25 mL
2	cloves garlic, minced	2
2 tbsp	canola oil	25 mL

Dry the racks well and score the outside layer of fat diagonally to make a small diamond pattern. Place the racks in a sturdy plastic bag. In a small bowl, combine the mint, sweet chili sauce, vinegar and garlic. Set aside half of the mixture in another small bowl. Stir the oil into the remaining mint mixture and pour over the lamb. Close the bag and knead gently to make sure the meat is coated with the marinade. Refrigerate for up to 4 hours. Remove from the refrigerator 30 minutes before roasting.

Place, bone side down, in a shallow, foil-lined roasting pan. (It is a good idea to intertwine the rib ends of the 2 racks, with the bones facing in and down, as it will make the meat cook more evenly.) Roast in a 450°F (230°C) oven for 10 minutes. Lower the temperature to 350°F (180°C) and roast until a thermometer registers 140°F (60°C), 20 to 30 minutes longer. Let stand, loosely covered with foil, for 10 minutes before carving between the ribs. To serve, drizzle each serving with some of the reserved mint-chili mixture. *Makes 4 servings.*

* Sweet chili sauce is a Thai sweet-sour sauce used for barbecues and dipping. It is available at most supermarkets.

LEMON-ROSEMARY GRILLED LAMB

Butterflied leg of lamb is great on the grill—tender and succulent, quick to cook and easy to carve. Rosemary remains a favourite seasoning.

1	butterflied leg of lamb (3 to 4 lb/ 1.5 to 2 kg)	1
2 tbsp	grated lemon zest	25 mL
1/4 cup	fresh lemon juice	50 mL
2 tbsp	olive oil	25 mL
4	cloves garlic, minced	4
2 tbsp	chopped fresh rosemary (or 2 tsp/10 mL dried)	25 mL
2 tsp	chopped fresh oregano (or 1/2 tsp/2 mL dried)	10 mL
1/2 tsp	black pepper	2 mL
•	Sea salt	•

Slash the lamb in several places on the meaty side so that it lies as flat as possible. In a shallow glass dish, combine the lemon zest, lemon juice, oil, garlic, rosemary, oregano and pepper. Add the lamb, making sure all the surfaces are coated with the marinade; cover and refrigerate for 4 to 8 hours, turning occasionally. Let stand at room temperature for 30 minutes before grilling.

Reserving the marinade, place the meat flat on a greased grill over medium-high heat. Place the marinade in a small saucepan and boil 3 minutes. Close the lid and cook the lamb, brushing occasionally with the marinade at the beginning and turning the meat twice, until a meat thermometer registers 140°F (60°C), 30 to 40 minutes. The meat should still be pink inside. Transfer to a cutting board, sprinkle with salt, cover with foil and let stand for 10 minutes. Slice the meat across the grain. *Makes about 8 servings.*

Lemon-Rosemary Grilled
Lamb (facing page)

LAMB KOFTAS *with* TOMATO YOGURT SAUCE

Koftas are small Indian meatballs, often served in a curry sauce. Here, I've made them bigger and serve them like burgers, topped with a fresh tomato yogurt sauce. Round out the menu with spicy skewered shrimp to start, a cucumber salad and mangoes or peaches for dessert.

3 tbsp	plain yogurt	45 mL	Pinch	cayenne		Pinch
2 tbsp	finely chopped fresh	25 mL	1 lb	lean ground lamb or beef		500 g
	coriander		4	pieces naan bread, chapatis		4
1 tsp	ground coriander	5 mL		or thick pita bread without		
1 tsp	ground cumin	5 mL		pockets		
½ tsp	curry powder	2 mL	•	Tomato Yogurt Sauce		•
½ tsp	salt	2 mL		(recipe follows)		

In a bowl, combine the yogurt, fresh coriander, ground coriander, cumin, curry powder, salt and cayenne. Gently mix in the ground lamb and lightly form into 4 round patties, about ¾ inch (2 cm) thick. (Burgers can be made ahead to this point, covered and refrigerated for up to 1 hour.)

Place the patties on a greased grill over medium heat and cook until the centres are no longer pink, 5 to 6 minutes per side, turning once. Meanwhile, warm the naan bread on the side of the grill. Enclose 1 patty in each and serve with Tomato Yogurt Sauce. *Makes 4 burgers.*

TOMATO YOGURT SAUCE

¼ cup	plain yogurt	50 mL	Pinch	granulated sugar	Pinch
1	clove garlic, minced	1	1 cup	seeded and diced	250 mL
½ tsp	ground cumin	2 mL		tomatoes	
¼ tsp	turmeric	1 mL	2 tbsp	chopped fresh coriander	25 mL
•	Salt	•			

In a small bowl, stir together the yogurt, garlic, cumin, turmeric, salt to taste and sugar. Gently stir in the tomatoes and coriander. Cover and refrigerate for 1 hour to allow the flavours to meld before serving. *Makes 1 cup (250 mL).*

THE FIRST NATIONS INHABITANTS of Ontario were farmers as well as hunters and gatherers, so in addition to harvesting wild foods, such as game, freshwater fish, maple sugar and forest greens like fiddleheads, they were also cultivating corn, beans and squash, Jerusalem artichokes and sunflowers in the province's fertile soil.

By the middle of the 18th century there were pockets of French and British colonists around their fur-trading forts, but the first major influx of settlers came with the United Empire Loyalists who arrived in the 1780s and took up residence along the St. Lawrence, around the Bay of Quinte and in the Niagara region. They were mostly British, but Germans and other Europeans, Iroquois allies of the British and some African Americans escaping slavery added their influences (including Southern American cookery) to the mix. Another group was the Pennsylvania German Mennonites who began farming in the Waterloo area in 1800 and are responsible for the region's passion for sauerkraut, smoked sausage, fresh pork and baked goods like shoofly pie.

By 1793 peach and cherry trees had already been planted at Niagara, and that area remains the tender fruit belt as well as the province's best-known wine region. Other wine-producing regions today are the Lake Erie north shore, Pelee Island and Prince Edward County. (Waterloo, Guelph, Cambridge and London all produce that other important beverage, beer.) By 1820, farms in the Bay of Quinte, Niagara and Windsor areas boasted well-cultivated gardens and orchards. The regions of Quinte and southwestern Georgian Bay are now home to the biggest apple orchards. Today, southern Ontario, with its rich, fertile soil in areas like the Holland Marsh and Essex County, remains the province's "salad bowl," producing

ONTARIO

a bounty of fresh vegetables including asparagus, tomatoes, corn, beans, carrots and other root vegetables.

After the War of 1812, British, Scottish and Irish immigrants working as loggers and in lumber shanties in the Ottawa Valley brought with them a tradition of baked beans and bread. The Scots tended to form tight-knit communities, but shared their taste for shortbread, oatmeal porridge, Black Bun (fruitcake) and haggis.

By the middle of the 19th century settlers in the backwoods were still roughing it, but colonists living on prosperous farms or in market towns enjoyed an abundance of foods. The traditional British diet of beef and pork, root vegetables, oats, white bread and tea was enriched with the harvest of the New World: corn, beans, pumpkin, squash, turkey, wild rice (native to Central and Northern Ontario) and maple syrup. Cooking was simple and seasonal, and farm wives made their own cheese, butter and preserves. In the last half of the 19th century, there began a transition to more refined foods and the beginnings of food processing industries. The first cheese factory was built in Ingersoll in 1864; by the 1880s, it was possible to buy packaged yeast, imported marmalades, bottled pickles and ketchup.

In the 19th and 20th centuries, ethnic communities established around the province included the Polish in Wilno (Renfrew County), Portuguese in Strathroy and Cambridge, Italians in Guelph, Scots in the Renfrew valley near Ottawa, Ukrainians and Eastern Europeans in Hamilton, and Finns in Thunder Bay (where abundant fish ensured that they would continue to enjoy their traditional smoked fish). There are many other cultural groups around the province, but these are the areas where the cuisine of the home country continues to be strong.

Thousands of immigrants enter Canada annually; half locate in Ontario, and the majority of these are drawn to the Toronto area, which has a rich international cuisine as a result. Since the 1970s, immigrants from such places as Southeast Asia, Africa, Southern Europe, Latin America, the Caribbean and the Middle East have contributed their culinary traditions, cooking styles and unique flavours. In our cosmopolitan cities, we are now just as familiar with pulled pork, sushi and designer pizzas as we are with the salt pork and potatoes that sustained some of the early settlers.

A MIDSUMMER GRILL

Many Ontarians own cottages on the endless shores of the province's lakes and rivers. This wonderful summertime menu can be orchestrated entirely from the barbecue, whether on a cottage deck or in a city garden. The menu reflects the long-time Italian settlements in cities like Toronto. Buy focaccia to toast on the grill or make the Gorgonzola Focaccia (page 13) ahead of time.

Antipasto Platter
(Marinated artichoke hearts,
shrimp, salami slices, olives)

Focaccia

Lemon-Rosemary Grilled Lamb
(page 120)

Garlicky Portobello Mushrooms
(page 154)

Sage New Potato Kabobs
(page 141)

Honey-Grilled Pears with
Ginger Mascarpone Cream
(page 222)

Hazelnut Biscotti (store-bought)

PASTA &
VEGETARIAN

CREAMY PENNE WITH
ASPARAGUS, MUSHROOMS
AND PROSCIUTTO ~ *127*

BAKED PENNE WITH MUSHROOMS
AND ARUGULA ~ *128*

PAD THAI ~ *129*

ZESTY THREE-CHEESE MACARONI ~ *130*

SPAGHETTI PUTTANESCA WITH CHERRY
TOMATO SAUCE ~ *130*

PENNE WITH GRILLED VEGETABLES ~ *132*

CARAMELIZED ONION AND PUMPKIN
VARENYKY (PEROGIES) ~ *135*

SQUASH AND BEAN STEW WITH
CHIPOTLE CREAM ~ *137*

ZARA'S
Italian Deli & Fresh Pasta

Fresh
Basil
2.00

CREAMY PENNE *with* ASPARAGUS, MUSHROOMS *and* PROSCIUTTO

In the 1950s, commercial cream of mushroom soup was the basis of many quick casseroles, especially with tuna. Here, light cream cheese and milk form a lovely, rich, low-fat sauce that's almost as easy to make. If you like, substitute a can of tuna for the prosciutto for old times' sake! Serve with crusty whole wheat rolls and a salad of greens.

1 lb	asparagus	500 g	¼ lb	light cream cheese, in pieces	125 g
2 tbsp	butter	25 mL	3 oz	thinly sliced prosciutto,	75 g
½ lb	mushrooms, sliced	250 g		slivered (1/2 cup/125 mL)	
	(2½ cups/625 mL)		4 cups	penne (about 12 oz/375 g)	1 L
2	cloves garlic, slivered	2	½ cup	freshly grated Parmesan	125 mL
¼ tsp	salt	1 mL		cheese	
¼ tsp	pepper	1 mL	•	Additional freshly grated	•
1 cup	skim or low-fat milk	250 mL		Parmesan cheese	

Snap off and discard any tough ends from the asparagus; cut the spears diagonally into 1-inch (2.5 cm) pieces. Set aside.

In a large deep skillet, melt the butter over medium heat; cook the mushrooms until golden, about 12 minutes, stirring occasionally. Add the garlic, salt and pepper; cook, stirring, for 2 minutes. Reduce the heat to medium-low; stir in the milk. Stir in the cream cheese, continuing to stir until the cheese melts. Stir in the prosciutto.

Meanwhile, cook the penne in a large pot of boiling, salted water for 6 minutes. Add the asparagus and cook until it's tender-crisp and the pasta is al dente (tender, but firm to the bite), 2 to 3 more minutes. Drain well but do not rinse.

Add the pasta and asparagus to the skillet; stir to coat with the mushroom mixture. Spoon into a warmed large pasta bowl or deep platter, and sprinkle with the Parmesan cheese. Serve at once with additional Parmesan on the side. *Makes 4 servings.*

BAKED PENNE *with* MUSHROOMS *and* ARUGULA

Canadians have had a love affair with lasagna for many years. This casserole is easier, has many of the same flavours and is also perfect for casual entertaining since it can be prepared entirely ahead of time. Offer a green salad and some artisanal bread. If you are opening a bottle of red wine to drink with the casserole, substitute wine for the water used in the sauce.

2 tbsp	olive oil	25 mL	Pinch	granulated sugar	Pinch
½ lb	cremini mushrooms, sliced (about 4 cups/1 L)	250 g	Pinch	hot pepper flakes	Pinch
			1 cup	whipping cream	250 mL
1½ lb	ground veal or beef (or a combination)	750 g	•	Salt and pepper	•
			1 lb	penne pasta (5 cups/1.25 L)	500 g
2	cloves garlic, minced	2	1 cup	freshly grated Asiago cheese	250 mL
1	can (28 oz/796 mL) crushed tomatoes	1	1 cup	freshly grated Parmesan cheese	250 mL
2 tbsp	tomato paste	25 mL			
½ cup	water	125 mL	3 oz	arugula, chopped (about 5 cups/1.25 L packed) (not baby arugula)	75 g
2 tsp	dried Italian herb seasoning	10 mL			

In a large saucepan, heat the oil over medium-high heat. Add the mushrooms and cook for 4 minutes. Remove to a bowl with a slotted spoon and set aside. Add the veal and cook until it's no longer pink, about 5 minutes, breaking the meat up with a spoon. Drain off any fat. Stir in the garlic and cook 1 minute. Add the tomatoes, tomato paste, water, Italian seasoning, sugar and hot pepper flakes. Return the mushrooms to the pan and bring to a boil. Reduce the heat and cook, stirring often, until thickened, 15 to 20 minutes. Stir in the cream and cook until it's thickened, 3 to 5 minutes. Season to taste with salt and pepper.

Meanwhile, cook the pasta in a large pot of boiling salted water until al dente, about 8 minutes. Drain well and add to the sauce.

Combine the cheeses in a bowl. Stir 1 cup (250 mL) into the pasta mixture along with the arugula. Spoon into a greased 13- × 9-inch (3 L) casserole dish. Sprinkle evenly with the remaining mixed cheeses. (The casserole can be cooled, covered with greased foil and refrigerated for up to 1 day. Remove from the fridge 30 minutes before baking.) Bake, covered, in a 375°F (190°C) oven for 25 minutes. Uncover and bake until bubbly and heated through, 20 to 30 minutes longer. *Makes 8 servings.*

PAD THAI

Not strictly a Thai dish, Pad Thai means "Thai fry" or "Thai-style stir-fried noodles" and was originally cooked up by immigrants from South China who arrived in Thailand after World War II. Whatever its origin, this dish is firmly established in our cuisine, appearing on many menus, both Thai and Western, and is a favourite of home cooks. Tamarind is used in the authentic version, but since it's not found readily in supermarkets, I've substituted rice vinegar and a bit of ketchup.

8 oz	rice stick noodles	250 g	8 oz	large shrimp, peeled and deveined	250 g
⅓ cup	fish sauce	75 mL	2 tsp	Asian chili sauce or hot pepper sauce	10 mL
¼ cup	fresh lime juice	50 mL			
¼ cup	ketchup	50 mL	2	eggs, lightly beaten	2
2 tbsp	brown sugar	25 mL	4 oz	tofu, cubed	125 g
1 tbsp	rice vinegar	15 mL	2 cups	bean sprouts	500 mL
1 tbsp	water	15 mL	6	green onions, sliced	6
2 tbsp	peanut or canola oil	25 mL	½ cup	fresh coriander leaves	125 mL
4	cloves garlic, minced	4	½ cup	roasted peanuts, coarsely chopped	125 mL
4	boneless, skinless chicken breast halves, cut into ½-inch (1 cm) pieces	4	•	Lime wedges	•

In a large bowl, soak the noodles in warm water until softened, about 7 minutes or according to package instructions. Drain well and set aside.

In a small bowl, combine the fish sauce, lime juice, ketchup, brown sugar, vinegar and water; set aside.

In a large wok, heat the oil over medium-high heat. Add the garlic and chicken; stir-fry for 1 minute. Add the shrimp and chili sauce; stir-fry for 2 to 3 minutes until the shrimp turn pink. Stir in the fish sauce mixture and bring to a boil; reduce the heat to medium. Stir in the eggs and cook 1 minute. Add the noodles and toss to coat well. Stir in the tofu, bean sprouts and green onions; toss until well combined. Garnish with the fresh coriander, peanuts and lime wedges. *Makes 6 to 8 servings.*

ZESTY THREE-CHEESE MACARONI

Macaroni and cheese was probably the first pasta dish many Canadians knew and it's still a hands-down favourite. I've made many versions with a white sauce, but our family prefers a tomato base with a bit of a custard topping. Here, I've used three different nippy cheeses, but feel free to use up little bits of cheese in your refrigerator, even Stilton for a really grown-up version.

2 cups	macaroni	500 mL
¼ lb	old Cheddar cheese	125 g
1	can (19 oz/540 mL) tomatoes (undrained)	1
¼ lb	Asiago cheese, grated	125 g
¼ lb	Portuguese São Jorge or provolone cheese, diced	125 g
2 tsp	dry mustard	10 mL
2 tsp	Worcestershire sauce	10 mL
1 tsp	granulated sugar	5 mL
½ tsp	dried thyme	2 mL
½ tsp	salt	2 mL
½ tsp	pepper	2 mL
½ tsp	Tabasco sauce	2 mL
1	egg, beaten	1
½ cup	milk	125 mL

In a large pot of boiling salted water, cook the macaroni until al dente, about 8 minutes. Drain and transfer to a greased 8-cup (2 L) deep casserole.

Cut the Cheddar cheese into thin slices; set aside. Stir together the tomatoes, Asiago cheese, São Jorge cheese, mustard, Worcestershire sauce, sugar, thyme, salt, pepper and Tabasco sauce. Pour over the macaroni and mix well. Top with the cheese slices.

In a small bowl, blend the egg and milk; pour over the cheese-covered macaroni, but do not stir. Bake, uncovered, in a 350°F (180°C) oven until the top is golden brown, 40 to 50 minutes. *Makes 4 to 6 servings.*

SPAGHETTI PUTTANESCA *with* CHERRY TOMATO SAUCE

Ripe cherry tomatoes are available all year round, thanks to our thriving greenhouse industry. They add a lovely sweetness and a rustic texture to this spicy pasta dish, said to be named after Italian "ladies of the night."

2 tbsp	olive oil	25 mL
4	cloves garlic, minced	4
¼ tsp	hot pepper flakes	1 mL
¼ tsp	dried oregano	1 mL
3 cups	whole cherry tomatoes	750 mL
•	Salt and pepper	•
4	anchovy fillets, chopped	4
¼ cup	pitted black or green olives, sliced	50 mL
2 tbsp	capers, rinsed and drained	25 mL
8 oz	spaghetti	250 g
¼ cup	chopped fresh parsley	50 mL

In a large deep skillet, heat the oil over medium heat. Add the garlic, hot pepper flakes and oregano; cook for 3 minutes, stirring. Add the tomatoes, ½ tsp (2 mL) salt and ¼ tsp (1 mL) pepper. Cook until the tomatoes start to split, 7 to 10 minutes, stirring often. Stir in the anchovies and cook for 5 minutes. Add the olives and capers; cook for 3 to 4 minutes longer until the sauce is thickened. Taste and adjust the seasoning if necessary.

Meanwhile, in a large pot of boiling salted water, cook the spaghetti until tender but firm. Drain well and toss with the sauce and parsley. *Makes 2 to 3 servings.*

Spaghetti Puttanesca with Cherry
Tomato Sauce (facing page)

PENNE *with* GRILLED VEGETABLES

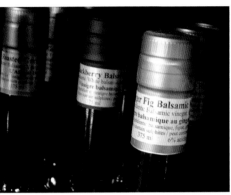

Grilling gives vegetables an extra dimension of smoky flavour. Have all the vegetables prepared ahead, ready to pop onto the grill with something like lamb leg or veal chops.

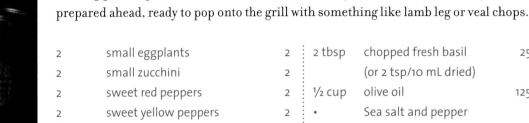

2	small eggplants	2	2 tbsp	chopped fresh basil	25 mL
2	small zucchini	2		(or 2 tsp/10 mL dried)	
2	sweet red peppers	2	½ cup	olive oil	125 mL
2	sweet yellow peppers	2	•	Sea salt and pepper	•
1	large red onion	1	6	firm ripe tomatoes	6
2 tbsp	chopped fresh thyme	25 mL	1½ lb	penne pasta	750 g
	(or 2 tsp/10 mL dried)			(about 7½ cups/1.9 L)	
2 tbsp	chopped fresh oregano	25 mL	1 tbsp	balsamic vinegar	15 mL
	(or 2 tsp/10 mL dried)				

Cut the eggplants and zucchini into ½-inch-thick (1 cm) diagonal slices. Quarter and seed the peppers. Cut the onion crosswise into 4 slices. Stir half the thyme, oregano and basil into the oil; brush over the vegetables on all sides. Reserve the remaining herbed oil. Sprinkle the vegetables with salt and pepper; set aside.

On a greased grill over medium-high heat, cook the tomatoes for 5 minutes, turning often; remove and let cool slightly. Working over a heatproof bowl or pot to retain the juices, peel, seed and dice the tomatoes; place in the bowl. Stir in the reserved herbed oil and salt and pepper to taste; keep warm at the side of the grill.

Place the onion slices on the grill; cook for 5 minutes. Add the eggplant, zucchini and peppers. Cook until tender, turning once, about 5 minutes longer.

Meanwhile, in a large pot of boiling salted water, cook the pasta until al dente, about 8 minutes. Drain well, return to the pot and add the tomato mixture; toss. Cut the grilled vegetables into large chunks. Mound the pasta on a large platter and top with the vegetables. Sprinkle the vegetables with the vinegar and remaining herbs. *Makes 8 generous servings.*

Ukrainian church on the Prairies >

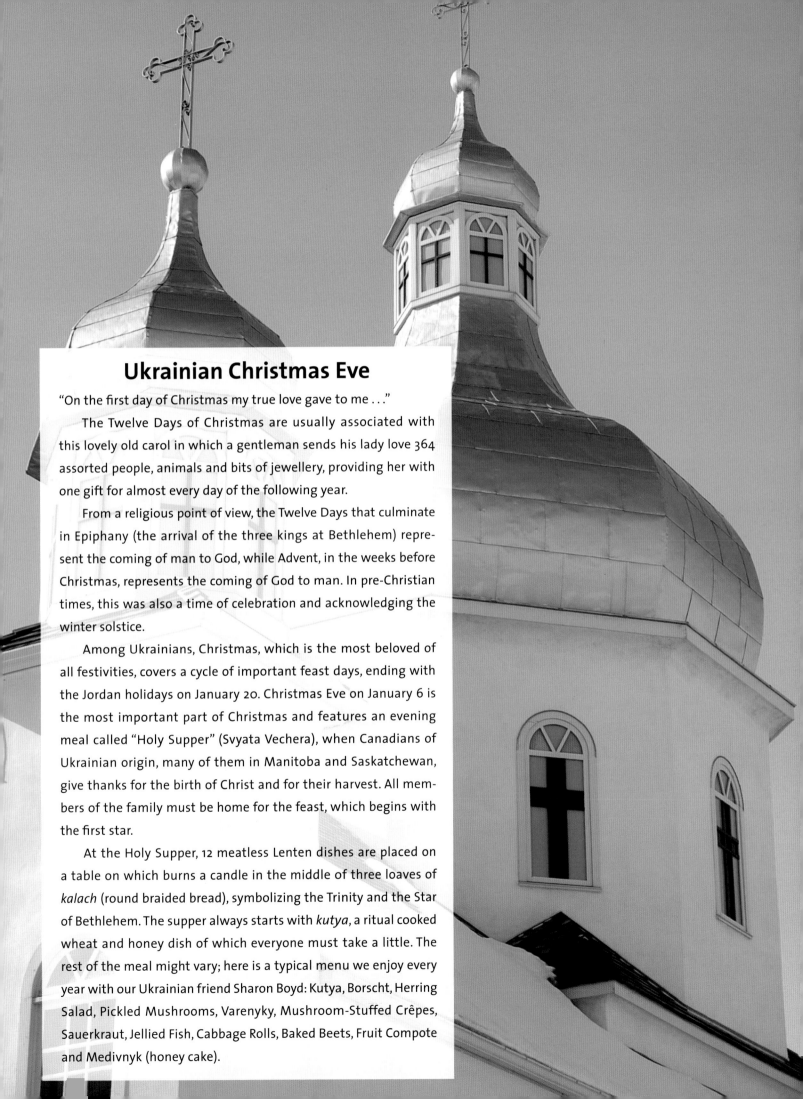

Ukrainian Christmas Eve

"On the first day of Christmas my true love gave to me . . ."

The Twelve Days of Christmas are usually associated with this lovely old carol in which a gentleman sends his lady love 364 assorted people, animals and bits of jewellery, providing her with one gift for almost every day of the following year.

From a religious point of view, the Twelve Days that culminate in Epiphany (the arrival of the three kings at Bethlehem) represent the coming of man to God, while Advent, in the weeks before Christmas, represents the coming of God to man. In pre-Christian times, this was also a time of celebration and acknowledging the winter solstice.

Among Ukrainians, Christmas, which is the most beloved of all festivities, covers a cycle of important feast days, ending with the Jordan holidays on January 20. Christmas Eve on January 6 is the most important part of Christmas and features an evening meal called "Holy Supper" (Svyata Vechera), when Canadians of Ukrainian origin, many of them in Manitoba and Saskatchewan, give thanks for the birth of Christ and for their harvest. All members of the family must be home for the feast, which begins with the first star.

At the Holy Supper, 12 meatless Lenten dishes are placed on a table on which burns a candle in the middle of three loaves of *kalach* (round braided bread), symbolizing the Trinity and the Star of Bethlehem. The supper always starts with *kutya*, a ritual cooked wheat and honey dish of which everyone must take a little. The rest of the meal might vary; here is a typical menu we enjoy every year with our Ukrainian friend Sharon Boyd: Kutya, Borscht, Herring Salad, Pickled Mushrooms, Varenyky, Mushroom-Stuffed Crêpes, Sauerkraut, Jellied Fish, Cabbage Rolls, Baked Beets, Fruit Compote and Medivnyk (honey cake).

CARAMELIZED ONION *and* PUMPKIN VARENYKY (PEROGIES)

These filled dumplings came to Canada with the Ukrainian and Polish settlers and are still made by their descendants, many of whom live on the Prairies or at Thunder Bay in Ontario. Fillings for varenyky, also known as perogies, might include mushrooms, potato and cheese, sauerkraut, cabbage or even fruit like plums or blueberries. Every year, I help my friend Sharon make the dumplings for her Ukrainian Christmas Eve supper. Along with the potato and cheese filling, we experimented with this modern version. We also confess to serving them with butter and sour cream, both of which would not be allowed in a true Lenten supper.

FILLING

1	large onion	1	¾ tsp	crumbled dried sage	4 mL
2 tbsp	olive oil	25 mL	½ tsp	dried thyme	2 mL
½ tsp	salt	2 mL	½ tsp	black pepper	2 mL
1½ cups	pumpkin purée (see page 206)	375 mL			

DOUGH

2 cups	all-purpose flour	500 mL	½ cup	cold water (approx)	125 mL
1 tsp	salt	5 mL	1 tbsp	canola oil	15 mL
1	egg	1			

FILLING: Cut the onion in half and slice each half thinly. In a large skillet, heat the oil over medium heat. Add the onion and salt, stirring to coat the onion well with oil. Cover and cook until softened, about 5 minutes. Uncover, reduce the heat to medium-low and cook, stirring often, until well browned, about 20 minutes.

Meanwhile, place the pumpkin in a sieve and drain well, especially if you use pumpkin you have baked yourself. Add to the onion with the sage, thyme, pepper and more salt if necessary. Cook and stir over medium heat until any liquid evaporates, about 5 minutes. Let cool.

DOUGH: In a deep bowl, stir the flour and salt together. In a small bowl, beat the egg with a fork and stir in the water and oil. Add to the flour mixture and stir gently to make a soft dough. (You may need a few more drops of water, but add it carefully as the dough should not be sticky.) Lightly flour the work surface and knead only until smooth (too much kneading will toughen the dough). Divide the dough in half; cover and let rest for 10 minutes.

(continued on next page)

CARAMELIZED ONION *and* PUMPKIN VARENYKY (PEROGIES) *(continued)*

Roll the dough very thinly on a lightly floured counter, working with half at a time. (Keep the remainder covered while you are not working with it to prevent it from drying out.) Cut rounds with a 3-inch (7.5 cm) cookie cutter or the top of a glass. Place a scant teaspoon (5 mL) of filling on each round, stretch the dough slightly and fold it over to form a half-circle; press the edges together with your fingers. (The edges should be free of any filling so they will seal properly.) As you fill the dumplings place them in a single layer on a baking sheet lined with a tea towel and cover with another tea towel. Do not crowd them. (If you reroll any scraps of dough, let the dough rest for 10 minutes, covered, before rerolling.)

Cook the varenyky, a few at a time, in a large pot of rapidly boiling salted water. The dumplings will come to the top when they are cooked, about 2 minutes, depending on the thickness of the dough. (The dumplings can be made ahead and frozen uncooked. Place frozen varenyky in boiling water and proceed as above.) *Makes 36 dumplings.*

NOTE: The dumplings are nice finished with sautéed onions. In a small skillet, sauté a small chopped onion in about ¼ cup (50 mL) butter (or canola oil if you want them as a Lenten dish). Place the cooked varenyky in a large baking dish and drizzle each batch with some of the butter and onion; keep warm in a low oven until all are done.

SQUASH *and* BEAN STEW
with CHIPOTLE CREAM

Squash and beans combine to create a rich vegetarian stew that's perfect served
with warm flour tortillas.

2 tbsp	canola or olive oil	25 mL	2 lb	buttercup, butternut or	1 kg
2	onions, coarsely chopped	2		hubbard squash, peeled,	
2 tsp	ground cumin	10 mL		seeded and cut into 1-inch	
1 tsp	salt	5 mL		(2.5 cm) cubes (about 5 cups/	
½ tsp	ground cinnamon	2 mL		1.25 L cubed squash)	
4	cloves garlic, minced	4	1	can (19 oz/540 mL) tomatoes	1
1	sweet green pepper,	1		(undrained)	
	seeded and thinly sliced		2	cans (19 oz/540 mL each) red	2
1 to 2	jalapeño peppers, seeded	1 to 2		kidney beans, drained and rinsed	
	and finely chopped		•	Chipotle Cream (recipe follows)	•
2 tbsp	chili powder	25 mL	•	Chopped fresh coriander	•

In a Dutch oven or large pot over medium heat, heat the oil. Add the onions, cumin, salt
and cinnamon. Cook for 5 minutes, stirring often, until the onions are soft. Reduce the
heat to low. Stir in the garlic, half the green pepper, the jalapeño and chili powder. Cover
and cook for 5 minutes, stirring occasionally.

Add the squash, stirring to coat it with the onion mixture. Chop the tomatoes in the can
using a knife or a pair of kitchen scissors; stir the tomatoes and their juice into the squash
mixture. Bring to a boil over medium-high heat, stirring to scrape up any browned bits
from the bottom. Reduce the heat to medium-low and cook until the squash is tender but
not mushy, about 20 minutes.

Gently stir in the beans and remaining green pepper. Cook, covered, for 5 minutes.
Taste and add more salt if necessary. Spoon into warmed wide bowls and top each portion
with a dollop of Chipotle Cream and a sprinkling of chopped coriander. Serve at once.
Makes 4 to 6 servings.

(continued on page 139)

137

SQUASH *and* BEAN STEW *with* CHIPOTLE CREAM *(continued)*

CHIPOTLE CREAM

1½ cups	sour cream	375 mL	2 tbsp	minced canned chipotle chilies (or more to taste)	25 mL

Whisk the sour cream and chipotle chilies together in a 2-cup (500 mL) serving bowl until well combined. Cover and refrigerate until ready to serve. *Makes about 1½ cups (375 mL).*

TIP: Chipotle chilies are smoked dried jalapeño peppers, usually packed in cans with adobo sauce. After opening, transfer any leftovers in the can to a tightly closed glass jar and store in the refrigerator for up to a week. Leftovers can also be frozen for up to 6 months. Pour the chilies and sauce into a freezer bag and seal well, gently pressing out the air. Manipulate the bag to separate the chilies so that it will be easy to break off a section of chili and sauce without thawing the whole package; then freeze.

∧   *Granville Island Market,*
    Vancouver

VEGETABLES, SIDES, SAUCES & PRESERVES

CREAMY POTATO-PARSNIP MASH ~ *141*

SAGE NEW POTATO KABOBS ~ *141*

DO-AHEAD SCALLOPED POTATOES WITH GRUYÈRE CRUST ~ *142*

WASABI MASHED POTATOES ~ *142*

SPICED SWEET POTATO PURÉE ~ *145*

GARLIC POTATO WEDGES ~ *145*

CUMIN-ROASTED CARROTS ~ *146*

CREAMED FIDDLEHEADS AND CARROTS ~ *146*

ROASTED ASPARAGUS WITH TARRAGON VINAIGRETTE ~ *148*

SAUTÉED SUGAR SNAPS WITH PROSCIUTTO CHIPS ~ *148*

SLOW-ROASTED TOMATOES ~ *149*

SHREDDED SPROUTS SAUTÉED WITH PANCETTA ~ *149*

A NEW-FASHIONED CORN ROAST ~ *151*

STIR-FRIED CORN AND SWEET PEPPERS ~ *152*

RAPINI SAUTÉED WITH WALNUTS AND ANCHOVIES ~ *152*

STIR-FRIED KALE ~ *154*

GARLICKY PORTOBELLO MUSHROOMS ~ *154*

RUTABAGA AND PEAR "CRISP" ~ *155*

ROASTED HARVEST VEGETABLES WITH SESAME-SAGE SAUCE ~ *156*

CARAMELIZED SQUASH ROUNDS ~ *157*

WILD RICE AND BARLEY PILAF ~ *157*

MUSHROOM YORKSHIRE PUDDINGS ~ *158*

SPICED CRANBERRY PORT SAUCE ~ *158*

PINK PEPPERCORN–MUSTARD SAUCE ~ *160*

CUCUMBER RAITA ~ *160*

PRESERVES ~ *162*
- Small-Batch Honey-Plum Jam
- Quick Pickled Beets
- Jewel Jam
- Tomato-Currant Chutney
- Small-Batch Spicy Peach Chutney

CREAMY POTATO-PARSNIP MASH

If you grow your own parsnips, try leaving a few in the garden until spring since freezing changes their carbo-hydrates to sugar, giving them a sweet, delicate, nutty flavour. This smooth mash is perfect for mopping up all the lovely gravy from a pot roast or stew.

4	large potatoes, peeled and quartered	4
4	large parsnips, peeled and cut into 1½-inch (4 cm) cubes	4
3	cloves garlic, peeled and left whole	3
¼ cup	light cream cheese	50 mL
¼ cup	light sour cream	50 mL
2 tbsp	butter	25 mL
¼ tsp	salt	1 mL
¼ tsp	black pepper	1 mL

Place the potatoes, parsnips and garlic in a large sauce-pan of salted water, cover, bring to a boil and cook until the vegetables are very tender, about 40 minutes. Drain well and return the saucepan to low heat for 30 seconds to dry the vegetables slightly.

Add the cream cheese, sour cream, butter, salt and pepper to the saucepan; mash the vegetables roughly. With an electric mixer, beat the mixture until smooth. Taste and add more salt and pepper if necessary. (The mash can be cooled, covered and refrigerated in a microwaveable dish for up to a day. Reheat in a microwave oven on High, stirring once, until piping hot. Transfer to a warm serving dish. Alternatively, cool, cover and refrigerate in an ovenproof dish; reheat in a 350°F/180°C oven until heated through, about 30 minutes.) *Makes 6 to 8 servings.*

SAGE NEW POTATO KABOBS

Tiny new waxy potatoes are perfect for kabobs. Boil them until just tender and grill them for a few minutes to reheat. If space on the grill is limited, thread all the potatoes on 3 or 4 skewers, and remove them to a plat-ter to serve.

24	small new potatoes (unpeeled)	24
¼ cup	olive oil	50 mL
¼ cup	finely chopped fresh sage	50 mL
1 tsp	paprika	5 mL
•	Sea salt and pepper	•

Scrub the potatoes well. In a saucepan of boiling salted water, cook the potatoes until barely tender, about 10 minutes. Drain well.

In a bowl, stir together the oil, sage and paprika. Add the potatoes and toss to coat well. Sprinkle with salt and pepper; toss again. (The potatoes can be prepared to this point and left at room temperature for up to 4 hours.)

Thread 8 skewers with 3 potatoes each. Place on a greased grill over medium-high heat and cook, turning often, until the skins are crisp and the potatoes are heated through, 3 to 4 minutes. *Makes 8 servings.*

DO-AHEAD SCALLOPED POTATOES *with* GRUYÈRE CRUST

Scalloped potatoes go so well with roast pork, ham or lamb and are a perfect make-ahead dish for company. These are rich and buttery without the use of cream.

¼ cup	butter	50 mL
4	large shallots, minced	4
8	large baking potatoes, peeled and thinly sliced	8
3 cups	milk	750 mL
¼ tsp	grated nutmeg	1 mL
•	Salt and pepper	•
1	clove garlic, halved	1
1½ cups	shredded Swiss Gruyère cheese	375 mL

In a large saucepan, melt the butter over medium heat; cook the shallots until softened, about 4 minutes. Add the potatoes and milk. Bring to a simmer over medium heat and cook, uncovered, for 20 minutes, lowering the heat as necessary and stirring often to prevent scorching. Season with nutmeg and salt and pepper to taste.

Meanwhile, rub the cut sides of the garlic over the inside of a greased shallow 8-cup (2 L) baking dish. Mince the garlic and sprinkle over the bottom. Top with the potato mixture and sprinkle with the cheese. (The potatoes can be cooled, covered and refrigerated for up to 2 days. Bring to room temperature before baking.)

Bake, uncovered, in a 375°F (190°C) oven until golden brown on top and bubbly, about 30 minutes. *Makes 8 servings.*

WASABI MASHED POTATOES

Mashed potatoes have been a long-time favourite accompaniment for the dark rich sauce of stews and roasts, but when I wanted to serve them with the Chinese-Style Roast Duck (page 86), I added wasabi paste for an interesting note. These mashed potatoes would pair well with any stew or roast.

4	potatoes, peeled	4
½ cup	whipping cream	125 mL
2 tbsp	butter	25 mL
2 tbsp	prepared wasabi	25 mL
•	Salt and pepper	•

Place the potatoes in a saucepan of cold salted water. Bring to a boil, reduce the heat, cover and cook until fork-tender, about 20 minutes. Drain; return to low heat for 2 minutes to dry. Mash or rice the potatoes.

Meanwhile, in a separate small saucepan or glass measure, heat the cream to steaming on the stovetop or in the microwave. Using a fork, gradually beat the cream into the mashed potatoes. Beat in the butter, wasabi, and salt and pepper to taste. *Makes 4 servings.*

Potatoes

Potatoes are our most important vegetable crop; 50 varieties are grown throughout the country. Although each province boasts of producing tonnes of the vegetable each year, the maritime provinces lead the way.

Native to Peru, the potato was brought back to Europe by explorers in the 16th century and became a staple food. The tuber has played a prominent role in Canada since potatoes were first cultivated at Port Royal, Nova Scotia, in 1623. Catharine Parr Traill wrote about it in *The Backwoods of Canada*, 1836: "The 'potatoe' is indeed a great blessing here; new settlers would otherwise be often greatly distressed, and the poor man and his family who are without resources, without the potatoe must starve." Pioneers planted potatoes as soon as they possibly could and relied on them for many things. They were used to make yeast for bread and mixed with flour for economy; starch squeezed from their pulp even found its way into the family laundry. They were used to soothe headaches, and small pieces of raw potato made good corks for bottles. Even in French Canada, where they were at first referred to disparagingly as "root" and eaten only when things were desperate, potatoes gradually started showing up at every meal.

A couple of so-called new varieties are appearing in supermarkets. Blue potatoes and fingerlings, those wee red or yellow potatoes that look like fingers, are both popular now, though I actually found fingerling potatoes at the Kitchener Farmers' Market almost 30 years ago.

Sweet Potatoes

Many shoppers are confused by the difference between a yam and a sweet potato. Actually, they are completely different vegetables. Yams originated in Africa and are found in our ethnic markets but do not grow here. Sweet potatoes, on the other hand, made their way north from South America and do grow well here. The best-known variety is the familiar orange-fleshed one that has made an appearance on Canadian holiday tables for years, often in an oversweet sauce or covered with marshmallows. I find them sweet enough on their own, and frequently bake them in their skins like white potatoes to enjoy split open to a bit of butter, salt and pepper.

Particularly good in soups and stews, sweet potatoes can be substituted in most recipes calling for regular potatoes. Sweet potato fries are currently the rage in many restaurants. If you make a cold salad with sweet potatoes, cook them a day ahead so the flesh is more solid and easier to slice or cube.

For dessert, why not try a sweet potato pie using cooked sweet potato purée in place of pumpkin?

SPICED SWEET POTATO PURÉE

This elegant and simple purée can be made ahead and set beside any number of roast meats. Depending on what you are serving, garnish the top with chopped fresh mint (great with lamb), coriander or parsley.

4	medium sweet potatoes	4
2 tbsp	butter	25 mL
1 tsp	ground cumin	5 mL
1 tsp	ground coriander	5 mL
Pinch	cayenne	Pinch
2 tbsp	sour cream or whipping cream	25 mL
•	Salt and pepper	•

Scrub the potatoes, but don't peel them. Pierce them in several places and arrange on a baking sheet. Roast in a 400°F (200°C) oven for about 1 hour or until very tender when pierced with a fork.

While they're still hot, peel the potatoes into a large bowl and mash them roughly. In a small skillet over medium heat, melt the butter and add the cumin, coriander and cayenne. Cook, stirring, until fragrant, about 2 minutes. Stir the mixture into the potatoes; add the sour cream, and salt and pepper to taste. Stir with a wooden spoon until smooth; or beat with an electric hand mixer if desired. Transfer to a greased 6-cup (1.5 L) shallow baking dish. (The potatoes can be cooled, covered and refrigerated for up to 1 day. Bring to room temperature before reheating.)

Reheat, covered, in a 350°F (180°C) oven for about 30 minutes or until hot throughout. *Makes 6 servings.*

GARLIC POTATO WEDGES

Vary the seasonings on these oven fries by substituting dried thyme, crumbled dried rosemary or even curry powder for the paprika. Use the flat side of a large chef's knife to crush the garlic.

4	large baking potatoes	4
2 tbsp	unsalted butter	25 mL
1 tbsp	canola oil	15 mL
1	clove garlic, crushed	1
1 tsp	paprika	5 mL
•	Salt	•

Preheat the oven to 450°C (230°C). Line a jelly roll pan or large rimmed baking sheet with foil. Scrub the potatoes well, then cut each lengthwise into 8 wedges, dropping the wedges into a bowl of cold water as you work. Melt the butter on the prepared pan in the oven for 1 minute, watching carefully to make sure it doesn't burn.

Remove from the oven and stir the oil, garlic and paprika into the melted butter. Drain the potatoes well and pat them dry. Add the potatoes to the butter mixture, turning to coat them well. Spread the potatoes out on the pan, return to the oven and bake for 15 minutes. Turn the wedges over and bake until golden and crisp, 10 to 15 minutes longer. Sprinkle with salt to taste. *Makes 4 servings.*

CUMIN-ROASTED CARROTS

Everyday carrots take on an exciting new look and flavour in this easy treatment that you can pop in the oven along with chicken or meat loaf. Substitute parsnips or do a combination of half carrots and half parsnips.

4	carrots	4
2 tbsp	fresh lemon juice	25 mL
2 tbsp	olive oil	25 mL
1 tsp	ground cumin	5 mL
½ tsp	salt	2 mL
¼ tsp	pepper	1 mL
¼ cup	chopped fresh parsley	50 mL
1	clove garlic, minced	1

Peel the carrots and cut them in half; cut each half into quarters and arrange in a small baking dish. Stir together the lemon juice, 4 tsp (20 mL) of the oil, cumin, salt and pepper. Pour over the carrots and toss to coat well. Cover with foil and roast in a 350°F (180°C) oven until tender, about 40 minutes.

Meanwhile, combine the parsley, garlic and remaining oil. Spoon over the carrots to serve.
Makes 4 servings. (Pictured on page 153.)

CREAMED FIDDLEHEADS *and* CARROTS

This delightful side dish is an abbreviated version of the traditional Maritime Hodge Podge, in which a colourful variety of new garden vegetables are cooked until just tender, then finished with cream. Fresh chervil arrives like magic early in the herb garden, and it is a wonderful addition here.

3	carrots, preferably new	3
2 tbsp	butter	25 mL
1 tbsp	finely chopped fresh chervil (or 1 tsp/5 mL dried)	15 mL
1 tsp	granulated sugar	5 mL
•	Salt and pepper	•
⅓ cup	water	75 mL
½ cup	whipping cream	125 mL
2 cups	fiddleheads*	500 mL

Cut the carrots into 2- × ½-inch (5 × 1 cm) strips. In a large heavy skillet, melt the butter over medium heat. Add the carrots; sprinkle with chervil, sugar, and salt and pepper to taste. Cook and stir the carrots to glaze them, 3 minutes.

Add the water and reduce the heat to medium-low; cover and simmer until almost tender, 6 to 8 minutes. Increase the heat to medium-high; uncover and cook until the water evaporates. Add the cream; cook until thickened, 2 to 4 minutes.

Meanwhile, in a saucepan of boiling water, cook the fiddleheads until tender, 5 to 7 minutes. Drain well and add them to the carrots. *Makes 4 servings.*

* See facing page for cleaning instructions.

Fiddleheads

The fiddleheads are up! That news sends wild-food enthusiasts into a frenzy of excitement. They know a delicious treat awaits them on the banks of rivers and streams where the tightly coiled spiral fronds (like the neck of a fiddle) of the ostrich fern are bursting forth.

As distinctly Canadian as wild rice and maple syrup, fiddleheads grow in every province and territory in the country, but the Maliseet Indians of New Brunswick are credited with having discovered these edible ferns and their nutritional value. (The ostrich is the only fern that's safe to eat, but their lovely, tropical-looking fronds are quite distinctive.) In New Brunswick, fiddleheads are harvested in large numbers and commercially frozen for distribution throughout the country.

Indeed, the fiddlehead is almost a provincial symbol in New Brunswick, where festivals, literary publications and radio stations proudly carry the name of this little harbinger of spring.

My first encounter with what is now one of my favourite greens was over 40 years ago along a stream near Collingwood, Ontario, when my husband's grandfather showed us the wild vegetable. He told us the story of how a Native person had introduced fiddleheads to his mother when her winter food supply was running low. Since then, my husband has always been lucky enough to find a good fern-picking spot wherever we have lived.

When in season, fresh fiddleheads are now available in some supermarkets, many farmers' markets and roadside stands. If you harvest your own, remember not to overpick so the ferns will continue to produce. They grow in clumps with the old fronds of the previous year still visible. Always leave about half the new fronds in each clump. Pick them in the morning while the plants are still crisp. Break off only tightly curled heads that are not higher than 6 inches (15 cm).

To clean fresh fiddleheads, uncurl each head and shake off the thin brown scaly husk. Wash ferns several times in cool water and trim off any dark stem ends. Two cups (500 mL) will make four servings.

Cook them, uncovered, in a large amount of boiling salted water, or steam them in a basket set over boiling water, until just tender, 5 to 8 minutes. Enjoy them hot with butter, salt, pepper and a squirt of lemon juice or serve them cold in a vinaigrette.

ROASTED ASPARAGUS *with* TARRAGON VINAIGRETTE

My favourite asparagus farmer, Tim Barrie, picks lovely big Jersey asparagus stalks for me to roast. I do them a few hours ahead, leave them at room temperature and drizzle on a simple herb vinaigrette just before serving. Never is there a stalk left on the platter!

5 lb	thick asparagus spears	2.2 kg
•	Olive oil	•
•	Salt and pepper	•
¼ cup	white wine vinegar	50 mL
⅔ cup	olive oil	150 mL
¼ cup	minced fresh tarragon leaves	50 mL

Trim the spears and arrange in a single layer on 2 baking sheets. Drizzle with olive oil (about 1 tbsp/15 mL per sheet), sprinkle with salt and pepper and roast in a 500°F (260°C) oven until just tender, about 8 minutes, stirring once. Remove to a large platter and let come to room temperature.

Meanwhile, combine the vinegar and salt and pepper to taste in a measuring cup; gradually whisk in the oil, then stir in the tarragon leaves. (The vinaigrette can be made a couple of hours ahead and left at room temperature.) Drizzle over the asparagus just before serving. *Makes 15 to 20 servings.*

SAUTÉED SUGAR SNAPS *with* PROSCIUTTO CHIPS

The first time I saw this edible-podded green pea, many years ago, I was visiting a farmers' market in Prince Edward Island. Although we were touring by car and had no means of cooking them, we couldn't resist buying a bag and eating them by the side of the road. When sugar snap peas are at our farmers' market, I buy them every week and cook them in the simplest ways . . . that is, if I cook them at all.

2 tbsp	olive oil	25 mL
4	slices prosciutto	4
3	cloves garlic, slightly crushed	3
1 lb	sugar snap peas, trimmed	500 g
1 tbsp	soy sauce	15 mL
1 tsp	granulated sugar	5 mL
•	Black pepper	•

In a large skillet, heat half the oil over medium-high heat and fry the prosciutto until crisp, about 3 minutes. Remove to drain on paper towels; break up into pieces and set aside.

In the same skillet, heat the remaining oil and stir-fry the garlic over medium-high heat until golden. Remove the garlic with a slotted spoon and discard. Add the peas to the skillet and stir-fry until tender and bright green but still crisp, about 2 minutes. Stir in the soy sauce, sugar and black pepper to taste. Serve immediately sprinkled with prosciutto pieces. *Makes 4 servings. (Pictured on page 153.)*

SLOW-ROASTED TOMATOES

Roasting makes plum tomatoes as sweet as candy. Serve as a side with grilled lamb chops or steak; top toasted baguette slices for an easy bruschetta; coarsely chop and stir into cooked pasta with lots of freshly grated Parmesan cheese; or make the Roasted Tomato and Cheese Tart (page 12).

8	plum tomatoes (about 2 lb/1 kg)	8
2	cloves garlic, thinly sliced	2
3	sprigs fresh rosemary	3
1 tbsp	brown sugar	15 mL
1 tbsp	balsamic vinegar	15 mL
1 tbsp	olive oil	15 mL

Line a shallow baking pan with parchment paper. Halve the tomatoes lengthwise and place, cut side up, in a single layer in the pan. Place a slice of garlic and a few rosemary leaves on each. Sprinkle with sugar; drizzle with vinegar and oil. Roast in a 250°F (120°C) oven until softened and lightly charred at the edges, about 2½ hours. *Makes 16 pieces.*

SHREDDED SPROUTS SAUTÉED *with* PANCETTA

Brussels sprouts are a favourite in our family. It's unfortunate many people avoid them because they have been subjected to overcooked grey versions of these little cabbage cousins. In this new fast way of cooking them, there is a lot of lively colour and flavour—sure to appeal to all.

1 lb	Brussels sprouts	500 g
1 tbsp	olive oil	15 mL
2 oz	pancetta,* diced (about ½ cup/125 mL)	50 g
½ tsp	hot pepper flakes	2 mL
2 tbsp	fresh lemon juice	25 mL

Trim the sprouts, cut them in half lengthwise and thinly slice across each half. (The sprouts can be shredded hours ahead of time and refrigerated.)

In a large skillet, heat the oil over medium heat. Add the pancetta and cook, stirring often, until crisp, about 4 minutes. With a slotted spoon, remove to drain on paper towels. Discard all but 2 tbsp (25 mL) of the drippings from the pan. Add the shredded sprouts and hot pepper flakes; sauté for 3 minutes. Cover the pan and cook until the sprouts are tender-crisp, 2 to 3 minutes longer. Stir in the lemon juice, sprinkle with the pancetta and serve immediately. *Makes 4 servings.*

* Pancetta is unsmoked Italian bacon available at most supermarket deli counters.

Corn

When Europeans came to Canada, Native peoples had long been growing corn, or maize. They valued it not only as a food, but also as currency, fuel, jewellery and a symbol in religious ceremonies. It was grown as part of the "three sisters," the other sisters being squash and beans.

The first settlers bartered with the local inhabitants for seed, and it was not unusual for settlers to grow corn even before they had their land cleared. Native people also taught them how to preserve corn by drying and powdering it. Fresh corn, dried corn and cornmeal were put to good use in countless ways to achieve some variety in an otherwise monotonous diet.

Today, corn is still valued across the country for its many uses, and when fresh corn starts to appear in the market people flock to buy it—one of the true rites of summer.

A NEW-FASHIONED CORN ROAST

The corn roasts I remember from my youth were actually corn "boils" accomplished in a huge metal drum. This updated version is done on the grill. It's easy and fun on the patio or even out in the field where the corn is grown. Just remember that appetites are big outdoors, and corn is always a favourite. Serve the grilled cobs with a choice of plain or flavoured butter. Each of the flavoured butters is enough for about 8 ears of corn; double the recipes if desired.

16	ears corn (husks on)	16			
CUMIN BUTTER					
⅓ cup	butter, at room temperature	75 mL	1 tsp	ground cumin	5 mL
			Pinch	hot pepper flakes	Pinch
ROSEMARY BUTTER					
⅓ cup	butter, at room temperature	75 mL	2 tsp	chopped fresh rosemary (or ½ tsp/2 mL dried)	10 mL
			Pinch	black pepper	Pinch

Leaving them attached at the base of the cob, carefully pull back the husks from each cob of corn. Remove all the silk and rewrap the corn in the husks, securing them at the tip with a string. Soak the corn in cold water for at least 15 minutes to moisten it well.

Grill over high heat for 20 to 30 minutes or until tender, turning occasionally. Remove the husks and serve hot with the butters.

CUMIN BUTTER: Cream together the butter, cumin and hot pepper flakes.

ROSEMARY BUTTER: Cream together the butter, rosemary and pepper. (The butters can be made up to 1 day ahead; pack each into a small ramekin, cover and refrigerate. Or, if desired, spoon each onto plastic wrap; shape into a log and wrap tightly. Refrigerate overnight. Slice into rounds to serve on the corn.) *Makes 8 servings (2 cobs each).*

TIP: Even with new strains of corn, the sooner you cook it after it's picked the better, and don't be tempted to pull back the husks when you buy it since that allows moisture to escape. Rely on your local farmer to know that it's good and feel the cobs yourself to be sure they are mature. Have a good look at the stems; they should be damp and pale green, not brown and dry.

STIR-FRIED CORN *and* SWEET PEPPERS

Our son and his wife were married at our house one lovely, warm September day. Both love fresh corn on the cob in season, but I thought eating it that way might be a challenge in wedding finery, so I made this stir-fry as a salad instead. Serve it hot, at room temperature or chilled as a salad on shredded lettuce.

4	ears corn, husked	4
1 tbsp	soy sauce	15 mL
1 tbsp	rice wine or sake	15 mL
1 tbsp	Worcestershire sauce	15 mL
1 tbsp	sesame oil	15 mL
1 tsp	granulated sugar	5 mL
1 tsp	Chinese hot chili sauce	5 mL
	(or ½ tsp/2 mL hot pepper flakes)	
1 tbsp	canola oil	15 mL
1 tbsp	minced fresh ginger	15 mL
2	cloves garlic, minced	2
2	sweet red peppers, coarsely diced	2
1	can (8 oz/227 g) water chestnuts, rinsed and coarsely chopped	1
1 cup	fresh coriander leaves	250 mL

Cut the kernels from the corn and set aside. (You should have about 2 cups/500 mL.)

In a small bowl, stir together the soy sauce, rice wine, Worcestershire sauce, sesame oil, sugar and chili sauce; set aside.

In a wok or large skillet over high heat, heat the canola oil. Add the ginger and garlic; stir-fry until fragrant, about 10 seconds. Add the corn and peppers; stir-fry for 2 minutes. Add the water chestnuts; stir-fry for 1 minute. Stir in the soy sauce mixture; stir-fry for 1 minute. Stir in the fresh coriander. *Makes 6 servings.*

RAPINI SAUTÉED *with* WALNUTS *and* ANCHOVIES

While early settlers relied on wild herbs for their greens, Canadians now have a wide choice of interesting and nutritious greens for our shopping carts—spinach, rapini, kale, Swiss chard, collards, dandelion, bok choy and a large selection of other Chinese greens. Also called broccoli raab, this skinny cousin of our more familiar broccoli is loaded with nutrients like its relative but hasn't been as popular because of its slightly bitter taste. Lately, however, more and more people are taking to its pungent, earthy flavour, especially when it's combined with interesting ingredients like nuts and anchovies.

1	bunch rapini (1 lb/500 g)	1
¼ cup	olive oil	50 mL
2	shallots, minced (about ½ cup/125 mL)	2
¼ tsp	hot pepper flakes	1 mL
½ cup	chopped walnuts	125 mL
•	Salt and pepper	•
3	anchovies, chopped	3
2 tbsp	fresh lemon juice	25 mL

Trim off 1 inch (2.5 cm) from the stalk bottoms and wash the rapini well. Cook, uncovered, in a large pot of boiling salted water until just tender, about 2 to 3 minutes. Drain and refresh under cold, running water to cool. Squeeze out any excess liquid and pat the rapini dry. Coarsely chop. (The blanched rapini can be refrigerated in a plastic bag for up to 24 hours.)

In a large skillet, heat the oil over medium-high heat. Sauté the shallots and hot pepper flakes until the shallots are soft, about 2 minutes. Add the walnuts; sauté for 2 minutes. Add the rapini; cook, stirring often, until heated through, about 3 minutes. Season with salt and pepper. Stir in the anchovies and lemon juice; serve immediately. *Makes 4 to 6 servings.*

CLOCKWISE, FROM TOP: *Cumin-Roasted Carrots (page 146).*
Sautéed Sugar Snaps with Prosciutto Chips (page 148) and
Rapini Sautéed with Walnuts and Anchovies (facing page)

STIR-FRIED KALE

Kale's frilly dark leaves are always so appealing in the farmers' market stalls, but few people know how nutrient-dense this member of the cabbage family actually is. It is starting to appear cut and ready to cook more often now in supermarkets. Often it is added to slow-cooking soups and stews. Here it is given a quick and easy stir-fry.

4 oz	kale	125 g
1 tbsp	canola oil	15 mL
1 tbsp	grated fresh ginger	15 mL
Pinch	salt	Pinch
1 tbsp	soy sauce	15 mL
¼ tsp	granulated sugar	1 mL
1 tsp	sesame oil	5 mL

Wash the kale well in several changes of water, but do not dry it. Remove any thick stalks and slice the leaves into thin strips. In a wok or large skillet over medium heat, heat the oil and stir-fry the ginger for 1 minute. Add the kale with the water that clings to it and the salt. Increase the heat, add the soy sauce and stir-fry until the kale is almost wilted, about 3 minutes. Stir in the sugar and drizzle with sesame oil. *Makes 2 to 3 servings.*

GARLICKY PORTOBELLO MUSHROOMS

Flavourful, meaty-textured portobellos are heavenly cooked on the grill.

16	small (or 8 large) portobello mushrooms	16
2 tbsp	olive oil	25 mL
1 tbsp	fresh lemon juice	15 mL
4	cloves garlic, minced	4
•	Salt and pepper	•

Cut the stems off the mushrooms just below the caps; reserve for another use, such as a stir-fry or soup. Wipe the top of each cap with a damp towel. Stir together the oil, lemon juice and garlic; brush all over the mushroom caps or toss together in a large bowl. Sprinkle with salt and pepper.

Place, underside down, on a greased grill over medium-high heat; cook for 5 minutes. Turn and cook until very tender when pierced, about 5 minutes longer. Slice or serve whole. *Makes 8 servings.*

RUTABAGA *and* PEAR "CRISP"

Rutabaga has been a traditional side dish at Christmas since early settlers started to grow this yellow-orange root that is often mistakenly called a turnip. Don't wait for the holidays to serve this lovely make-ahead casserole.

4	pears	4		½ tsp	ground ginger	2 mL
¼ cup	apple juice or cider	50 mL		•	Salt and pepper	•
1	rutabaga (about 3 lb/1.5 kg)	1		•	Lemon-Parsley Crumbs	•
4	carrots	4			(recipe follows)	
2 tbsp	butter	25 mL				

Peel, core and coarsely chop the pears. Combine with the apple juice in a small saucepan; bring to a boil, reduce the heat, cover and cook 10 minutes. Uncover, increase the heat to medium and cook until the pears are very soft, about 10 minutes longer.

Meanwhile, peel and cut the rutabaga and carrots into large chunks. In a saucepan of boiling water, cook the rutabaga and carrots until tender, about 20 minutes. Drain well.

Transfer the vegetables and pears to a food processor or blender; purée until smooth. Blend in the butter, ginger, and salt and pepper to taste. Transfer to a 6-cup (1.5 L) baking dish. (The casserole can be cooled, covered and refrigerated for up to 1 day. Bring to room temperature for 30 minutes before proceeding.)

Sprinkle lemon-parsley crumbs evenly over the rutabaga purée. Grease foil and cover the casserole with it, greased side down. Bake in a 350°F (180°C) oven for 20 minutes. Uncover and bake until the purée is heated through and the crumb topping is golden, another 20 to 30 minutes. *Makes 8 servings.*

LEMON-PARSLEY CRUMBS

1	lemon	1		1 tbsp	olive oil	15 mL
½ cup	fresh parsley leaves	125 mL		•	Salt and pepper	•
4	slices bread, preferably homemade-style white	4				

Cut the zest from the lemon in strips with a vegetable peeler or zester and combine in a food processor with the parsley. Pulse to finely chop. Remove the crusts and break up the bread; add to the food processor and pulse to make coarse crumbs. With a fork, stir in the oil and season with salt and pepper. (The mixture can be refrigerated in a plastic bag for a day or 2.)

ROASTED HARVEST VEGETABLES *with* SESAME-SAGE SAUCE

Roasting root vegetables at a high temperature brings out all their sweetness. The sauce is a delicious accompaniment, and it is also great with a medley of grilled vegetables or makes a lovely dip for raw vegetables and cooked shrimp.

24	tiny red potatoes (1 lb/500 g)	24	1 tbsp	finely chopped sage	15 mL
4	carrots	4		(or 1 tsp/5 mL crushed	
4	parsnips	4		dried sage)	
½	rutabaga	½	1 tsp	salt	5 mL
¼ cup	olive oil	50 mL	¼ tsp	pepper	1 mL
1 tbsp	finely chopped fresh	15 mL	2 tbsp	fresh lemon juice	25 mL
	rosemary (or 1 tsp/5 mL		•	Sesame-Sage Sauce	•
	crushed dried rosemary)			(recipe follows)	

Scrub the potatoes, but do not peel them. Cut the large ones into quarters. Cut the carrots and parsnips into 1½-inch (4 cm) pieces. Peel and cut the rutabaga into ¼-inch (5 mm) slices, then cut each slice into 5 wedges.

In a large, greased shallow baking dish, combine the vegetables, oil, rosemary, sage, salt and pepper. Toss to coat well. Drizzle with lemon juice. Cover and roast in a 450°F (230°C) oven for 30 minutes. Uncover and roast until the vegetables are tender and browned, about 25 minutes, stirring after 15 minutes. Serve hot with cold Sesame-Sage Sauce on the side. *Makes 6 servings.*

SESAME-SAGE SAUCE

1 cup	good-quality mayonnaise	250 mL	1 tbsp	soy sauce	15 mL
2 tbsp	fresh lemon juice	25 mL	1 tbsp	Dijon mustard	15 mL
2 tbsp	finely chopped fresh sage	25 mL	2	cloves garlic, minced	2
2 tbsp	toasted sesame seeds	25 mL	1	jalapeño pepper, minced	1
1 tbsp	rice vinegar	15 mL	•	Salt and pepper	•

In a bowl, stir together the mayonnaise, lemon juice, sage, sesame seeds, vinegar, soy sauce, mustard, garlic, jalapeño, and salt and pepper to taste. Cover and refrigerate for up to 3 days. *Makes about 1 ½ cups (375 mL).*

CARAMELIZED SQUASH ROUNDS

Look for butternut squash with long necks for this simple side dish.

2	butternut squash	2
2 tbsp	olive oil	25 mL
1 tbsp	butter, melted	15 mL
1 tsp	crumbled dried sage	5 mL
1 tsp	brown sugar	5 mL
Pinch	ground cinnamon	Pinch
•	Salt and pepper	•

Cut the neck from each squash and reserve the remainder for another use. Cut off the stems and slice the necks into twelve 3/4-inch (2 cm) rounds; peel.

Place the rounds in a single layer on a parchment-lined baking sheet. In a small bowl, stir together the oil, butter, sage, sugar and cinnamon. Brush over both sides of the rounds and sprinkle the tops with salt and pepper. (The squash can be prepared a couple of hours ahead and left at room temperature. The rounds can be cut and peeled up to a day ahead of this.) Bake in a 375°F (190°F) oven until tender, 20 to 25 minutes. Serve hot, 2 to a plate. *Makes 6 servings.*

WILD RICE *and* BARLEY PILAF

Pilafs are traditionally made with rice, but here I've used two Canadian-grown grains to make an interesting side dish for beef or lamb. Dried wild mushrooms are now available in most supermarkets and require no soaking before you add them to the barley mixture.

1 tbsp	olive oil	15 mL
1	onion, chopped	1
1 tbsp	chopped fresh rosemary or thyme	15 mL
½ cup	barley	125 mL
½ cup	wild rice, rinsed	125 mL
1	pkg (0.5 oz/14 g) dried morels or other dried mushrooms, rinsed	1
4 cups	beef or chicken stock	1 L
•	Salt and pepper	•
¼ cup	dried cranberries	50 mL
½ cup	chopped fresh parsley	125 mL

In a large saucepan, heat the oil over medium-low heat. Add the onion and rosemary and cook, stirring often, until softened, about 5 minutes. Add the barley and wild rice; stir to coat. Stir in the mushrooms, stock, and ½ tsp (2 mL) each salt and pepper. Bring to a boil; stir, cover, reduce the heat to low and cook until the liquid has almost been absorbed and the grains are tender, about 60 minutes. (You don't want the barley too dry, but if there is too much liquid, simmer uncovered for a few minutes.) Stir in the cranberries, cover, remove from the heat and let stand for 5 minutes.

Stir in the parsley and transfer to a heated serving dish. *Makes 6 servings.*

MUSHROOM YORKSHIRE PUDDINGS

Our British settlers brought us the tradition of puddings, both sweet and savoury. Now our Sunday roast doesn't seem complete without airy Yorkshire puddings, and these, with their mushroom fillings, are extra special.

2 tbsp	butter	25 mL
8 oz	mushrooms, coarsely chopped	250 g
½ tsp	dried thyme	2 mL
¼ tsp	crumbled dried sage	1 mL
•	Salt and pepper	•
2	eggs	2
1 cup	all-purpose flour	250 mL
1 cup	milk	250 mL
2 tbsp	canola oil	25 mL

In a large skillet, melt the butter over medium heat. Add the mushrooms, thyme, sage, and ¼ tsp (1 mL) each salt and pepper. Cook, stirring occasionally, until the mushrooms are golden, about 10 minutes. Remove from the heat and let cool. (The mushrooms can be covered and refrigerated for up to 24 hours.)

In a blender or food processor, place, in order, the eggs, ½ tsp (2 mL) salt, flour and milk. Blend just until smooth. Refrigerate for at least 1 hour and up to 6 hours.

Spray 8 muffin cups with cooking oil and divide the canola oil among them, brushing the sides to grease well. (It is important the cups be well greased.) Stir the batter briefly; pour into the cups, dividing it evenly. Spoon the mushroom mixture into the centre of each, dividing it evenly. Bake in a 400°F (200°C) oven until golden brown and puffy, 30 minutes. Serve at once. *Makes 8 puddings.*

SPICED CRANBERRY PORT SAUCE

It is seldom a beautiful roast turkey is put on a table without cranberry sauce. Why not make it an elegant one?

¾ cup	port (ruby)	175 mL
½ cup	water	125 mL
¾ cup	granulated sugar	175 mL
1	strip lemon zest (5 inches/12 cm long)	1
4	whole cloves	4
3	whole star anise	3
1	cinnamon stick (3 inches/8 cm)	1
12 oz	cranberries, fresh or frozen, unthawed (about 3½ cups/875 mL)	375 g

In a medium saucepan, combine the port, water, sugar, lemon zest, cloves, star anise and cinnamon stick. Bring to a boil, stirring to dissolve the sugar. Reduce the heat to low and simmer, uncovered, for 10 minutes. Remove from the heat, cover and let stand for 5 minutes.

Strain the syrup and return to the saucepan, discarding the solids. Bring to a boil, stir in the cranberries and reduce heat to medium-low; simmer, uncovered and stirring occasionally, until most of the cranberries have burst and the sauce is slightly thickened, about 8 minutes. Let cool. (The sauce will thicken more upon cooling.) The sauce can be cooled, covered and refrigerated for up to 1 week or frozen for up to 1 month. *Makes 2 cups (500 mL).*

Cranberries

As my flight took off from Vancouver, British Columbia, the beautiful crimson carpet thousands of feet below took my breath away. The young couple sitting beside me were intrigued, and I explained that it was, in fact, a sea of cranberries, from vines that had been flooded just before harvest. (There are two ways of harvesting, this wet method and a dry harvest in which berries are combed from the vines.) After a machine beats the vines to release the fruit, labourers in hip waders corral the glistening berries with rakes and booms, pushing them toward conveyor belts that pick them up and load them onto waiting wagons. This region, Richmond, just south of Vancouver, and others in the Fraser Valley produce 80 percent of Canada's cranberries.

Nova Scotia was once the leading cranberry-producing area in Canada, shipping as far away as London, England, in 1874. Now the province has only one major commercial grower, whose crop is primarily sold on the fresh market throughout the Maritimes. Prince Edward Island's wild berry harvest is mostly for residents of the province. In Newfoundland, it's not the wild cranberry that's harvested but a relative close enough to mention—the partridgeberry (called foxberry in the Maritimes and lingonberry in Scandinavia). Commercial cranberry crops are relatively recent in Quebec, although both small and large cranberries grow wild there in abundance. Ontario boasts two good-sized commercial bogs in Muskoka: Johnston's Cranberry Marsh at Bala and the Iroquois Cranberry Growers near Mactier.

Before early settlers arrived in this country, Native inhabitants used cranberries (which they called *assamanesh*, or bitter fruit) for a rich red dye and also for food, especially combined with ground venison and fat to make a dried staple called pemmican. They also found the fruit's acidity made it a good poultice for wounds.

Cranberries contain benzoic acid, a natural preservative, which allows them to retain their high nutritive content and to stay whole and separate when frozen. This unique characteristic, discovered by Natives in a cold climate, allows you to treat the frozen fruit exactly as you would fresh berries, making it a year-round treat.

PINK PEPPERCORN– MUSTARD SAUCE

This zesty cold sauce would be great on any cold meat, especially beef. Pink peppercorns are available at most delis.

4 tsp	pink peppercorns	20 mL
½ cup	mayonnaise	125 mL
½ cup	sour cream	125 mL
2 tbsp	Dijon mustard	25 mL
1	clove garlic, minced	1
2 tsp	icing sugar	10 mL

Crush the peppercorns with a mortar and pestle or in a mini chopper or pepper grinder. (Or place in a sturdy plastic bag and crush with a heavy skillet.) Set aside.

In a bowl, whisk together the mayonnaise, sour cream, mustard, garlic and sugar until smooth. Stir in the peppercorns. Sprinkle any pink flakes left in the bag on the top for garnish. Cover and refrigerate at least 1 hour and up to 24 hours before serving. *Makes 1¼ cups (300 mL).*

CUCUMBER RAITA

This is the perfect accompaniment to the spicy Beef and Tomato Curry (page 107), but I enjoy it on its own as a salad, to which I might add a few halved cherry tomatoes.

1	piece (8 inches/20 cm) English cucumber	1
•	Salt	•
1 cup	thick plain yogurt	250 mL
1	small shallot, minced	1
2 tbsp	chopped fresh coriander	25 mL
1 tbsp	fresh lemon juice	15 mL
½ tsp	ground cumin	2 mL
Pinch	cayenne	Pinch
•	Black pepper	•

Dice the unpeeled cucumber and toss with 1 tsp (5 mL) salt in a colander; let stand for 30 minutes to drain. Press out any moisture.

In a bowl, combine the yogurt, shallot, coriander, lemon juice, cumin, cayenne and pepper to taste; stir in the cucumber. *Makes 2 cups (500 mL).*

Preserving Pleasures

I look forward each year to spending a day with my daughter-in-law making chili sauce, an afternoon with my friend Diane canning beans for Waterloo County's Schnippled Bean Salad and a whole day with friends in Waterloo making relish. It doesn't seem like work when you can chat and visit while you chop and stir.

There is not the same necessity as when I helped my mother preserve the food from our garden and woods so we could have something to see us through the meagre months of winter, but there is a nostalgic pleasure.

Before canning became widespread with the 1858 patenting of the Mason jar, long cold winters forced early Canadian settlers to rely on brine-curing, smoking, drying and their less-than-effective root cellars in order to preserve the harvest.

I've included a few simple preserves in this book, most of them small batches that can be kept in the refrigerator for a few weeks. In case you do wish to keep them longer on the shelf, use canning jars with new two-piece lids. Wash them well, rinse and if the filled jars are to be processed in a boiling water bath for fewer than 10 minutes, sterilize the empty jars by placing them in the rack of your boiling water canner filled with cold water. Let the jars fill with water, bring to a boil and boil for 10 minutes. Heat the flat metal disks in hot water to soften the sealing compound. Fill the hot empty jars with the hot preserves leaving the recommended headspace, and apply the screw band until just fingertip-tight. Have the canner two-thirds full of boiling water and place the jars in the canner rack; lower the rack and pour in enough boiling water to come 1 inch (2.5 cm) above the top of the jars. Cover; bring back to a boil and time.

PRESERVES

SMALL-BATCH HONEY-PLUM JAM

Make a batch of this quick, fresh-tasting jam every time you want something special to spread on morning toast or hot tea biscuits. You can make jam all winter long by freezing the plums and sugar needed for each batch in small freezer bags.

3 cups	pitted and coarsely chopped purple plums (about 1 lb/500 g)	750 mL
⅓ cup	granulated sugar	75 mL
⅓ cup	water	75 mL
2 tbsp	fresh lemon juice	25 mL
2 tbsp	liquid honey	25 mL

In a heavy medium saucepan, combine the plums, sugar, water and lemon juice. Bring to a boil over medium-high heat. Reduce the heat to medium; boil, stirring and mashing occasionally with the back of a spoon, until thickened, about 15 minutes.

Remove from the heat; stir in the honey. Let cool to room temperature. Refrigerate in tightly covered jars for up to 2 weeks. *Makes 2 cups (500 mL).*

QUICK PICKLED BEETS

I recently saw a jar of commercially pickled beets noted in an upscale food magazine. That was enough to convince me I wasn't the only person who loved this old-fashioned preserve. If you have a craving for this but don't have the resources or time to "put down" ten sealers, here is a quick and easy taste.

1 lb	small (1-inch/2.5 cm) beets	500 g
½ cup	cider vinegar	125 mL
½ cup	water	125 mL
3 tbsp	packed brown sugar	45 mL
½ tsp	coarse pickling salt	2 mL
¼ tsp	ground cinnamon	1 mL
¼ tsp	dry mustard	1 mL
Pinch	ground cloves	Pinch
Pinch	black pepper	Pinch

Wash the beets and remove all but 1 inch (2.5 cm) of the stems. Leave the roots on. In a medium saucepan of boiling salted water to cover the beets, cook the beets until tender when pierced with a fork, 15 to 18 minutes. Peel and place in a small bowl or jar.

In a small saucepan, combine the vinegar, water, sugar, salt, cinnamon, mustard, cloves and pepper. Bring to a boil, reduce the heat and simmer, uncovered, 5 minutes. Pour over the beets, let cool, cover and refrigerate at least 1 day before using. The beets will keep in the refrigerator for 2 weeks. *Makes about 8 servings.*

JEWEL JAM

The traditional fruits for this stunning jam are a combination of cherries, gooseberries, red currants and raspberries. This version substitutes easier-to-find cranberries (now available all year either fresh or frozen) for the gooseberries and leaves out the cherries.

2 cups	cranberries	500 mL
3 cups	granulated sugar	750 mL
2 cups	raspberries	500 mL
2 cups	red currants, stemmed	500 mL

Combine the cranberries and 1 cup (250 mL) of the sugar in a large saucepan. Bring to a boil over medium-high heat, then boil rapidly for 5 minutes, stirring constantly. Stir in the raspberries, red currants and the remaining 2 cups (500 mL) sugar. Bring back to a boil, then boil, uncovered, over medium-high heat, stirring constantly, for 10 to 15 minutes, until thickened and set (see TIP on next page). Pour the jam into hot, sterilized jars, leaving ½-inch (1 cm) headspace. Seal by placing on the disc and screwing on the band firmly without forcing it. Leave at room temperature overnight. Refrigerate for up to 1 month or freeze for up to 1 year. Or, for storage at a cool room temperature, process

(continued on page 164)

LEFT TO RIGHT: *Tomato-Currant Chutney (page 164),*
Small-Batch Spicy Peach Chutney (page 164),
Spiced Cranberry Port Sauce (page 158)

PRESERVES *(continued)*

immediately for 5 minutes in a boiling water bath (see page 161). *Makes about 3½ cups (875 mL).*

TIP: To test for setting point, place 2 small plates in the freezer before you start cooking. Drop ½ tsp (2 mL) thickened jam onto 1 cold plate; leave for 1 minute to cool. Tilt the plate and if the jam flows slowly, it's set. Or when you run your finger through the mixture and the surface wrinkles, the jam is set. If it is too runny, return the plate to the freezer; continue cooking and testing every few minutes with the colder plate. Alternatively, use a candy thermometer; at 220°F (104°C) the jam is set.

TOMATO-CURRANT CHUTNEY

Chili sauce with tomatoes, onions, peppers and celery is a Canadian culinary icon for which most serious cooks have a favourite family recipe. This thick, spicy-sweet chutney is reminiscent of chili sauce and goes well with pâté, cheese or meat pies.

3 lb	tomatoes (about 8)	1.5 kg
2	onions, chopped	2
⅔ cup	cider vinegar	150 mL
1 tbsp	grated lemon zest	15 mL
⅔ cup	packed brown sugar	150 mL
⅓ cup	dried currants	75 mL
1 tbsp	minced fresh ginger	15 mL
1½ tsp	mustard seeds	7 mL
½ tsp	salt (preferably pickling)	2 mL
¼ tsp	cayenne	1 mL
¼ tsp	each of ground cloves and cinnamon	1 mL

Cut an X in the bottom of each tomato; place in a large heatproof bowl. Cover with boiling water and let stand until the skins begin to split, about 30 seconds. Drain and cool in cold water. Remove from the water. Peel, cut out the cores and chop.

Combine the tomatoes, onions, vinegar and lemon zest in a large heavy saucepan. Bring to a boil over high heat, then reduce the heat to medium-low and cook,

partially covered, for 10 minutes. Stir in the sugar, currants, ginger, mustard seeds, salt, cayenne, cloves and cinnamon. Increase the heat to medium and cook uncovered, stirring often, for 30 minutes. Reduce the heat to low and simmer, stirring often, until thickened, 30 to 40 minutes. Pour the chutney into hot jars, leaving ½-inch (1 cm) headspace. Seal with discs and bands and leave at room temperature overnight. Refrigerate for up to 1 month or freeze for up to 1 year. Or, for storage at a cool room temperature, process immediately for 15 minutes in a boiling water canner (see page 161). *Makes about 4 cups (1 L).*

SMALL-BATCH SPICY PEACH CHUTNEY

Once you've tasted this spicy, amber-coloured chutney, you'll make several batches when you have a few spare minutes since it's quick to put together, easy to handle and will not heat up your house as it cooks to a thick richness in the microwave oven. Use it to accompany meat, as a glaze for poultry and ham, or as a topping on bagels and cream cheese for breakfast.

2	small red chilies, seeded and chopped	2
½	onion, chopped	½
1 tbsp	pickling spice	15 mL
1 tbsp	chopped fresh ginger	15 mL
¾ cup	cider vinegar	175 mL
1½ cups	packed brown sugar	375 mL
½ tsp	pickling salt	2 mL
6	large peaches, peeled and coarsely chopped (about 2½ lb/1.25 kg)	6

Tie the chilies, onion, pickling spice and ginger in a rinsed cheesecloth bag. Add to the vinegar in an 8-cup (2 L) measuring cup or large microwaveable bowl. Cook, uncovered, at the High setting for 2½ to 3 minutes or until the vinegar boils. Stir in the sugar and salt until dissolved, about 2 minutes. Stir in the peaches. Cook, uncovered, at the Medium setting for about 1 hour or until the mixture is dark and thickened, stirring about every 10 minutes. Discard the bag and pack the chutney into hot sterilized jars. Seal, cool and refrigerate for up to one month. *Makes 2 cups (500 mL).*

SALADS

MUSTARD VINAIGRETTE ~ *168*

MAPLE CABBAGE SLAW ~ *168*

BROCCOLI SLAW ~ *169*

FIESTA THREE-BEAN SALAD ~ *169*

HORSERADISH POTATO SALAD ~ *170*

WARM POTATO AND ARUGULA SALAD ~ *170*

WILD RICE AND CRANBERRY SALAD ~ *172*

FRESH PEACH, GORGONZOLA
AND PROSCIUTTO SALAD ~ *172*

LENTIL AND HAZELNUT SALAD ~ *174*

ROASTED BEET AND BARLEY SALAD
WITH WALNUT VINAIGRETTE ~ *175*

BEET AND STILTON SALAD ~ *176*

ROAST PLUM AND SWEET ONION SALAD ~ *176*

GRILLED MELON AND ARUGULA SALAD ~ *177*

BAKED CHÈVRE ON MESCLUN
WITH FIG VINAIGRETTE ~ *177*

TOMATO AND MARINATED
BOCCONCINI SALAD ~ *179*

WARM CHICKEN LIVER SALAD
WITH PARSLEY ~ *180*

SUMMER TOSSED SUSHI SALAD ~ *181*

RICE NOODLE CUCUMBER SALAD ~ *182*

QUEBEC ~ *183*
A SOPHISTICATED SUPPER ~ *184*

Great Greens

Christopher Columbus is given credit for introducing lettuce to the New World 500 years ago. In Canada, though, wild herbs were more generally used as greens, and only the most progressive settlers or those who could afford servants were likely to cultivate lettuce. In 1836, Susanna Moodie still used dandelion, convinced "it makes an excellent salad, quite equal to endive, and is more hardy and requires less care." By the middle of the 19th century, however, numerous settlers show lettuce in their garden plans and even in Canada's (so-called) first cookbook, *The Cook Not Mad; or Rational Cookery*, published in 1831, there is a reference to preserving lettuce, roots and all, in dry sand.

Today, there is a green revolution. One thriving business is Ontario's Cookstown Greens, started over 20 years ago by vegetarian chef and food writer David Cohlmeyer and his wife, Barbara. It has catered to the increased demand for interesting and flavourful salad basics (as well as a myriad of other vegetables) by raising as many as 25 different varieties of lettuce, plus another 35 or so types of other greens (kales, cresses and mustards) over the course of a single year. Indeed, all across Canada, salads are now one of the most frequently ordered foods in restaurants, and Canadians in general are nibbling on an astounding variety of greens, both cultivated and wild.

Basic lettuces, such as Boston, head, leaf and romaine, are in all our markets as well as a host of other salad greens that technically aren't lettuces: arugula, Belgian endive, escarole and curly endive, mâche, radicchio and watercress. Mesclun (sometimes referred to as "spring mix") is made up of young leaves of many different salad greens, with a variety of flavours, textures and colours. It can include arugula, chervil, an assortment of young lettuces and sometimes radicchio, frisée, chicory, dandelion greens and purslane. Other versions include tatsoi and mustards such as mizuna. Whatever the mix, mesclun has become exceedingly popular—probably satisfying our yearning for eternal spring!

Other sturdier greens are catching on as well, probably because people not only want something different, but also realize the great nutritional worth of such vegetables as kale, collard, rapini, Swiss chard, bok choy and broccolini (a cross between broccoli and Chinese kale). Other Asian greens to consider are *gai lan* (Chinese broccoli), broccoli raab or *ong choy* (water spinach). Their flavours vary from mild to pungent and lend themselves to a variety of cooking methods, everything from steaming to stir-frying to long braising in soups and stews.

MUSTARD VINAIGRETTE

When you have the freshest and most tender salad greens, proper dressing is particularly important. A good dressing complements rather than masks the flavours of your greens. Use it sparingly so it lightly coats each leaf—about ¼ cup (50 mL) for 6 cups (1.5 L) of lightly packed leaves. Always dress green salads just before serving. Good wine vinegars are well worth the investment, and the oil should be an aromatic, fruity, extra virgin olive oil or a combination of olive oil and a lighter canola. Many other oils are now on the market—walnut, hazelnut, brazil nut, sesame seed, grape seed and the like. Be sure the flavour complements the greens. Mustard vinaigrette is my everyday dressing. Sometimes I omit the garlic.

1	clove garlic, minced	1
Pinch	salt	Pinch
1 tsp	Dijon mustard	5 mL
1 tbsp	white or red wine vinegar	15 mL
¼ cup	extra virgin olive or canola oil	50 mL
•	Black pepper	•

In a small bowl, mash the garlic with the salt. With a fork or small whisk, stir in the mustard until smooth; then add the vinegar. Whisking constantly, add the oil in a stream and season with pepper to taste. *Makes ¼ cup (50 mL).*

MAPLE CABBAGE SLAW

This creamy coleslaw is a winner, especially with pork and baked beans.

6 cups	finely shredded green cabbage	1.5 L
½ cup	diced red onion	125 mL
½ cup	shredded carrot	125 mL
½ cup	coarsely chopped fresh parsley	125 mL
⅔ cup	light mayonnaise	150 mL
3 tbsp	maple syrup	45 mL
1 tbsp	cider vinegar	15 mL
•	Salt	•
Pinch	paprika	Pinch

In a large bowl, toss together the cabbage, onion, carrot and parsley. In a small bowl, whisk together the mayonnaise, syrup, vinegar, salt to taste and paprika. Pour over the vegetables and toss to coat well. Cover and refrigerate for at least 1 hour or up to 4 hours. *Makes 6 to 8 servings.*

BROCCOLI SLAW

This salad adds crunch and colour to your menu and can be made ahead.

1	bunch broccoli	1
½ cup	slivered red onion	125 mL
½ cup	thinly sliced celery	125 mL
½	sweet red pepper, slivered	½
⅓ cup	white vinegar	75 mL
⅓ cup	canola oil	75 mL
3 tbsp	granulated sugar	45 mL
1 tsp	paprika	5 mL
½ tsp	salt	2 mL
¼ tsp	pepper	1 mL
½ cup	roasted unsalted sunflower seeds	125 mL

Trim and peel the broccoli stalks; chop coarsely. Cut the florets into small pieces. In a large salad bowl, stir together the broccoli, onion, celery and red pepper.

In a 2-cup (500 mL) liquid measure, whisk together the vinegar, oil, sugar, paprika, salt and pepper. Continue to whisk until the sugar dissolves and the dressing thickens slightly. Pour the dressing over the broccoli mixture and toss well. Refrigerate the salad, covered, for at least 4 hours or up to 24 hours.

Just before serving, add the sunflower seeds to the salad; toss well and serve at once. *Makes 8 servings.*

FIESTA THREE-BEAN SALAD

Bean salad has long been a staple at family reunions and picnics. It remains popular at potlucks and casual meals because it is easy, can be made far in advance and is not perishable when it sits out on a buffet. This one is enlivened with popular green soybeans (edamame, pronounced "ed-ah-mah-may"), which are available frozen in most supermarkets now.

8 oz	frozen shelled edamame (about 1½ cups/375 mL)	250 g
1	can (19 oz/540 mL) black beans, drained and rinsed	1
1	can (19 oz/540 mL) white kidney beans, drained and rinsed	1
2	sweet peppers, preferably 1 red and 1 orange, diced	2
2 cups	thinly sliced celery	500 mL
½ cup	chopped red onion	125 mL
½ cup	chopped fresh coriander or parsley	125 mL
¼ cup	fresh lime juice	50 mL
1 tbsp	ground cumin	15 mL
1	clove garlic, minced	1
1 tsp	salt	5 mL
1 tsp	pepper	5 mL
3 tbsp	olive oil	45 mL

Cook the edamame in boiling salted water, uncovered, until tender, about 4 minutes. Drain and rinse under cold water; drain well again. In a large bowl, combine the edamame, black beans, kidney beans, peppers, celery, onion and coriander.

In a measuring cup, whisk together the lime juice, cumin, garlic, salt and pepper. Gradually whisk in the oil. Pour the dressing over the bean mixture and gently mix to combine. Let sit 10 minutes before serving to allow the flavours to blend, or cover and refrigerate for up to 2 days. *Makes about 12 servings.*

HORSERADISH POTATO SALAD

Colourful and delicious, this easy salad goes particularly well with roast or grilled beef.

4½ lb	small new red potatoes	2 kg
2 tbsp	white wine vinegar	25 mL
1½ cups	good-quality mayonnaise	375 mL
½ cup	sour cream	125 mL
½ cup	bottled horseradish	125 mL
1 tbsp	icing sugar	15 mL
•	Salt and pepper	•
2 cups	diced celery	500 mL
⅔ cup	snipped fresh chives	150 mL

Scrub the potatoes, but do not peel them. In a large pot of boiling salted water, cook the potatoes just until tender but not mushy, 10 to 15 minutes. Drain well and return to the saucepan; cut into quarters. Sprinkle with the vinegar and toss gently. Let cool to room temperature. (The potatoes can be cooked up to 1 day ahead, covered and refrigerated.)

Meanwhile, stir together the mayonnaise, sour cream, horseradish, icing sugar, and salt and pepper to taste. (The dressing can be made up to 1 day ahead, covered and refrigerated.)

Stir the celery and chives into the potatoes; add the dressing and gently stir to coat the vegetables well. Taste and adjust the seasoning. Cover and refrigerate for about 4 hours to allow the flavours to blend. *Makes about 15 servings.*

WARM POTATO *and* ARUGULA SALAD

Of the Waterloo, Ontario, traditional salads, Dandelion Salad and Hot German Potato Salad are probably the best known. I had both in mind when I concocted this simple warm dish. Arugula has the same bite as dandelion greens and is more readily available (at least in stores). Plan to cook extra potatoes the night before—they slice more easily when cold. Actually, sautéed new potatoes are so delicious just by themselves that I often cook more than I need for dinner so that I can slice and sauté them the next day. For a true Waterloo region treat, grill thick farmer's sausage to serve alongside.

1 lb	small new potatoes, cooked	500 g
4	slices side bacon or pancetta*	4
2 tbsp	olive oil	25 mL
½ cup	chopped red onion	125 mL
•	Salt and pepper	•
2	cloves garlic, crushed	2
2 tbsp	white wine vinegar	25 mL
4 cups	baby arugula or regular arugula, torn	1 L
1 cup	freshly grated Romano or Parmesan cheese	250 mL

Slice the potatoes and set aside.

In a large skillet over medium heat, cook the bacon until crisp. With a slotted spoon, remove the bacon and drain on paper towels.

Add the oil to the pan; cook the onion with a sprinkle of salt and pepper until softened, 3 to 5 minutes. Add the potatoes and garlic; cook, stirring often, until the potatoes are browned and crisp, about 5 minutes. Add the vinegar and cook, stirring, for 1 minute. Transfer the mixture to a large bowl. Add the arugula and cheese; toss until the arugula starts to wilt. Sprinkle with the reserved bacon and serve warm. *Makes 4 servings.*

* Pancetta is unsmoked Italian bacon available at most supermarket deli counters.

Wild Rice

Food fads come and go like weeds in a well-kept garden, but certain trends do become firmly rooted. Wild rice is one—it fits well into the current fashion of fresh, healthful and natural foods.

Wild rice, actually a member of the grass family and our only native cereal, is a gourmet food whose interesting nutty flavour is appreciated around the world. Grown in northwestern Ontario, northern Manitoba and northern Saskatchewan, this ancient food (or *manomin,* as the Ojibway call wild rice) was once harvested by hand. In 1985, I had the privilege of seeing first-hand the traditional method of gathering wild rice. From the single-prop seaplane, I could see a lone canoe in the middle of nowhere, weaving its way through a thick, lime-green carpet on a small river north of Kenora, Ontario. There were two people in the canoe—one poling it from the bow and the other bending the stalks of rice over the canoe with a stick and beating the ripe grain into the boat with a second stick. The Native people would set up camp on remote lakes and pick every day as the rice ripened, over the two- or three-week period of the harvest.

Years ago, processing the green rice would have been accomplished right on the spot by "dancing the rice"— treading the seeds in a pit after parching it over open fires. Today, machines do the harvesting and seaplanes pick up bags of the green rice to take to processing plants where other sophisticated machines turn it into the glossy black grains we buy.

A natural product, wild rice has never been sprayed with insecticides and is never fertilized. Easy to digest and low in fat, it is a good source of protein and is rich in vitamins and minerals.

Although it has a gourmet reputation and hefty price tag, a little goes a long way since it swells to three to four times its volume upon cooking. To cook, simply rinse in a sieve and combine in a pot of boiling salted water (at least three times the quantity of the rice). Bring back to a boil, reduce the heat to a dancing simmer and cook, covered, for 30 to 45 minutes or until the kernels are tender, then drain well.

WILD RICE *and* CRANBERRY SALAD

This is the kind of salad I like to make for buffets because it can be made ahead, suits any season, will hold well at room temperature and is so delicious everyone will enjoy it.

1 cup	wild rice, rinsed	250 mL
•	Salt	•
½ cup	dry orzo pasta	125 mL
¼ cup	white wine vinegar	50 mL
1 tbsp	granulated sugar	15 mL
¼ cup	olive oil	50 mL
2	cloves garlic, minced	2
⅓ cup	finely chopped red onion	75 mL
1 tbsp	minced fresh ginger	15 mL
1 cup	dried cranberries	250 mL
½ cup	sliced celery	125 mL
½ cup	coarsely chopped fresh parsley	125 mL

In a fine sieve, rinse the rice under cold water. In a medium saucepan, combine the rice, 3 cups (750 mL) water and ½ tsp (2 mL) salt. Bring to a boil, reduce the heat to medium-low, cover and cook until the rice is tender and beginning to burst, about 45 minutes. Drain and place in a large bowl.

In a separate saucepan of boiling salted water, cook the orzo until tender, about 5 minutes. Drain and stir together with the rice.

In a small bowl, stir together the vinegar and sugar until the sugar is dissolved; set aside.

In a small saucepan, heat the oil over medium heat; add the garlic, onion, ginger and ¼ tsp (1 mL) salt. Cook, stirring often, for 3 minutes. Add the cranberries and ⅓ cup (75 mL) water. Cook, uncovered, until the cranberries are soft, about 5 minutes. Remove from the heat and stir in the vinegar mixture. Stir the cranberry mixture and celery into the rice. Let cool, cover and refrigerate for at least 4 hours or up to 2 days. Just before serving, taste for seasoning and stir in the parsley. *Makes 8 servings.*

FRESH PEACH, GORGONZOLA *and* PROSCIUTTO SALAD

When peaches are in season, I love to have them raw in salads. Don't peel them since the skin adds more colour. The crisp, salty prosciutto contrasts nicely with the soft, sweet peaches, then the simple salad gets a wonderful lift of flavour from creamy Gorgonzola and peppery arugula.

¼ cup	olive oil	50 mL
1 tbsp	balsamic vinegar	15 mL
½ tsp	black pepper	2 mL
4	peaches, pitted and sliced	4
4	slices prosciutto	4
4 cups	arugula or watercress	1 L
1 cup	Gorgonzola, crumbled (about 3½ oz/100 g)	250 mL

In a medium bowl, whisk together 3 tbsp (45 mL) of the oil with the vinegar and pepper. Add the peaches and toss to coat.

In a skillet, heat the remaining oil over medium-high heat and fry the prosciutto until crisp, about 3 minutes. Break into pieces.

Place the arugula on a platter or individual plates. Arrange the peach slices on top and drizzle with the dressing. Sprinkle with the prosciutto pieces and cheese. Serve immediately. *Makes 4 servings.*

Fresh Peach, Gorgonzola and Prosciutto Salad (facing page)

LENTIL *and* HAZELNUT SALAD

Big bouquets of fresh basil appearing at our farmers' market and a bag of in-shell hazel-nuts lingering in my freezer were the inspirations for this pretty, do-ahead salad.

2½ cups	green or brown lentils (1 lb/500 g)	625 mL	¼ cup	canola oil	50 mL
			•	Sea salt and coarsely ground black pepper	•
5	cloves garlic	5			
1	onion, halved	1	1 cup	shelled hazelnuts	250 mL
1	bay leaf	1	3	sweet peppers, 1 red, 1 yellow and 1 orange, diced	3
⅓ cup	white wine vinegar	75 mL			
1 cup	dry orzo pasta	250 mL	4	green onions, thinly sliced	4
½ cup	hazelnut or olive oil	125 mL	½ cup	slivered fresh basil	125 mL

Rinse the lentils well and place in a large saucepan with water to cover by 1 inch (2.5 cm). Slightly crush 3 of the garlic cloves and add with the onion, bay leaf and 1 tbsp (15 mL) of the vinegar. Bring to a boil, reduce the heat and cover and simmer until just tender, 15 to 20 minutes. Drain and transfer to a large bowl; discard the onion, crushed garlic and bay leaf.

Meanwhile, in another saucepan of boiling salted water, cook the orzo until tender, about 5 minutes. Drain well. Stir into the drained lentils.

Make the dressing by combining the remaining vinegar, hazelnut oil and canola oil in a food processor. With the motor running, drop in the remaining 2 cloves of garlic and process until smooth. Season with salt and pepper. Pour over the hot lentil mixture and stir to coat well. Let cool to room temperature.

Spread the hazelnuts out on a baking sheet and toast in a 350°F (180°C) oven until fragrant, about 8 minutes. Wrap immediately in a clean tea towel and rub well to remove most of the skins. Coarsely chop the nuts and set aside.

Stir the peppers and onions into the lentil mixture, cover and refrigerate overnight. Let stand at room temperature for 30 minutes. Stir in the hazelnuts and basil to serve. *Makes 15 to 20 servings.*

TIP: To sliver basil, stack several leaves together, roll them up tightly like a cigar and thinly slice across the roll.

ROASTED BEET *and* BARLEY SALAD
with WALNUT VINAIGRETTE

Homey barley and earthy beets get a sophisticated boost from walnut oil and tangy arugula.
For entertaining, the beets and barley can be prepared separately ahead of time and put
together with the cheese, walnuts and arugula at the last minute.

8	small beets	8	½ cup	dry white wine	125 mL
¼ cup	red wine vinegar	50 mL	2½ cups	vegetable or	625 mL
3	cloves garlic, minced	3		chicken stock	
1 tbsp	Dijon mustard	15 mL	½ lb	feta cheese, coarsely	250 g
•	Salt and pepper	•		crumbled	
¼ cup	olive oil	50 mL	1 cup	coarsely chopped	250 mL
⅓ cup	walnut oil	75 mL		walnuts, toasted	
1 cup	pearl barley	250 mL	6 cups	torn arugula or baby arugula	1.5 L

Cut the tops from the beets, leaving a 1-inch (2.5 cm) stem on each. Scrub well, then
place in a shallow non-metallic baking dish large enough to hold them in a single layer.
Add ½ inch (1 cm) of water to the dish, cover tightly with foil, then roast in a 375°F (190°C)
oven until the beets feel tender when pierced with a sharp knife, 50 to 60 minutes. When
the beets are cool enough to handle, peel them, cut into ¼-inch (5-mm) slices and put
in a medium bowl.

Whisk together the vinegar, garlic, mustard, and ¼ tsp (1 mL) each salt and pepper in
a small bowl. Gradually whisk in 2 tbsp (25 mL) of the olive oil and the walnut oil to make
a creamy dressing. Add ¼ cup (50 mL) of the dressing to the warm beets; toss gently. Let
cool to room temperature.

Heat the remaining 2 tbsp (25 mL) olive oil in a heavy saucepan over medium-high
heat. Add the barley and cook for about 4 minutes, stirring almost constantly, until
toasted. Stir in the wine; cook, stirring, for 1 minute. Stir in the stock and bring to a boil
over high heat. Reduce the heat to medium-low; simmer, covered, until the barley is tender and most of the liquid has been absorbed, 40 to 45 minutes. Remove from the heat
and let stand, uncovered, for 10 minutes. The barley will still be quite moist.

Spoon the barley into a large bowl and fluff it with a fork. Add the remaining dressing
to the warm barley, tossing to coat well. Let cool to room temperature.

Add the cheese, walnuts and arugula to the barley; toss gently. Taste and add more salt
and pepper if necessary. Mound the barley on a large platter; arrange the beets on top,
drizzling with any remaining dressing. Serve at once. *Makes 8 servings.*

BEET *and* STILTON SALAD

Stilton gives a tangy creaminess to this colourful salad, but if you have another blue cheese on hand, give it a try. Remember that fresher beets cook faster and are easier to peel than those stored for a while. Both have good flavour.

6	medium beets	6
1 tbsp	red wine vinegar	15 mL
•	Salt and pepper	•
1 cup	light mayonnaise	250 mL
1 tbsp	Dijon mustard	15 mL
1 tbsp	olive oil	15 mL
4 oz	Stilton cheese, coarsely crumbled	125 g
2	stalks celery, sliced	2
½ cup	toasted walnut pieces	125 mL
•	Lettuce leaves, arugula or watercress	•

Scrub the beets well and remove all but 1 inch (2.5 cm) of the stems. In a large pot of boiling salted water, cook the beets until tender when pierced, 15 to 20 minutes. Cool just enough to handle, then peel and cut into bite-sized cubes. Toss with the vinegar and salt and pepper to taste. (The salad can be prepared up to 24 hours ahead to this point, cooled, covered and refrigerated.)

In a small bowl, whisk together the mayonnaise, mustard, olive oil, and salt and pepper to taste. Pour over the beet mixture and toss gently to coat. Gently stir in the cheese and celery. (The salad can be covered and refrigerated for up to 4 hours.) Just before serving, toss in the walnuts and arrange on a lettuce-lined platter or individual plates. *Makes 8 servings.*

ROAST PLUM *and* SWEET ONION SALAD

Since you need to let the onion marinate, start to prepare this salad well in advance. Use large dark plums like Valor, Blue Fre, Grand Duke or one of the prune varieties. The salad would be lovely with Corn-Crusted Roast Salmon (page 64), which could share the oven.

1	small Spanish onion	1
•	Salt and pepper	•
¼ cup	white wine vinegar	50 mL
¼ cup	olive oil (more for the plums)	50 mL
2 tbsp	water	25 mL
2 tbsp	liquid honey	25 mL
2 tbsp	chopped fresh parsley	25 mL
1 tbsp	chopped fresh thyme (or 1 tsp/5 mL dried)	15 mL
4	plums	4
1 tsp	granulated sugar	5 mL
•	Arugula or watercress	•
½ cup	toasted pine nuts	125 mL

Peel the onion, then slice very thinly into rings. Put the rings in a non-metallic bowl and sprinkle generously with salt and pepper. Whisk together the vinegar, ¼ cup (50 mL) olive oil, water, honey, parsley and thyme. Pour over the onion, cover and refrigerate for at least 5 hours, stirring occasionally.

Meanwhile, cut the plums in half and remove the pits. Arrange, cut side up, in a baking dish just large enough to hold them in a single layer. Drizzle them with a little olive oil, then sprinkle with sugar, salt and pepper. Roast in a 450°F (230°C) oven until tender, about 20 minutes. Let cool slightly, then cut into bite-sized pieces. Drain most of the liquid from the onion; stir in the plums and any cooking juices.

Line a shallow salad bowl or 4 individual plates with arugula; mound the plum mixture on top and sprinkle with pine nuts. *Makes 4 servings.*

GRILLED MELON *and* ARUGULA SALAD

Fragrant melon slices wrapped in slightly salty prosciutto make an appetizing starter. The melon is grilled just long enough to accent the flavour, then served atop peppery arugula or watercress.

⅓ cup	olive oil	75 mL
4 tsp	balsamic vinegar	20 mL
2 tsp	chopped fresh thyme (or ½ tsp/2 mL dried)	10 mL
1	firm, ripe cantaloupe or other melon	1
8	slices prosciutto	8
2	bunches arugula or watercress	2
•	Freshly ground black pepper	•
½ cup	toasted pine nuts	125 mL
•	Herb blossoms or edible flowers (optional)	•

Whisk together the oil, vinegar and thyme; set aside. Cut the melon in half lengthwise, remove the seeds and cut into 16 lengthwise slices. Peel each slice. Cut the prosciutto in half lengthwise and wrap one piece around the middle of each melon slice. (The melon and prosciutto can be prepared a few hours ahead, covered and refrigerated. Bring to room temperature for 30 minutes.) Brush each lightly with dressing.

Grill over medium heat, turning once, just until heated through, about 5 minutes.

Meanwhile, in a large bowl, toss the arugula with the remaining dressing and a few grindings of pepper. Divide among 8 salad plates. Sprinkle with pine nuts and arrange the grilled melon on top. Garnish with blossoms if desired. *Makes 8 servings.*

BAKED CHÈVRE *on* MESCLUN *with* FIG VINAIGRETTE

Melting cheese, crisp greens and a slightly sweet dressing make a tantalizing first course or a lovely segue into dessert.

4 oz	goat cheese or Brie or Camembert	125 g
¼ cup	good-quality olive oil	50 mL
¼ tsp	coarsely ground black pepper	1 mL
⅓ cup	fine fresh breadcrumbs	75 mL
2 tbsp	fresh orange juice	25 mL
1 tbsp	fresh lemon juice	15 mL
2	fresh figs or dried figs, stemmed and diced	2
5 cups	mesclun or torn mixed greens such as a combination of escarole, leaf lettuce, radicchio and arugula	1.25 L
•	Salt	•

Cut the cheese into 4 wedges or slices. Combine the oil and pepper in a shallow bowl and place the breadcrumbs in a separate bowl or on waxed paper. Dip each piece of cheese in the oil mixture, turning to coat it well; place one at a time in the breadcrumbs, patting on the crumbs to coat the cheese. Reserve the remaining oil. Leaving plenty of space between the pieces, place the cheese in a small baking dish, cover and refrigerate for at least 1 hour or overnight.

Stir the orange juice, lemon juice and figs into the reserved oil, cover and set aside to macerate for 1 hour at room temperature. Refrigerate overnight if using dried figs.

Just before serving, bake the cheese in a 450°F (230°C) oven for about 8 minutes or until the cheese begins to bubble but still holds its shape. Meanwhile, toss the greens with half the fig dressing and salt to taste; divide among 4 salad plates. Top with the hot cheese pieces and drizzle the cheese with the remaining dressing; serve immediately. *Makes 4 servings.*

TOMATO *and* MARINATED BOCCONCINI SALAD

My son, Allen, and his wife, Cherrie, are very fond of the popular Caprese Salad that appears so often on restaurant menus. I wanted to include all their favourites in their wedding dinner at our house and used the salad as a sit-down starter. To make it special, we served everyone a beautifully ripe smallish tomato on a bed of greens with the cheese slices standing up in the tomato. Since it was tomato season, Cherrie and my daughter approached one of my favourite vendors at the Cambridge Farmers' Market to see if they could choose 85 perfect tomatoes from his bushels! He agreed and the result was a luscious salad. Choose bocconcini balls that are almost the size of the tomatoes.

¼ cup	olive oil	50 mL	1 tbsp	tiny basil leaves or finely	15 mL
2 tsp	chopped fresh oregano	10 mL		chopped fresh mint	
	(or ½ tsp/2 mL dried)		2 tsp	capers, coarsely chopped	10 mL
¼ tsp	red pepper flakes	1 mL	•	Kosher or sea salt	•
1	clove garlic, minced	1	6	medium tomatoes	6
6 oz	bocconcini (fresh	175 g	6 cups	mesclun (spring mix)	1.5 L
	mozzarella balls), drained		6	sprigs fresh basil	6
1 tbsp	chopped fresh parsley	15 mL			

In a small saucepan, heat the oil, oregano, red pepper flakes and garlic over medium heat until the garlic sizzles and just begins to colour, 1 to 2 minutes. Remove and cool to room temperature. Cut each ball of mozzarella into 4 slices and place in a bowl. Cover with the oil mixture. Add the parsley, basil leaves and capers; stir gently to coat well and let stand several hours in the refrigerator, stirring occasionally. Bring out to room temperature and season with salt.

Core the tomatoes and cut 3 or 4 slits from the top almost through. Place a cheese slice in each slit. Arrange some mesclun on each salad plate, place a cheese-filled tomato on top and drizzle with the dressing. Arrange a basil sprig on top of each. *Makes 6 servings.*

VARIATION:

Substitute 2 cups (500 mL) cherry or grape tomatoes for the larger ones and mini bocconcini for the bigger mozzarella balls. Arrange mesclun on a large shallow bowl or platter. Lift out the cheese with a slotted spoon and arrange in the centre. Add 1 tbsp (15 mL) balsamic vinegar to the marinade. Toss the tomatoes in this mixture and arrange around the cheese. Drizzle any remaining marinade over the tomatoes to serve.

WARM CHICKEN LIVER SALAD *with* PARSLEY

Two wonderful but often overlooked ingredients, lowly chicken livers and parsley, come together in this rich salad, best served with lots of crusty bread on the side.

1 lb	chicken livers	500 g		8 oz	baby spinach	250 g
2	hard-cooked egg yolks*	2			(about 14 cups/3.5 L)	
2 tbsp	fresh lemon juice	25 mL		¼ cup	chopped fresh parsley	50 mL
1 tsp	Dijon mustard	5 mL		3 tbsp	red wine vinegar	45 mL
½ tsp	salt	2 mL		2 tbsp	minced shallots	25 mL
½ tsp	pepper	2 mL			(about 1 shallot)	
½ cup	olive oil	125 mL		12	large seedless red grapes, halved	12

Put 5 dinner plates in a 250°F (120°C) oven to warm. Trim the livers, then cut each into 2 pieces. Pat dry with paper towels. Set aside.

In a very large bowl, mash the egg yolks with the lemon juice, mustard and half of the salt and pepper. Very gradually whisk in ⅓ cup (75 mL) of the oil. Add the spinach; stir gently to coat with the egg-yolk mixture.

Heat the remaining oil in a large skillet over medium-high heat. Add the livers and cook, stirring, until brown on the outside but still pink in the centre, 3 to 5 minutes. Remove the livers to a warm plate and place in the oven to keep warm.

Add the parsley, vinegar, shallots and remaining salt and pepper to the skillet; cook over medium heat for 20 seconds, scraping up any brown bits from the bottom. Return the livers to the skillet; toss quickly to coat with the parsley mixture. Divide the spinach among the 4 remaining warm plates. Spoon the hot liver mixture on top of the spinach, dividing it evenly. Garnish each salad with grape halves. Serve at once. *Makes 4 servings.*

* Hard-cook whole eggs, then peel, cut in half and remove the yolks, reserving the white parts for another use.

> *Trout Lake Farmers' Market,*
> *Vancouver (top and bottom)*

SUMMER TOSSED SUSHI SALAD

Many Japanese immigrants have entered Canada through the Pacific gateway of British Columbia, resulting in such a Canadian love affair with sushi that it's almost a supermarket staple. As well as freshly made takeout sushi, most stores have a supply of its ingredients. Here, the rice is cooked and treated in the Japanese sushi method, then tossed with seasonal local ingredients for a colourful hot-weather salad. Such a dish is called *chirashi* in Japanese households, where they might combine any cooked leftovers as well as raw ingredients with the rice.

I like the crunch of the raw vegetables, but feel free to use whatever you have on hand, whether cooked or raw. Sliced green beans, cooked green peas, mushrooms, carrots, radishes are all good. Sushi rice and rice vinegar are now available in most supermarkets.

1½ cups	sushi rice	375 mL	8 oz	sugar snap or snow peas	250 g
2 cups	cold water	500 mL		(approx 2 cups/500 mL),	
⅓ cup	rice vinegar	75 mL		trimmed and thinly	
2 tsp	granulated sugar	10 mL		sliced on a diagonal	
1 tsp	sea salt (approx)	5 mL	⅔ cup	diced red onion	150 mL
2	cobs corn, uncooked	2	2 tsp	canola oil	10 mL
1	sweet red pepper, diced	1	1 cup	peeled, seeded	250 mL
1	stalk celery, diced	1		cucumber, diced	
			½ cup	chopped fresh coriander	125 mL

Place the rice in a sieve in a large bowl of cold water. Swish it around with your hands. Drain and repeat several times until the water is almost clear. Transfer to a medium saucepan, add the cold water and let stand for 20 minutes.

Bring the rice to a boil, cover, reduce the heat to low and cook for 20 minutes. Remove from the heat and let stand, covered, for 10 minutes.

Meanwhile, in a glass measuring cup, stir together ¼ cup (50 mL) of the rice vinegar, sugar and salt. Fluff the rice with a fork; then transfer to a large glass bowl. Pouring on a little at a time, add the vinegar mixture to the rice, tossing the rice carefully with the fork. Continue tossing the rice until it is fairly cool and glistens, about 5 minutes.

Break each corncob in half. Place, flat side down, in another large bowl and cut the kernels into the bowl. (You should have about 1½ cups/375 mL of kernels.) Add the sweet red pepper, celery, peas and onion and toss with the oil, remaining 2 tbsp (25 mL) of vinegar and more sea salt to taste. Let stand for 30 minutes, then toss with the rice. Mix in the cucumber and coriander. *Makes about 8 servings. (Pictured on page 23.)*

RICE NOODLE CUCUMBER SALAD

Because of extensive greenhouse operations in Canada, we can buy homegrown cucumbers year-round. Teamed with popular Thai flavours, they add a refreshing note to this pretty salad. A Thai cook would use a slivered hot red chili instead of the sweet red pepper. Serve as part of an Asian meal or as a side with barbecued chicken. Rice noodles are readily available in supermarkets.

3 oz	rice or bean vermicelli noodles	75 g	3 tbsp	fish sauce	45 mL
			3 tbsp	fresh lime juice	45 mL
2 tbsp	canola oil	25 mL	1 tbsp	soy sauce	15 mL
¼ lb	ground pork	125 g	2 tsp	packed brown sugar	10 mL
3	cloves garlic, minced	3	2 tsp	sesame oil	10 mL
1	green onion	1	¼ tsp	hot pepper flakes	1 mL
1	stalk celery, thinly sliced on the diagonal	1	•	Lettuce leaves	•
½	small sweet red pepper, slivered	½	½	English cucumber, thinly sliced	½
1 cup	loosely packed fresh coriander leaves	250 mL	1	lime, in wedges	1

In a large bowl, soak the noodles in warm water for 20 minutes. Drain well; cut into 2-inch (5 cm) lengths with scissors. Bring a pot of water to a boil over high heat. Drop the noodles into the boiling water and cook for 1 minute. Drain well. Rinse under cold running water; drain again. Gently squeeze dry. Put into a large bowl; set aside.

In a wok or large skillet, heat the oil over medium heat. Add the pork and garlic; stir-fry until the pork is no longer pink, 2 to 3 minutes, breaking up the meat with the back of the spoon. Remove the wok from the heat; let cool.

Thinly slice the green onion lengthwise; cut it crosswise into 1-inch (2.5 cm) lengths. Add to the noodles, along with the celery, red pepper, ¾ cup (175 mL) of the fresh coriander and the cooled pork mixture.

In a small bowl, stir together the fish sauce, lime juice, soy sauce, brown sugar, sesame oil and hot pepper flakes for the dressing. (The salad and dressing can be covered and refrigerated for up to 24 hours. Bring to room temperature for 30 minutes before proceeding.)

Just before serving, toss the noodle mixture well with the dressing. Line a serving platter with lettuce leaves; mound the salad on top and sprinkle with the remaining coriander. Arrange the cucumber slices in an overlapping row around the edge of the salad and garnish with lime wedges. Serve immediately. *Makes 4 servings.*

IT'S A 400TH BIRTHDAY BASH for Quebec City in 2008. In early July 1608, Samuel de Champlain sailed up the St. Lawrence River looking for the right location to build a permanent settlement he hoped would become the capital of New France. This was the first French colony in Quebec, although Jacques Cartier had claimed New France in 1534 and had selected this same location to build a short-lived settlement in 1535.

Fish was already being caught and smoked along the south shore of the St. Lawrence at least a century before Cartier claimed Quebec for France. Louis Hébert was the first Frenchman to cultivate land in 1617, and thus began the strong agricultural tradition of the province. Along the St. Lawrence, the land was divided by the old seigneurial system, with habitant families farming long narrow strips stretching back from the river.

Fortunately, the early settlers from the northwest of France were a hardy rural bunch that learned to use wild game, fish and berries, adopted the Native methods of tapping maple trees, and gradually adapted many old-country dishes like pâtés and fish stews to available ingredients. They learned to cope with food shortage, and long, cold winters. To add flavour to their winter cooking, they mixed together fresh herbs like chives and onions, layered them in jars with lots of salt (*herbes salées*) and used them to season soups and stew. One can now buy commercially made herbes salées.

The original French dishes—the tourtières, ragoûts, pea soup, *cretons* (potted pork), baked beans, *cipaille* (a layered meat pie) and tartes (maple syrup and sugar pies) that were common all over the province—changed as settlers moved from the old seigneurial lands along the St. Lawrence to new regions and had

QUEBEC

A SOPHISTICATED SUPPER

Quebec leads the way in taking fine food seriously. A salad featuring its own wonderful chèvre is part of this elegant menu that starts with an easy pâté. The province has a long history of pâtés, the favourite called cretons made with ground pork.

Quick Brandied Chicken Liver Pâté
(page 15)
with Baguette Slices

Toasted Garlic Soup
(page 33)

New World Coq au Vin
(page 79)
with Buttered Fingerling Potatoes

Baked Chèvre on Mesclun
with Fig Vinaigrette
(page 177)

French Lemon Tart
(page 232)

to use the local foods they found. (This explains why there are so many versions of dishes like tourtière.) As a result, Quebec has a distinctive regional cuisine.

After the British conquest at Quebec in 1759, there was lack of contact with France, so many traditional dishes resemble those from medieval and early Renaissance France. For example, tourtière was seasoned with cinnamon and cloves, spices traditionally used in medieval cooking. The *trenchers* of medieval cuisine gave French Canadians a taste for dried bread soaked in liquid, so there was a fondness for bread pudding and French toast.

Scottish and Irish immigrants introduced oatmeal and potatoes, while the English fishermen in the Gaspé contributed bubble and squeak along with rice, bread and lemon puddings. The Loyalists who settled in the Eastern Townships made up the greatest number of non-French settlers.

From early colonial times, food has always been more than just fuel in Quebec, and the rest of us know and buy their specialties, everything from foie gras, farm-raised game and smoked fish to maple syrup and cheese. Eighty percent of the world's maple syrup comes from Quebec. The province produces a stunning array of more than 350 specialty cheeses made from the milk of cows, goats and sheep. Most are unique and have lately earned Quebec cheese makers an international reputation. Cranberries are grown on a large scale here. The Montérégie Valley is known for its apples and cider (including ice cider), and Quebec producers have recently established a "cider route" so tourists can visit the orchards and cider-making facilities.

Young chefs experiment with the local ingredients, but Quebec cuisine still shows its French roots.

˄   *Parc Forillon, a national park*
on the Gaspé Peninsula

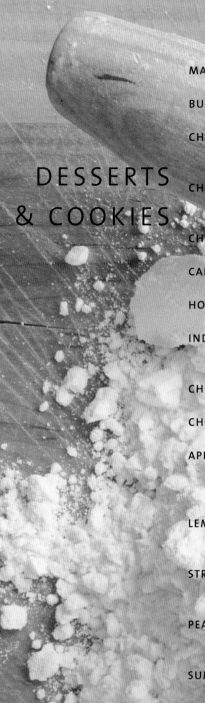

DESSERTS
& COOKIES

MAPLE YOGURT MOUSSE ~ *187*

BUTTER TARTS IN PHYLLO ~ *190*

CHOCOLATE PAVLOVA WITH MINTED
STRAWBERRIES ~ *192*

CHOCOLATE-HAZELNUT BOMBE WITH
RASPBERRY SAUCE ~ *193*

CHOCOLATE MOLTEN CAKES ~ *194*

CARAMEL SAUCE ~ *195*

HOT CHOCOLATE SOUFFLÉ ~ *196*

INDIVIDUAL MINCEMEAT
CHEESECAKES ~ *197*

CHOCOLATE-ALMOND TORTE ~ *198*

CHOCOLATE CHIP COFFEE CAKE ~ *199*

APRICOT COFFEE CAKE WITH
BUTTERSCOTCH WALNUT
FILLING ~ *200*

LEMON MOUSSE CAKES WITH RASPBERRY
SAUCE ~ *201*

STRAWBERRY OR PEACH
SHORTCAKE ~ *202*

PEACH-BLACKBERRY UPSIDE-DOWN
CAKE ~ *203*

SUMMER PLUM CAKE WITH COGNAC
CREAM ~ *204*

PUMPKIN ROLL WITH PRALINE
FILLING ~ *207*

LIGHT ORANGE ALMOND FRUITCAKE ~ *211*

CHOCOLATE PECAN FRUITCAKE ~ *212*

RASPBERRY PUDDING ~ *213*

WHITE CHRISTMAS PUDDING ~ *214*

BLUEBERRY BREAD PUDDING WITH
WHISKY SAUCE ~ *216*

LAYERED ALMOND-PLUM TRIFLE ~ *217*

PEAR AND BLACKBERRY HAZELNUT
CRUNCH ~ *219*

RHUBARB RED WINE MOUSSE WITH
POACHED RHUBARB ~ *221*

HONEY-GRILLED PEARS WITH GINGER
MASCARPONE CREAM ~ *222*

TEA-INFUSED WINTER FRUITS WITH
PRUNE BRANDY CREAM ~ *222*

LAVENDER CRÈME BRÛLÉE ~ *223*

SPICED ROASTED ORCHARD FRUIT
PIES ~ *225*

ALMOND CHERRY GALETTE ~ *226*

STRAWBERRY RHUBARB TART ~ *227*

APRICOT TARTLETS ~ *228*

COCONUT PUMPKIN PIE ~ *228*

FRENCH APPLE TART ~ *231*

FRENCH LEMON TART ~ *232*

PLUM SORBET ~ *234*

BLACK FOREST BROWNIES ~ *235*

RASPBERRY NANAIMO BARS ~ *236*

CRANBERRY GINGER OAT SQUARES ~ *237*

CHOCOLATE ALMOND BARS ~ *238*

CAPE BRETON PORK PIES ~ *239*

LEMON SHORTBREAD STARS ~ *241*

ORANGE PECAN CRESCENTS ~ *242*

COCONUT GINGER MACAROONS ~ *242*

NEWFANGLED HERMITS ~ *243*

THE MARITIMES ~ *244*
A MARITIME COMPANY BUFFET ~ *246*

NEWFOUNDLAND AND LABRADOR ~ *247*
CHRISTMAS DINNER ~ *249*

MAPLE YOGURT MOUSSE

This light-and-easy dessert is creamy-textured but low in fat. Yogurt adds a pleasant tang that balances the sweetness of the maple syrup.

1	envelope unflavoured gelatin	1	½ cup	2% milk	125 mL	
			⅓ cup	whipping cream	75 mL	
½ cup	cold water	125 mL	•	Additional whipped cream,	•	
1 cup	maple syrup	250 mL		walnut halves (optional)		
¾ cup	plain low-fat yogurt	175 mL				

In a small saucepan, sprinkle the gelatin into the cold water. Let stand for 5 minutes, then stir over low heat until the gelatin is dissolved. Stir in the maple syrup and remove from the heat.

Add the yogurt and milk, stirring with a whisk until smooth. Pour into a large bowl and refrigerate, stirring occasionally, until slightly thickened, about 20 minutes.

In a small bowl, whip the cream to soft peaks; fold into the maple mixture. Pour into stemmed glasses and refrigerate until set, about 2 hours. If desired, garnish each serving with a small dollop of whipped cream and top with a walnut half. *Makes 6 servings.*

Liquid Gold (Maple Syrup)

It's maple syrup's unique and earthy sweet flavour that makes the sugaring-off season such a special rite of spring in Canada. The ritual of collecting and boiling down the clear sap of maple trees to make our most luxurious and versatile of sweeteners is as important today as it was more than 300 years ago when settlers learned about it from First Nations peoples. And although we no longer need to use maple sugar and syrup as our sole form of sugar, as did pioneer settlers, we have acquired a taste for the irresistible amber liquid.

Equipment has come a long way since early inhabitants accidentally discovered "sweet water" flowing from a gash in a maple tree. They extracted the syrup either by throwing heated rocks into a wooden trough of sap to evaporate the excess water or by freezing the sap over a period of several nights and throwing away the ice. Early settlers soon replaced the log with an iron kettle, and the Acadians perfected this method by 1699.

Madame de Repentigny on Montreal Island started the first Canadian commercial operation in 1705, but it wasn't until the 19th century that it became a viable industry. Quebec still leads the way, producing 90 percent of the Canadian market, which is, in turn, about 80 percent of the world's supply of maple syrup. Ontario and the Maritimes (New Brunswick, Nova Scotia and Prince Edward Island) each contribute about four percent.

Although you may still find maple sap collected in the traditional way, drop by drop into buckets hung from trees, you're more likely to see bright plastic tubing that runs from tree to tree and carries the sap eventually to oil-fired stainless steel evaporators.

However modern the method, the results still vary from producer to producer, tree to tree, year to year and day to day. Sunny summers with adequate moisture, late fall frosts, cold winters with lingering snow covers, and a spring of frosty nights and warm days will provide the optimum conditions for superlative syrup. Maple syrup makers have much in common with winemakers, who are also at the mercy of the weather. As well, just as the variety of grapes dictates the wine, so does the kind of tree dictate the syrup. All trees produce sap, but sugar maple trees produce the most and the sweetest, only exceeded by black maples. However, these are harder to tap since they don't grow in stands and are not found as far north as sugar maples. Less productive are red maples; occasionally, silver maples are tapped.

Just as you would taste wine, consider the colour, bouquet and flavour of syrups. The top grade—extra light, light or medium in colour—should be clear, with a delicate bouquet and mild flavour. The second grade is amber in colour and has a strong maple flavour; the third is dark in colour with a strong molasses-like flavour. All grades must meet the minimum density of 66 percent sugar with no additives, achieved by boiling down 40 litres of sap to make one litre of syrup, and since the average tree yields 35 to 50 litres of sap during the sugaring season, there is good reason to name this treat liquid gold.

BUTTER TARTS *in* PHYLLO

Uniquely Canadian, butter tarts were probably adapted from old-fashioned sugar or maple syrup pies. There is constant controversy as to how runny they should be, or whether they should include currants, raisins or nuts. Everyone is in agreement, however, over the pastry. If it is too thick, the tarts just aren't as good as they could be. I thought I would eliminate this problem and create a recipe for even those who don't make pastry by using readily available and easy to use phyllo pastry. They even look prettier than usual.

6	sheets frozen phyllo pastry, thawed	6	3 tbsp	melted butter	45 mL

FILLING

1	egg	1	1 tsp	vanilla	5 mL
½ cup	packed brown sugar	125 mL	1 tsp	fresh lemon juice	5 mL
½ cup	corn syrup	125 mL	⅓ cup	coarsely chopped pecans	75 mL
2 tbsp	melted butter	25 mL			

Place the phyllo pastry between two sheets of waxed paper and cover with a damp tea towel. Place 1 sheet on a work surface, keeping the remaining sheets covered. Brush the phyllo with some of the melted butter; top with a second sheet. Continue stacking the sheets of phyllo, brushing each with melted butter, until you have a stack of 6. Brush the top sheet well with butter. Cut into 12 even squares. Press the squares evenly into 12 muffin cups.

FILLING: In a bowl, beat the egg well with a whisk, then whisk in the sugar, corn syrup, butter, vanilla and lemon juice. Stir in the nuts. Spoon the filling evenly into the prepared phyllo cups, being careful not to let the filling come up above the pastry. (They will appear about half full.) Bake in the bottom third of a 375°F (190°C) oven until the pastry is golden, about 15 minutes. Place the pan on a rack to cool completely. *Makes 12 tarts.*

CHOCOLATE PAVLOVA *with* MINTED STRAWBERRIES

This meringue dessert from Australia and New Zealand has become a Canadian favourite. My New Brunswick friend Catherine Betts shared with me a recipe she gathered when she lived in Tasmania years ago. It is one of my best desserts for entertaining. Not only is it easy, showy and delicious, but it also utilizes the egg whites I have tucked away in the freezer after making custards or hollandaise. The resurrected classic has a new chocolate interest that goes so well with any of the fruit you might set on top.

4	egg whites	4	1 oz	semi-sweet chocolate, chopped	25 g
Pinch	cream of tartar	Pinch			
1 cup	granulated sugar	250 mL	1 cup	whipping cream	250 mL
2 tsp	cornstarch	10 mL	2 cups	small strawberries or	500 mL
2 tsp	white vinegar	10 mL		large strawberries, halved	
1 tsp	vanilla	5 mL	•	Slivered fresh mint	•
¼ cup	sifted unsweetened cocoa powder	50 mL			

Line a baking sheet with parchment paper and draw a dark 9-inch (23 cm) circle on the paper. Turn the paper over.

In a large bowl, beat the egg whites and cream of tartar until foamy. Reserving 2 tbsp (25 mL) of the sugar, very gradually beat the remainder into the eggs until stiff and glossy. In a small bowl, stir together the cornstarch, vinegar and vanilla. Fold into the beaten whites, then gently fold in the cocoa and chocolate. Mound the mixture inside the circle on the parchment. Make an indentation in the middle and swirl the mixture up at the sides. Place on the middle rack in a 350°F (180°C) oven and immediately reduce the temperature to 300°F (150°C). Bake for 1¼ hours. Turn the oven off and let the meringue cool slowly in the oven with the door ajar, if possible. (The meringue can be made a day or two ahead and left at room temperature.)

Just before serving, whip the cream with the 2 tbsp (25 mL) reserved sugar until it holds soft peaks. Pile into the meringue's centre and arrange the strawberries on top. Sprinkle with mint. *Makes 6 to 8 servings.*

VARIATION:

CHOCOLATE RASPBERRY PAVLOVA

Fold 2 tbsp (25 mL) raspberry liqueur into the whipped cream and substitute fresh raspberries for the strawberries and mint.

CHOCOLATE-HAZELNUT BOMBE *with* RASPBERRY SAUCE

This is my favourite type of dessert: it looks sophisticated but is a cinch to make and tastes totally decadent. Any leftovers (as if!) will keep for up to one week in the refrigerator. If you wish, leftovers can be cut into tiny squares and served in foil cups as truffles. Since we now have a wider choice of chocolate (in percentage of pure chocolate liquor), use the best chocolate you can for this dessert, perhaps one with 70 percent.

¾ cup	whole hazelnuts (3½ oz/100 g pkg)	175 mL	¼ cup	icing sugar	50 mL
			2 tbsp	butter	25 mL
12 oz	bittersweet chocolate, coarsely chopped	375 g	1 tsp	vanilla	5 mL
			•	Raspberry Sauce (see page 201)	•
1 cup	whipping cream	250 mL	•	Fresh mint sprigs	•

Spread the hazelnuts out on a baking sheet and toast in a 350°F (180°C) oven until fragrant, 8 to 10 minutes. Immediately enclose in a clean tea towel and rub vigorously with the towel to remove most of the skins. Chop the nuts coarsely and set aside.

In a small heavy saucepan, combine the chocolate, cream, icing sugar and butter; place over low heat until the chocolate is almost melted, stirring occasionally. Remove from the heat and stir until smooth. Stir in the vanilla and hazelnuts.

Line a 3-cup (750 mL) bowl with enough plastic wrap to leave an overhang large enough to wrap over the top of the dessert. Pour the chocolate mixture into the bowl; fold the excess plastic wrap over it, pressing so that the plastic wrap touches the top of the mixture. Refrigerate until set, at least 3 hours or overnight.

To serve, remove the plastic wrap from the top; invert the bombe onto a serving plate and remove the bowl and plastic wrap. Cut into wedges. Spoon raspberry sauce onto each of 8 dessert plates; arrange a wedge of bombe in the centre of the sauce. Garnish each with a sprig of mint. *Makes 8 servings.*

CHOCOLATE MOLTEN CAKES

One of our country's most respected culinary experts, Monda Rosenberg has been food editor at *Chatelaine* for 30 years. I knew her years before that when she developed recipes for Maple Leaf Mills and taught me a great number of classic cooking techniques on weekends. This recipe for molten, or lava, cakes is a perfect example of her well-tested, flavourful recipes—each warm mini chocolate cake with an orange-chocolate truffle melted in the middle. Pure heaven.

TRUFFLES

2 oz	semi-sweet or bittersweet chocolate	50 g	2 tbsp	whipping cream	25 mL
			1 tbsp	finely grated orange rind	15 mL

CAKES

8 oz	semi-sweet chocolate	250 g	6	eggs	6
½ cup	unsalted butter, cubed	125 mL	¾ cup	granulated sugar	175 mL
2 tbsp	orange liqueur	25 mL	½ cup	all-purpose flour	125 mL
1 tbsp	vanilla	15 mL	¼ tsp	salt	1 mL

TRUFFLES: Finely chop the chocolate and place in a glass bowl. Pour the cream overtop and microwave on Medium until the chocolate starts to melt, 1 to 2 minutes. Remove and stir until smooth. Stir in the orange rind and refrigerate until firm, about 1 hour. Scoop out teaspoons (5 mL) of the mixture, form into nuggets and place on waxed paper. Refrigerate while making the cakes.

CAKES: Generously spray a 12-cup muffin tin with cooking oil. Chop the chocolate and place in a large glass bowl. Add the butter and microwave on Medium until the chocolate is almost melted, 2 to 3 minutes. Stir until smooth and the butter is mixed in. Alternatively, combine the chocolate and butter in a heatproof bowl set over hot water. Stir until melted and smooth, about 5 minutes. Stir in the liqueur and vanilla.

Separate 3 of the eggs, placing the whites in a medium bowl and the yolks in a large bowl. Add the 3 remaining whole eggs to the yolks. Using an electric mixer on high, gradually beat the sugar into the yolks. Continue beating until pale yellow and thick, about 4 minutes. Beat in the chocolate mixture, flour and salt.

Wash and dry the beaters well. Beat the egg whites until soft peaks form when the beaters are lifted. Stir half of the whites into the chocolate mixture, then gently fold in the remaining whites until no streaks remain.

CHOCOLATE MOLTEN CAKES *(continued)*

Spoon the mixture into the muffin cups, filling them almost to the rims. Press a truffle into the centre of each. (It's fine if it is not completely submerged.) Bake in the centre of a 400°F (200°C) oven until the sides are crusty and the tops almost set, 8 to 10 minutes. The cakes will jiggle slightly, but they should be set on the sides and tops. Let stand 2 minutes, then run a knife around the inside of the muffin cups and gently lift each one out and place, bottom side up, on dessert plates. Serve warm. (The cakes can be made up to 1 day ahead. Turn them out onto a foil-lined baking sheet. Cover and refrigerate. Before serving, bring to room temperature, then reheat in a 400°F/200°C oven until warm, 2 to 4 minutes. Alternatively, turn the cakes out onto individual plates and refrigerate. Microwave the cakes individually on Medium for 30 to 60 seconds.) *Makes 12 cakes.*

CARAMEL SAUCE

Enjoy this deep, rich golden sauce as it is on ice cream, cake or Christmas pudding. Add a large pinch of sea salt flakes to it and you have a Salted Caramel Sauce that is wickedly delicious with individual hot chocolate soufflés (next page). For a thicker sauce, decrease the amount of cream.

1 cup	granulated sugar	250 mL
¼ cup	water	50 mL
1 cup	whipping cream	250 mL
2 tbsp	butter	25 mL
1 tsp	vanilla	5 mL

In a medium-sized heavy saucepan, combine the sugar and water; place over low heat until the sugar is dissolved. Raise the heat to medium-high and bring to a boil without stirring. Boil until the sugar starts to colour around the edges. Leaving the pan on the element, gently swirl to even out the colour and continue to cook until the mixture turns a medium amber colour, 5 to 8 minutes. Watch carefully that it doesn't darken too much and burn.

Immediately remove from the heat and cool a minute or two. At arm's length, gradually whisk in the cream; it will bubble up and the sugar may clump to the whisk. Put back on the heat and bring to a boil, whisking. Remove from the heat again; whisk in the butter and vanilla until smooth. (The sauce can be cooled, covered and refrigerated for up to 5 days. To serve, gently reheat in the microwave oven or over low heat on the stovetop.) *Makes 1½ cups (375 mL).*

HOT CHOCOLATE SOUFFLÉ

Since my son-in-law, Rob Loxton, always orders a dessert soufflé if it is on the menu, he was delighted when I delivered a new soufflé dish to their cupboard with the promise of making a chocolate soufflé during my visit. This light hot dessert looks so impressive yet is surprisingly simple to make using ingredients you probably have on hand.

1 tbsp	softened butter (approx)	15 mL	½ tsp	vanilla	2 mL
•	Granulated sugar	•	4	egg yolks	4
1 cup	milk	250 mL	2 tbsp	chocolate liqueur	25 mL
½ cup	granulated sugar	125 mL		(optional)	
⅓ cup	unsweetened cocoa	75 mL	5	egg whites	5
	powder		¼ tsp	salt	1 mL
3 tbsp	all-purpose flour	45 mL	¼ tsp	cream of tartar	1 mL
1 tbsp	butter	15 mL	1 tbsp	icing sugar (approx)	15 mL

Generously butter a 6-cup (1.5 L) soufflé dish. Cut a piece of waxed paper long enough to encircle the dish with a 2-inch (5 cm) overlap; fold in half lengthwise. Wrap the paper around the outside of the dish so that it extends 2 inches (5 cm) above the rim. Tie string tightly around the dish to hold the paper in place. Butter the inside of the paper that extends above the dish; sprinkle the dish and paper with sugar.

In a large saucepan, heat ½ cup (125 mL) of the milk over medium-high heat until tiny bubbles appear around the edge; remove from the heat. In a small bowl, stir together the remaining ½ cup (125 mL) milk, the sugar, cocoa and flour until smooth. Whisk the cocoa mixture into the hot milk; cook over medium-high heat, stirring constantly, until the mixture boils and thickens. Let boil, stirring constantly, for 30 seconds. Remove from the heat; stir in the butter and vanilla. Let cool 3 minutes.

In a medium bowl, beat the egg yolks with an electric mixer until light and foamy; stir into the cocoa mixture until well combined. Stir in the liqueur, if using.

In a large bowl, beat the egg whites until foamy, using clean beaters. Add the salt and cream of tartar; beat until the whites are stiff but not dry, adding 1 tbsp (15 mL) icing sugar during the last couple of minutes of beating.

Fold one-quarter of the whites into the cocoa mixture to lighten it. Carefully fold in the remaining whites until thoroughly combined. Do not overmix.

Pour into the prepared dish; place in the centre of a preheated 400°F (200°C) oven. Immediately reduce the heat to 375°F (190°C); bake 20 minutes without opening the door. Quickly sprinkle the top of the soufflé with a little icing sugar and bake until a long, thin knife inserted in the side of the soufflé where it has risen above the top of the dish comes clean, 5 to 10 minutes more. Serve immediately. *Makes 4 to 6 servings.*

VARIATION:

INDIVIDUAL HOT CHOCOLATE SOUFFLÉS
Mascarpone cheese or Salted Caramel Sauce (page 195) adds a special touch to these little desserts.

Grease six 1-cup (250 mL) individual soufflé dishes with butter, then sprinkle sugar over the base and sides. Alternatively, grease and sugar six ¾-cup (175 mL) ramekins, then tie a folded strip of waxed paper around each one to make a collar. Butter the inside of the paper that protrudes above each dish and sprinkle it with sugar.

Prepare the Hot Chocolate Soufflé recipe as above and divide the mixture among the dishes. Bake for 15 minutes; sprinkle with icing sugar. Bake until a long, thin knife inserted in the side of the soufflé where it has risen above the top of the dishes comes clean, 5 to 10 minutes more. Place a soufflé in front of each guest. Carefully break open the top of each soufflé. Spoon 1 tbsp (15 mL) mascarpone cheese into each or pour in some Salted Caramel Sauce.

Makes 6 servings.

INDIVIDUAL MINCEMEAT CHEESECAKES

A crown of warm mincemeat is the perfect foil for tiny frozen cheesecakes, a taste of Christmas that is not overly sweet.

1¼ cups	fine vanilla wafer crumbs	300 mL
½ cup	finely chopped pecans	125 mL
½ cup	butter, melted	125 mL
8 oz	cream cheese, at room temperature	250 g
½ cup	sour cream	125 mL
⅓ cup	icing sugar	75 mL
1 tsp	vanilla	5 mL
½ cup	whipping cream, whipped	125 mL
1½ cups	mincemeat	375 mL
¼ cup	dark rum	50 mL
1 tbsp	grated orange zest	15 mL
•	Orange slices	•

Line the 12 cups of a muffin pan with plastic wrap. Set aside.

In a bowl, stir together the crumbs, pecans and butter until well combined. Press into the bottom and up the sides of the muffin cups. Place in the freezer.

In a big bowl, beat the cream cheese until smooth. Beat in the sour cream, sugar and vanilla. Fold in the whipped cream. Fill the muffin cups, cover and place in the freezer for at least 30 minutes or up to 3 days.

In a glass measure or small saucepan, combine the mincemeat, rum and orange zest. Heat in a microwave oven or on top of the stove until just warm. Remove cheesecakes from the freezer and invert onto dessert plates. Top each with a couple of spoons of mincemeat and garnish the plates with orange slices.

Makes 12 servings.

CHOCOLATE-ALMOND TORTE

Over the years, there has been a chocolate cake in every recipe collection in the country. There was even one called "Wacky Cake" that was popular when butter and eggs were scarce—it contained neither and was made right in the baking pan. This one, however, has lots of eggs and butter and is quite decadent. It's perfect for a special party because it freezes very well.

4	eggs, separated	4	¼ cup	all-purpose flour	50 mL
¾ cup	granulated sugar	175 mL	2 tbsp	ground blanched almonds	25 mL
¾ cup	unsalted butter, cut in pieces	175 mL	Pinch	cream of tartar	Pinch
			Pinch	salt	Pinch
6 oz	bittersweet chocolate, coarsely chopped	175 g			

FROSTING

1 cup	whipping cream	250 mL	½ cup	toasted sliced almonds	125 mL
4 tsp	instant coffee granules	20 mL	•	Chocolate-covered coffee beans (optional)	•
½ cup	icing sugar	125 mL			

Grease and flour a 9-inch (2.5 L) springform pan; line the base with a circle of parchment.

In a medium bowl, beat together the egg yolks and ½ cup (125 mL) of the sugar using an electric mixer until pale yellow. In a heatproof bowl that's set over a saucepan of very hot—but not boiling—water, melt the butter and chocolate, stirring until smooth. Remove from the heat. Slowly beat the chocolate mixture into the egg yolk mixture. Then slowly beat in the flour and almonds until just combined.

In a large bowl and using clean beaters, beat the egg whites until foamy. Add the cream of tartar and salt; beat until soft peaks form. Gradually beat in the remaining sugar until stiff but not dry peaks form. Fold the chocolate mixture into the egg whites until no white streaks remain.

Pour the batter into the prepared pan, shaking the pan back and forth to level the top. Bake in a 375°F (190°C) oven until the top is firm, crisp and cracked, about 30 minutes. Do not overbake. Let cool completely in the pan on a wire rack. Remove the cake from pan. (Cake can be frozen for up to 3 months; wrap it well in plastic wrap and foil. Remove the cake from the freezer and let stand at room temperature for 2 hours before frosting.)

FROSTING: In a glass measure, heat ¼ cup (50 mL) of the cream in the microwave oven on High for 30 seconds or until boiling. Stir in the coffee granules until coffee dissolves. Transfer to a medium bowl and refrigerate until cold. Using a whisk or electric mixer, beat in the remaining cream and icing sugar until soft peaks form. Spread the frosting over the top and sides, making decorative swirls with a knife. Press sliced almonds around the sides of the torte. Decorate the top with chocolate-covered coffee beans. *Makes 8 servings.*

CHOCOLATE CHIP COFFEE CAKE

Sour cream coffee cakes have been around for a long time because they are easy to make and stay moist for days. You can make this kid-pleaser version ahead and freeze if you wish. To reheat, wrap the frozen cake in foil and put in a 350°F (180°C) oven for 35 minutes.

TOPPING

²/₃ cup	packed brown sugar	150 mL	½ cup	all-purpose flour	125 mL
⅓ cup	butter, softened	75 mL	½ cup	finely chopped pecans	125 mL
2 tsp	grated orange zest	10 mL			

BATTER

2 cups	all-purpose flour	500 mL	2	eggs	2
1 tsp	baking powder	5 mL	1 tsp	grated orange zest	5 mL
1 tsp	baking soda	5 mL	1 tsp	vanilla	5 mL
¼ tsp	salt	1 mL	1 cup	light sour cream	250 mL
½ cup	butter, softened	125 mL	1½ cups	semi-sweet chocolate	375 mL
1 cup	granulated sugar	250 mL		chips (10 oz/300 g pkg)	

Grease a 13- × 9-inch (3.5 L) baking pan; line the base and two long sides with parchment paper, leaving an overhang on both sides.

TOPPING: In a medium bowl, stir together the sugar, butter and orange zest until they are combined. Stir in the flour (using your fingertips if necessary) and pecans until well combined; set aside.

BATTER: In a medium bowl, whisk together the flour, baking powder, baking soda and salt; set aside. In a large bowl, beat the butter and sugar until light. Beat in the eggs, one at a time; beat in the orange zest and vanilla.

Stir half the flour mixture into the butter mixture; stir in the sour cream. Stir in the remaining flour mixture just until well combined. Stir in the chocolate chips.

Spread the batter in the prepared pan; sprinkle evenly with the topping. Bake in the centre of a 350°F (180°C) oven until a tester inserted in the centre of the cake comes out clean, about 40 minutes. Cool in the pan on a rack for 15 minutes. Use the parchment paper to lift the cake from the pan onto a cutting board. Cut into squares and serve warm. *Makes 15 squares.*

APRICOT COFFEE CAKE *with* BUTTERSCOTCH WALNUT FILLING

This moist cake has bursts of flavour from the apricots and toasted walnuts. A delightful ending to a festive brunch, it is also just great with coffee or tea any time of the year or day.

FILLING

1 cup	packed brown sugar	250 mL	½ cup	finely chopped	125 mL
¼ cup	cold butter, in bits	50 mL		toasted walnuts	
½ tsp	vanilla	2 mL			

CAKE

½ cup	butter, softened	125 mL	2¼ cups	all-purpose flour	550 mL
¾ cup	granulated sugar	175 mL	1 tbsp	baking powder	15 mL
3	eggs	3	½ tsp	salt	2 mL
1 tsp	vanilla	5 mL	1 cup	milk	250 mL
2 cups	finely chopped dried apricots (10 oz/300 g)	500 mL			

GLAZE

½ cup	icing sugar	125 mL	2 tsp	whipping cream or	10 mL
½ tsp	vanilla	2 mL		milk (approx)	

^   *Coffee at Halifax's Farmer's Market*

Grease and flour a 10-inch (3 L) Bundt pan; set aside.

FILLING: In a bowl, combine the sugar, butter and vanilla; stir in the walnuts. Set aside.

CAKE: In a large bowl, beat the butter and sugar until light and fluffy. Beat in the eggs, one at a time. Beat in the vanilla. In a separate bowl, toss the apricots with ¼ cup (50 mL) of the flour; set aside. Whisk together the remaining 2 cups (500 mL) flour, baking powder and salt; add to the butter mixture alternately with the milk, making 3 additions of dry ingredients and 2 of milk. Stir in the apricots.

Spread one-third of the batter in the prepared pan; sprinkle with half the filling. Repeat the layers once. Top with the remaining batter, spreading it to cover the filling. Bake in the centre of a 350°F (180°C) oven until a cake tester inserted in the centre comes out clean and the top springs back when lightly touched, about 1 hour. Let cool in the pan for 10 minutes. Remove from the pan; cool completely on a rack. (The cake can be wrapped in plastic wrap and stored in an airtight container at room temperature for up to 2 days or frozen for up to 2 weeks.) Transfer to a cake plate.

GLAZE: Stir the sugar, vanilla and cream together, adding more cream if needed to make a thin glaze. Drizzle over the cake, letting the glaze run down the side. *Makes 12 servings.*

LEMON MOUSSE CAKES *with* RASPBERRY SAUCE

These light-tasting and not overly sweet little pudding cakes are easy to make and a pretty picture for company when served with raspberry sauce. Use the versatile sauce for other cakes and puddings as well.

2	eggs, separated	2	¼ cup	fresh lemon juice	50 mL
¼ tsp	salt	1 mL	¼ cup	all-purpose flour	50 mL
¾ cup	granulated sugar	175 mL	2 tbsp	butter, melted	25 mL
1 cup	milk	250 mL	•	Raspberry Sauce	•
1 tbsp	grated lemon zest	15 mL		(recipe follows)	

Put six greased ¾-cup (175 mL) custard cups in a 13- × 9-inch (3.5 L) baking pan.

With an electric mixer, beat the egg whites with the salt until soft peaks form. Gradually beat in half the sugar until the whites are stiff but not dry. Set aside.

Using the same beaters on medium speed, beat the yolks and remaining sugar in a large bowl until light in colour. Beat in the milk, lemon zest and juice, flour and butter until combined. Carefully fold the egg whites into the mixture until no white streaks remain.

Ladle the batter into custard cups, dividing it evenly. Transfer the pan containing the custard cups to the centre of a 350°F (180°C) oven, then carefully pour hot water into the baking pan to a depth of 1 inch (2.5 cm). Bake until the tops are set and golden brown, about 40 minutes. Wearing oven mitts, or using a pair of tongs, remove the custard cups from the pan. Let the puddings stand for 20 minutes before serving.

To serve, drizzle some of the Raspberry Sauce onto each of 6 dessert plates. Run a knife around the inside edge of each custard cup, then invert a warm pudding onto each plate, centering the desserts on the plates. Serve at once with the remaining raspberry sauce on the side. *Makes 6 servings.*

RASPBERRY SAUCE

1	pkg (10 oz/300 g) frozen unsweetened raspberries, partially thawed	1	⅓ cup	icing sugar	75 mL
			2 tbsp	fresh lemon juice	25 mL

Purée the raspberries in a food processor until smooth. Rub the purée through a fine sieve into a bowl, discarding the seeds. Whisk the icing sugar and lemon juice into the purée until smooth. *Makes about 1 cup (250 mL).*

STRAWBERRY *or* PEACH SHORTCAKE

The beloved Canadian author Edna Staebler made Mennonite country cooking famous in *Food That Really Schmecks* (1968 and commemorative edition, 2007). From that book comes this "old-fashioned biscuit-dough shortcake recipe" that remains a favourite because it is so quick and easy. You can update it with fancy creams or add interesting flavours to the fruit, but the shortcake itself is delicious. When Edna was well enough to travel, we would visit friends on a farm near Owen Sound each year during peach season. Edna would make her shortcake and take along a lovely basket of Niagara peaches from the farmers' market. For years I have made it for my Canada birthday parties, to which Edna would always come wearing her red and white capri pants! So, partly in her unique prose, here is the shortcake that I will continue to make (although I do like to split it and add whipped cream with the fruit).

4 cups	all-purpose flour	1 L		1 tsp	salt	5 mL
1 cup	granulated sugar (approx)	250 mL		1 cup	shortening	250 mL
2 tbsp	baking powder	25 mL		2 cups	well-shaken buttermilk	500 mL
1 tsp	baking soda	5 mL			or sour milk*	

In a large bowl, whisk together the flour, sugar, baking powder, baking soda and salt. With 2 knives or a pastry blender, cut in the shortening until the mixture is crumbly. Add the buttermilk and mix just enough to make sure the dry part is moistened. Spread the dough out in a greased 13- × 9-inch (3.5 L) pan—"quite a large flat one—or you can use half the recipe and put the batter into a 9- × 9-inch (2.5 L) square one." Sprinkle with additional sugar and bake in the centre of a 400°F (200°C) oven until a tester inserted in the centre comes out clean, about 20 minutes. "Serve warm and smothered with sugared berries or sliced peaches. You don't need to split it and butter it or slather it with whipped cream." *Makes 12 servings.*

* In Mennonite country cooking, nothing was wasted, and if the milk was past its prime, it was used in shortcake. If you don't have buttermilk, you can sour milk by placing a table-spoon (15 mL) lemon juice or white vinegar in a glass measure; fill it with milk to the 1 cup (250 mL) mark and let it stand for 15 minutes.

∧ *Peach tree orchard, Niagara-
on-the-Lake*

PEACH-BLACKBERRY UPSIDE-DOWN CAKE

Upside-down cakes made with pineapple rings and maraschino cherries were popular in the early 20th century. I still make a fresh peach version every summer as a treat for my husband. This cake is pretty like the old-fashioned pineapple-cherry one but much fresher and lighter, with just a tiny bit of batter and lots of fruit. It is best served warm with sweetened whipped cream.

3 tbsp	butter	45 mL		½ tsp	vanilla	2 mL
⅓ cup	brown sugar	75 mL		½ tsp	almond extract	2 mL
5	ripe peaches	5		1¼ cups	cake and pastry flour,	300 mL
1 cup	blackberries	250 mL			sifted before measuring	
⅓ cup	butter, softened	75 mL		2 tsp	baking powder	10 mL
½ cup	granulated sugar	125 mL		¼ tsp	salt	1 mL
1	egg	1		½ cup	milk	125 mL

Place the 3 tbsp (45 mL) butter and the brown sugar in a deep 9-inch (1.5 L) round cake pan and set it in the oven while you are preheating it to 350°F (180°C). As soon as the butter melts, remove the pan and stir well, spreading the mixture evenly in the bottom.

Meanwhile, blanch the peaches, slip off the skins, halve, remove the pits, and cut into 1-inch (2.5 cm) slices. Scatter the blackberries in the bottom of the prepared pan and nestle the peach slices, rounded side down, around them in circles.

In a large bowl, cream together the ⅓ cup (75 mL) butter and the granulated sugar. Stir in the egg, vanilla and almond extract, beating until well combined. Sift the flour, baking powder and salt together, then sift again. Stir one-third of the flour mixture, then half the milk into the butter mixture. Repeat, ending with the remaining flour mixture. Spoon evenly over the peaches and berries; smooth the top.

Bake in the centre of a 350°F (180°C) oven until the cake is well browned and springs back when lightly touched, 55 to 60 minutes. Let cool in the pan on a rack for 10 minutes. Run a knife around the edges and invert onto a plate. *Makes about 6 servings.*

SUMMER PLUM CAKE *with* COGNAC CREAM

When a friend gave me a basket of plums, she passed along this simple plum cake recipe her mother had been making for years. I entertain in plum season just so I can make it because it is super easy and delicious, looks pretty and highlights one of my favourite fruits. Cognac Cream lifts it to company status, but it's good on its own or with vanilla ice cream. Use purple prune plums since they keep their shape in baking.

1 cup	granulated sugar	250 mL	1 tsp	baking powder	5 mL
½ cup	butter, softened	125 mL	¼ tsp	salt	1 mL
2	eggs	2	12 to 14	plums, halved and pitted	12 to 14
1 tsp	vanilla	5 mL	•	Icing sugar	•
1 cup	all-purpose flour	250 mL	•	Cognac Cream (recipe follows)	•

Set aside 1 tbsp (15 mL) of the sugar. In a large bowl, cream the remaining sugar with the butter until light and fluffy. Beat in the eggs, one at a time, until well incorporated. Beat in the vanilla. Sift or stir together the flour, baking powder and salt; gradually stir into the butter mixture. Spread the batter evenly in the bottom of a greased 9-inch (2.5 L) spring-form pan.

Top with plum halves in a single layer, skin side up. Sprinkle with the reserved sugar and bake in the centre of a 350°F (180°C) oven until a tester inserted in the cake portion comes out clean, about 1 hour. Cool on a rack and dust with icing sugar to serve warm, or serve at room temperature with Cognac Cream. *Makes 6 to 8 servings.*

COGNAC CREAM

1 cup	whipping cream	250 mL	2 tbsp	cognac or brandy	25 mL
2 tbsp	icing sugar	25 mL			

In a medium bowl, whip together the cream, icing sugar and cognac. *Makes 1½ cups (375 mL).*

Plums

When I was growing up, we had the most marvellous plum tree beside our house. Its trunk was very dark and gnarled, its branches erratic and the fruit big, dark purple and deliciously warm and sweet on a late summer afternoon.

I knew that almost every farm harboured at least one old knotted tree like this, but I didn't realize that the plum is one of the world's most widely distributed fruits, growing on almost every continent and encompassing more than 2,000 varieties. The plum thrives best in an equable climate free from extremes of heat and cold, wet and dry. In Canada it's confined to favoured localities on the Atlantic seaboard, in the Great Lakes region, on the Pacific coast and in the Okanagan and related valleys, with British Columbia, Ontario and Nova Scotia the biggest commercial growers.

The fruit itself can be elliptical, heart-shaped, oblong, ovate or round, small as a cherry or big as a peach, and ripening in a rainbow of colours—purple, blue, black, scarlet, yellow or green.

There are about 18 plum species that are horticulturally important. These include two main types—the Japanese varieties and the European varieties. The Japanese start the season, are favoured for their juiciness and are generally more for eating out of hand than for cooking. Although a variety of shapes and colours, they are usually not blue or purple and are not freestone. European varieties include the most common one, prune plum, and are always blue or purple. Usually smaller than Japanese varieties, they are oval or roundish with a milder flavour and firmer texture so they hold their shape in tarts and cakes. French colonists brought European plums to the Maritimes, and Japanese plums were introduced to North America around 1870. It is no wonder plum trees took early root on many farms, including ours near Georgian Bay.

Pumpkins

The pumpkin is, in fact, a winter squash and is native to North America. Following the example of local First Nations, settlers grew pumpkins in their cornfields and sliced and dried them to keep over the winter. Now, we are able to cook pumpkin and freeze the purée for use year-round.

Although big pumpkins make great grinning Halloween faces, small varieties are better for cooking because they are less stringy, smoother-textured, darker in colour and sweeter. To bake, cut the pumpkin in half and scoop out the seeds. Place halves cut side down on a greased pan and bake in a 375°F (190°C) oven until tender, about 1 hour. To steam, cut into 2-inch (5 cm) chunks and cook over boiling water until tender, 15 to 20 minutes. To make pumpkin purée, drain in a sieve for 10 minutes if the pumpkin looks watery and purée in a food processor or blender until smooth. The purée will keep for 5 days in a container in the refrigerator or up to a year in the freezer. Canned pumpkin may be substituted for home-made pumpkin purée in recipes, but be sure to buy plain pumpkin, not pumpkin pie filling.

In Canada, we are more apt to use this member of the squash family as a Halloween jack-o-lantern or for dessert, but it is considered a vegetable elsewhere in the world, so don't neglect trying it in soups, stews and the like. (See Pumpkin Bisque with Cranberry Oil Swirl, page 33.) The United Empire Loyalists developed that fall treat, the pumpkin pie.

PUMPKIN ROLL *with* PRALINE FILLING

When flour became finer and more readily available, early cookbooks, including those put out by the flour companies themselves, abounded with cake recipes. The 1877 *Canadian Home Cook Book*, "Compiled by the Ladies of Toronto and other chief cities and towns in Canada," contains no fewer than 105 recipes for cakes and cookies. Jelly roll was a standard in many homes for decades. They were often white with jam or lemon curd filling, but a favourite at Christmas was the Yule Log (Bûche de Noël), especially in Quebec. Here, a new fall take on the traditional jelly roll features a moist, spicy cake filled with a nut- and caramel-laced cream.

∧ *Pumpkin harvest, Nova Scotia*

PRALINE

½ cup	granulated sugar	125 mL	½ cup	toasted nuts (pecans, and/or walnuts), coarsely chopped	125 mL
3 tbsp	water	45 mL			

CAKE

1 cup	cake and pastry flour, sifted before measuring	250 mL	6	eggs, separated	6
1 tsp	ground cinnamon	5 mL	⅓ cup	granulated sugar	75 mL
1 tsp	ground ginger	5 mL	⅓ cup	packed brown sugar	75 mL
½ tsp	freshly grated nutmeg	2 mL	¾ cup	pumpkin purée (see facing page)	175 mL
¼ tsp	ground cloves	1 mL	Pinch	salt	Pinch

TOPPING

¼ cup	icing sugar	50 mL	½ tsp	ground cinnamon	2 mL

FILLING

1 cup	whipping cream	250 mL	•	Liquid honey and toasted chopped nuts	•
2 tbsp	icing sugar	25 mL			
1 tbsp	brandy	15 mL			

PRALINE: Butter a baking sheet and set aside. Put the sugar in a small heavy-bottomed saucepan; pour the water over the sugar. Cook over medium heat, without stirring, until the sugar is completely dissolved. Increase the heat to medium-high; cook, without stirring, until golden, 6 to 8 minutes. Remove the saucepan from the heat and stir in the nuts. Return the saucepan to the heat just until the caramel melts, then immediately pour it onto the prepared baking sheet and spread it quickly with a wooden spoon into a thin layer. Let cool completely. Break the praline into chunks; then chop it coarsely with a large knife.

(continued on next page)

PUMPKIN ROLL WITH PRALINE FILLING *(continued)*

CAKE: Grease the bottom of a 15- × 10-inch (40 × 25 cm) jelly roll pan; line the pan with parchment paper. Grease the paper and the sides of the pan very well. Set aside. Sift the flour, cinnamon, ginger, nutmeg and cloves together into a small bowl. Set aside.

Using an electric mixer on high speed, beat the egg yolks with the granulated and brown sugars in a large bowl until the mixture is very thick, about 3 minutes. Reduce the mixer speed and beat in the pumpkin. Beat in the flour mixture until smooth.

In a separate large bowl, using clean beaters, beat the egg whites with the salt until they form stiff but not dry peaks. Pour the pumpkin mixture over the egg whites and fold in just until no white streaks remain. Pour the batter into the prepared pan, spreading it evenly into the corners. Bake in the centre of a 375°F (190°C) oven until the cake is lightly browned around the edges and a toothpick inserted in the centre comes out clean, about 15 minutes. Cool on a rack.

TOPPING: While the cake is still hot, stir the icing sugar and cinnamon together in a small bowl. Sift the mixture evenly over the hot cake. Run a knife around the edges of the pan to loosen the cake. Place a clean tea towel over the cake in the pan, then invert the pan and tea towel together. Remove the pan and carefully peel the paper off the base of the cake.

Starting at one narrow end, immediately and loosely roll up the cake and towel together. Lift it onto a rack, then let it cool completely.

FILLING: Just before serving, whip the cream and icing sugar in a medium bowl until stiff peaks form. Fold in the brandy and praline until well combined.

Unroll the cake and remove the towel. Spread the cream mixture evenly over the cake and then roll it up again. Lift onto a serving plate, placing the seam side down. Trim the ends neatly. Brush lightly with honey and sprinkle with nuts. To serve, cut the cake into slices with a serrated knife. (The cake can be loosely covered with plastic wrap and refrigerated for up to 2 hours before serving.) *Makes 8 to 10 servings.*

Fruitcakes

Our custom of having cakes and other sweets at Christmas originated in England, when cakes were given to the poor women who sang carols in the streets. British settlers introduced fruitcakes to Canada as Christmas treats, while settlers from other countries brought their own traditional Christmas recipes with them. Recipes such as Christmas Medivnyk (Honey Cake) from the Ukraine, Vinaterta from Iceland and the French Bûche de Noël were well established in provinces such as Manitoba, Saskatchewan and Quebec.

Various customs came along with the traditional Christmas cakes. On Christmas Eve in Nova Scotia, for instance, village people would participate in the Dutch and German custom of Bell Snicklers. Dressed in costumes, they would call on their neighbours, announcing the holiday season with bells and horns and wishing all "Merry Christmas and Happy New Year." The callers would then be invited in for singing and Christmas cakes and wine. And in Newfoundland, the mummers, a troupe of professional entertainers, were served cake and drinks at each village on their holiday season tour.

To the British settlers of the 19th century, finding the right fruit and nuts for their fruitcakes was very important and a symbolic link to the homeland. Today, it is still worthwhile seeking out the best ingredients for fruitcakes since not only are fresh ingredients vital to the taste of the cake, but these cakes are stored much longer than most baked goods. Years ago, everything had to be chopped and seeded; now we have a vast array of pre-chopped candied fruit and seeded raisins, but be sure to choose these ingredients in stores that have a brisk business and look for fruit and peel that are moist and clear in colour. Taste any nuts you use to be sure they are absolutely fresh as well.

(continued on next page)

Fruitcakes have had a bad rap in Canada over recent years, but I think those awful jokes about them originated from those who have had poorly made commercial versions of the cakes. Whenever I serve homemade pieces of fruitcake, they disappear first from any tray of Christmas cookies.

In the era in which my friends and I were being married, fruitcake was the cake of choice for a wedding feast. Although I made chocolate cake for both my children when they were married, my good friend Elizabeth Baird always arrived with an absolutely delicious fruitcake to be cut and individually wrapped for each guest. There were never any pieces of it left behind!

There are generally two distinct types of fruitcakes. There is a dark, rich version with seeded raisins, nuts and loads of fruit all held together with a tiny bit of batter. These need to be made about six weeks ahead so they can ripen—mellow in flavour and achieve a texture that ensures easy cutting. The other is a light version, which is much cakier in texture and usually contains golden raisins, light-coloured fruit and often almonds. I developed a third cake, a Chocolate Pecan Fruitcake (page 212) that is a new twist on the other two holiday favourites.

LIGHT ORANGE ALMOND FRUITCAKE

Even those who claim they don't like fruitcake won't be able to resist this delicious orange-accented one. Make this one about three weeks before you cut it.

3 cups	mixed candied fruit	750 mL	½ tsp	salt	2 mL
2 cups	golden raisins	500 mL	½ cup	butter, softened	125 mL
1½ cups	halved candied cherries	375 mL	1 cup	granulated sugar	250 mL
1½ cups	coarsely chopped candied pineapple	375 mL	3	eggs	3
			1 tbsp	coarsely grated orange zest	15 mL
1½ cups	finely chopped blanched almonds	375 mL			
			1 tsp	almond extract	5 mL
1 cup	candied citron peel	250 mL	½ cup	orange liqueur or orange juice	125 mL
2 cups	all-purpose flour	500 mL			
2 tsp	baking powder	10 mL			

Grease two 9- × 5-inch (2 L) loaf pans; line the bases and sides with a double thickness of brown or parchment paper. Grease the paper. Set aside.

In a large bowl, combine the mixed candied fruit, raisins, cherries, pineapple, almonds and citron peel; toss with ½ cup (125 mL) of the flour and set aside.

Stir together the remaining flour, baking powder and salt; set aside.

In a large bowl, beat the butter with the sugar until fluffy. Beat in the eggs, one at a time, then the orange zest and almond extract, beating well. Add the flour mixture alternately with the liqueur, making three additions of dry and two of liqueur and mixing just until the flour is incorporated. Fold in the fruit mixture. Scrape into the prepared pans, smoothing the tops.

Set a shallow baking dish half full of boiling water on the bottom rack of the oven. Bake the cakes on the centre rack in a 250°F (120°C) oven for 2½ hours or until a cake tester inserted into the centre comes out clean, covering loosely with foil if the cakes begin to crack.

Let the cakes cool completely in their pans on racks before removing them from the pans. When cool, the cakes can be wrapped in cheesecloth moistened with brandy or another spirit, then in waxed paper, then foil and stored in an airtight container in the refrigerator for several weeks. *Makes 2 cakes, about 90 small pieces.*

TIP: It's easy to slice fruitcake if you refrigerate it for a few hours before serving. Always slice with a very sharp knife and wipe the blade with a damp cloth between slices. An electric knife works well.

CHOCOLATE PECAN FRUITCAKE

Chocolate adds a luxurious new twist to a traditional holiday cake. Be sure to chop the chocolate very finely or even grate it for better texture.

4½ cups	mixed candied pineapple and cherries (about 2 lb/1 kg)	1.125 L	2 cups	all-purpose flour	500 mL
			2 tsp	baking powder	10 mL
2 cups	coarsely chopped toasted pecans	500 mL	½ tsp	salt	2 mL
			¾ cup	unsalted butter, softened	175 mL
4 oz	unsweetened chocolate, finely chopped	125 g	1 cup	granulated sugar	250 mL
			6	eggs	6
3 oz	semi-sweet chocolate, finely chopped	90 g	¾ cup	brandy	175 mL
			1 tsp	vanilla	5 mL
1 cup	golden raisins	250 mL	•	Additional brandy	•

In a large bowl, toss together the pineapple, cherries, pecans, unsweetened and semi-sweet chocolate and raisins; toss with 1 cup (250 mL) of the flour. Stir together the remaining 1 cup (250 mL) of flour, the baking powder and salt. Set aside.

In a large bowl, beat the butter and sugar until light and fluffy; beat in the eggs, one at a time, beating thoroughly. Beat in ¼ cup (50 mL) of the brandy and the vanilla. Gradually stir in the dry ingredients until well blended. Stir in the fruit mixture. Scrape into a greased 13- × 9-inch (3.5 L) cake pan, tapping the pan on the counter to eliminate air pockets; smooth the top.

Bake in a 300°F (150°C) oven for 1½ hours or until a cake tester inserted into the centre comes out clean. Cool in the pan on a rack.

Cut the cake crosswise into 6 bars. Heat the remaining ½ cup (125 mL) brandy but do not boil. With a skewer, make several holes through the cake; pour in the brandy.

Moisten pieces of cheesecloth with additional brandy; wrap around the individual bars. Wrap in waxed paper, then foil; store in an airtight container in a cool, dry place for at least 1 week or up to 2 months, checking occasionally and adding more brandy if the cake begins to dry. *Makes 6 small cakes, about 14 slices each.*

TIP: To toast the pecans, spread them out on a baking sheet and toast in a 350°F (180°C) oven for about 10 minutes or until lightly browned and fragrant.

RASPBERRY PUDDING

Elizabeth Baird remembers sitting on the terrace of Le Lapin Sauté, a charming restaurant in Quebec City, on a warm May day in 2001. Why does she remember all these details? Of course, they are centred on food, especially a sensational raspberry pudding that she persuaded me to include since she felt it was part of the Great Canadian Pudding Tradition. When I made it to rave reviews from my family, I didn't need much persuasion.

2	pkg (10 oz/300 g each) frozen raspberries, thawed	2	½ cup	granulated sugar	125 mL

CAKE TOPPING

½ cup	butter, softened	125 mL	1¼ cups	all-purpose flour	300 mL
¾ cup	granulated sugar	175 mL	1½ tsp	baking powder	7 mL
2	eggs	2	Pinch	salt	Pinch
½ tsp	vanilla	2 mL	½ cup	milk	125 mL

Drain the raspberries, reserving the juice in a measure; add enough water to make 1 cup (250 mL). Set aside. In a greased 8-inch (2 L) square metal cake pan, toss the raspberries with ¼ cup (50 mL) of the sugar; set aside.

CAKE TOPPING: In a large bowl, beat the butter and sugar until light and fluffy. Beat in the eggs, one at a time; beat in the vanilla. In a separate bowl, whisk together the flour, baking powder and salt; add to the butter mixture alternately with the milk, making three additions of flour mixture and two of milk. Scrape the batter evenly over the raspberries, smoothing the top. Set aside.

In a small saucepan, bring the reserved raspberry juice and the remaining sugar to a boil; pour over the batter. Bake in the centre of a 350°F (180°C) oven until the edges are bubbly and the cake is firm to the touch, about 50 minutes. Let cool slightly before serving. (The pudding can be stored at room temperature for up to 8 hours; reheat if desired.) *Makes 8 servings.*

WHITE CHRISTMAS PUDDING

When the first British settlers came to Canada, Plum Pudding seemed to be an important link to the old country and their Christmas celebrations there, but they often lacked the ingredients to make a successful pudding. In *Early Days in Upper Canada: Letters of John Langton*, he explains that "currants and suet were scarce, the eggs entirely wanting, and flour by much the preponderating ingredient" so it was a decided failure, although it was eaten.

When carrots appeared in pioneer gardens, they were sometimes grated and added to the pudding to add moisture and flesh out the other ingredients; thus was born the Carrot Pudding, which Canadians continued to make for several years despite the availability of dried fruit and eggs. This cool, creamy version of Christmas pudding has the same traditional ingredients and flavours as Plum Pudding, but it's lighter, easier to make and needs no sauce.

½ cup	dried currants	125 mL	1 tsp	vanilla		5 mL
¼ cup	dark rum	50 mL	½ tsp	grated nutmeg		2 mL
¼ cup	orange juice	50 mL	½ tsp	ground cinnamon		2 mL
1	envelope unflavoured gelatin	1	½ cup	chopped candied fruit (cherries and/or pineapple)		125 mL
¾ cup	granulated sugar	175 mL	⅓ cup	diced candied orange peel		75 mL
1½ cups	milk	375 mL	¼ cup	diced crystallized ginger		50 mL
3	eggs	3	1 cup	whipping cream		250 mL

In a small bowl, soak the currants in the rum. In a separate bowl, stir together the orange juice and gelatin; set aside.

In the top of a double boiler or heatproof bowl, stir together the sugar and milk. Heat over simmering water until bubbles start to appear around the edge.

Meanwhile, in a large bowl, beat the eggs until thick and pale. Gradually pour in the hot milk, beating constantly. Pour the mixture back into the double boiler and cook over simmering water, stirring constantly, until the mixture thickly coats a spoon, about 7 minutes; do not boil. Stir in the gelatin mixture. Remove from the heat. Stir in the vanilla, nutmeg, cinnamon, currants and rum. Cool slightly, stirring occasionally. Stir in the candied fruit, peel and ginger. Transfer to a large bowl, place plastic wrap directly on the surface and refrigerate until slightly thickened, about 20 minutes.

Whip the cream to soft peaks; fold into the custard. Pour into an oiled 6-cup (1.5 L) mould or Bundt pan (it will not be filled completely), or use individual moulds. Cover and refrigerate for at least 8 hours or up to 2 days. To serve, dip the mould briefly in warm water and invert onto a plate. Cut into slices to serve. *Makes about 10 servings.*

BLUEBERRY BREAD PUDDING
with WHISKY SAUCE

This was inspired by a delicious bread pudding served at Pictou Lodge Resort one cool September day when Elizabeth Baird and I went in search of Nova Scotia's finest fare for a *Canadian Living* story. Elizabeth had worked up an appetite for a hearty dessert or two after flying one of the resort's many kites before dinner.

The Whisky Sauce brings back memories of our stop at Cape Breton's Glenora Inn and Distillery in Glenville in the Mabou Highlands. It is Canada's only single malt whisky distillery and Donnie Campbell, the inn's whisky ambassador, coached Elizabeth and me on the fine technique of nosing whisky.

6	eggs	6	12 cups	cubed white sandwich	3 L
2 cups	18% cream	500 mL		bread, about 1¼ loaves,	
1 cup	granulated sugar	250 mL		crusts trimmed off	
1 cup	whipping cream	250 mL	2 cups	fresh blueberries	500 mL
1 cup	milk	250 mL	½ cup	finely chopped pecans	125 mL
1 tbsp	maple extract	15 mL	•	Whisky Sauce	•
1 tsp	vanilla	5 mL		(recipe follows)	

In a large bowl, whisk the eggs. Whisk in the 18% cream, all but 2 tbsp (25 mL) of the sugar, the whipping cream, milk, maple extract and vanilla. Add the bread and blueberries; stir gently but thoroughly to moisten evenly. Scrape into a lightly greased 13- × 9-inch (3 L) glass baking dish. (The pudding can be made ahead, covered and refrigerated for up to 8 hours; add 10 minutes to the baking time.)

Toss the pecans with the remaining sugar; sprinkle over the surface of the pudding. Bake in the centre of a 375°F (190°C) oven until puffed and golden brown and the tip of a knife inserted in the centre comes out clean, about 45 minutes. Let cool on a rack for 15 minutes to serve hot or for up to 1 hour to serve warm. Serve with Whisky Sauce. *Makes 8 to 10 servings.*

WHISKY SAUCE

1	egg	1	⅓ cup	unsalted butter, melted	75 mL
½ cup	granulated sugar	125 mL	¼ cup	whisky	50 mL
1 tsp	cornstarch	5 mL			

In a heatproof bowl, whisk together the egg, sugar and cornstarch until smooth; whisk in the butter. Set over a saucepan of simmering water; cook, whisking, until thickened enough to coat the back of a spoon, about 4 minutes. Remove from the heat; whisk in the whisky. (The sauce can be made ahead, cooled, covered and refrigerated for up to 24 hours. Reheat in a heatproof bowl over hot but not boiling water.) *Makes about 1¼ cups (300 mL).*

LAYERED ALMOND-PLUM TRIFLE

When plums are in season, I love using them in all kinds of desserts and sauces. Easier to make than a traditional trifle with a cooked custard, this pretty little dessert seems just as decadent. Amaretti are almond-flavoured Italian cookies available in Italian grocery stores, gourmet shops and some large supermarkets.

1 lb	large red or purple plums (about 7)	500 g	¼ cup	brandy	50 mL
			8 oz	light cream cheese	250 g
½ cup	granulated sugar	125 mL	2 tbsp	light sour cream	25 mL
¼ cup	water	50 mL	1 cup	whipping cream	250 mL
1½ cups	coarsely chopped amaretti cookies (about 26 cookies)	375 mL	2 tbsp	icing sugar	25 mL
			⅓ cup	toasted sliced almonds	75 mL

Pit and slice the plums; combine in a large skillet with the sugar and water. Cook over medium-low heat, stirring occasionally, until the sugar dissolves. Bring to a boil, reduce the heat to low, cover and simmer until the plums are soft, 8 to 12 minutes.

With a slotted spoon, transfer the plums to a bowl, draining well. Boil the cooking syrup for about 5 minutes or until it is reduced to ¼ cup (50 mL). Refrigerate the plums and syrup separately for at least 1 hour or up to 3 days, covering them after they cool.

Moisten the cookie crumbs with 3 tbsp (45 mL) of the brandy and set aside.

In a food processor or using an electric mixer, blend the cream cheese, reserved plum syrup and sour cream until smooth.

In a separate bowl, whip the cream with the icing sugar until soft peaks form; blend in the remaining brandy.

Sprinkle half the amaretti mixture in the bottom of a 4-cup (1 L) straight-sided glass dish. Spread with half the cream cheese mixture, half the plums and then half the whipped cream. Repeat the layers, cover with plastic wrap and refrigerate for at least 3 hours and up to 6 hours before serving. Sprinkle the almonds overtop just before serving. *Makes 6 servings.*

TIP: To toast almonds, spread them out in a small heavy skillet; cook over medium heat, stirring occasionally and watching carefully, for 3 to 5 minutes, until golden and fragrant.

Blackberries

The farm on which I was raised had a huge hardwood bush a mile back from our house. In it was a wealth of wild berries, the most prized of which were huge, juicy blackberries. Although we grew raspberries, strawberries, gooseberries and all colours of currants in our garden, my mother and I, along with our dear friend and neighbour Ethel Milne, would tie honey pails to our belts and head off to the bush for those treasures. They were exquisite in pies, trifles, jams, pancakes, shortcake, cobblers or crisps.

The other vivid memory I have of these luscious berries comes from arriving in Vancouver by train and seeing endless canes of wild blackberries along the track. I wanted to grab a pail and jump off the train right there. Cultivated in North America since the 1800s, they are best known in British Columbia, where the Himalayan blackberry has gone wild in that relatively mild climate and grows well throughout town and country. Here, we can always find them in August at our local Cambridge, Ontario, farmers' market. Since they freeze so well, I usually quickly rinse them off and lay them out in a single layer on a cookie sheet. After they're frozen, I pop them into freezer bags and use them in cooking without even thawing them. Lately, I have noticed there are bags of frozen commercial blackberries available in the supermarket.

PEAR *and* BLACKBERRY HAZELNUT CRUNCH

Throughout the decades, baked fruit desserts topped with biscuit dough, crumbs or pastry have appeared on Canadian tables under names like cobblers, crisps, betties, buckles and grunts (particularly common in the Maritimes and topped with dumplings). Crisp, crunch or crumble all imply a crunchy topping usually made with rolled oats or breadcrumbs (for Brown Betty), butter, and brown sugar. Cobblers wear sweet biscuit topping, and pandowdies feature a pie crust covering.

These desserts all have a lot in common with pies and tarts, but they are not as precise and are easier to make. This one is particularly easy and versatile since you can try endless combinations of fruit—peaches and blueberries or raspberries, apples and blackberries or cranberries, nectarines and berries or cherries—whatever you have on hand. If hazelnuts are not available, try almonds or pecans. It's great with whipped cream or ice cream.

2 cups	pears, peeled, cored and sliced	500 mL	¼ cup	brown sugar	50 mL
			¼ cup	granulated sugar	50 mL
2 cups	blackberries, fresh or frozen (unthawed)	500 mL	2 tbsp	all-purpose flour	25 mL

NUT TOPPING

½ cup	all-purpose flour	125 mL	¼ cup	brown sugar	50 mL
⅓ cup	rolled oats	75 mL	½ tsp	ground cinnamon	2 mL
⅓ cup	coarsely chopped hazelnuts	75 mL	¼ cup	butter, softened	50 mL

In a greased 8-inch (2 L) square baking dish, combine the pears, blackberries, brown and granulated sugars and flour.

NUT TOPPING: In a large bowl, stir together the flour, oats, nuts, sugar and cinnamon. Rub in the butter until well combined. Sprinkle over the filling and bake in a 350°F (180°C) oven until the topping is brown and the filling is bubbling, 35 to 45 minutes. It is best served warm. *Makes 6 servings.*

Rhubarb

Every spring, I recall the long row of vigorous green leaves that marked the rhubarb patch running along the garden's edge on our farm. I'm sure I'm not the only Canadian with rural roots to have a similar rhubarb patch in her memory bank. A true harbinger of spring in our cold climate where it thrives, rhubarb has adapted well to the Maritimes, Quebec, Ontario and even the Prairies, where severe winters rule out many tree fruits. Horticulturally speaking, rhubarb is a vegetable, but from the beginning, it was more apt to finish a meal—so often in the form of pie that it was dubbed "pie plant."

Native to Central Asia, rhubarb was introduced to the Western world via Russia, probably entering Britain in the 16th century and Canada late in the 18th century. From pioneer days, when it was clearly part of the Canadian culinary tradition recorded in early cookbooks, rhubarb has been popular not only in pies, but in crisps, cobblers, compotes, sauces, cakes, drinks (its other nickname is "wine plant"), jams, relishes, chutneys, muffins, bread puddings and soufflés. It's the tart or tangy flavour of rhubarb that makes it such a versatile ingredient, winning it another moniker: "lemon of the north."

There are many varieties of this old reliable perennial that appears untended every spring in the corner of the garden. We would call this field rhubarb, but there are a number of growers who supply greenhouse or forced rhubarb for winter consumption. Roots are lifted from the field before freeze-up and placed in a forcing shed, where they're covered with soil and heated; the plant is ready for harvest in about a month. This type, with its pale red or pink stalks and yellowish leaves, is generally sweeter than field rhubarb, so will require less sugar than that picked from your garden later on.

When picking it from a garden, remember to pull the stalks out, then remove the leaves and dispose of them. The only edible part of the plant is the celery-like stalk. Pretty as they are, the leaves contain oxalic acid and can be highly toxic.

RHUBARB RED WINE MOUSSE *with* POACHED RHUBARB

Rhubarb is a much-loved Nova Scotia ingredient, and never is it more elegant than in this new take on a rhubarb-strawberry dessert by Chef Ray Bear at Gio in Halifax. If you wish, garnish each dessert plate with extra whipped cream and a sprig of mint. Perfect for a dinner party, the mousse can be made days ahead.

POACHED RHUBARB

1 cup	water	250 mL	½ tsp	vanilla	2 mL
¾ cup	granulated sugar	175 mL	6 to 8	stalks thin pink rhubarb,	6 to 8
3 tbsp	fresh lemon juice	45 mL		cut into 2-inch (5 cm) pieces	
1	cinnamon stick	1		(about 8 oz/250 g)	
	(3 inches/8 cm)				

RHUBARB AND RED WINE MOUSSE

2 cups	chopped rhubarb	500 mL	1 tsp	vanilla	5 mL
	(about 8 oz/250 g)		1	envelope unflavoured gelatin	1
½ cup	granulated sugar	125 mL	¼ cup	cold water	50 mL
⅓ cup	red wine	75 mL	¾ cup	whipping cream	175 mL
1 tbsp	unsalted butter	15 mL	1 cup	sliced strawberries	250 mL
1	cinnamon stick	1			
	(3 inches/8 cm)				

POACHED RHUBARB: In a saucepan, bring the water, sugar, lemon juice and cinnamon stick to a boil; reduce the heat and simmer until syrupy, about 10 minutes. Remove from the heat. Stir in the vanilla, then the rhubarb pieces. Let cool. Transfer to a container, cover and refrigerate for 24 hours.

RHUBARB AND RED WINE MOUSSE: In a saucepan, bring the rhubarb, sugar, wine, butter and cinnamon stick to a boil; reduce the heat, cover and simmer until mushy, about 10 minutes. Let cool slightly. Discard the cinnamon stick; stir in the vanilla. Purée in a blender or a food mill; pour into a bowl.

Meanwhile, in a small saucepan, sprinkle the gelatin over the cold water; let soften for 5 minutes. Warm over low heat until dissolved; stir into the warm rhubarb purée. Refrigerate until the mixture can mound on a spoon, about 30 minutes.

In a bowl, whip the cream. Whisk one-third into the rhubarb mixture, then fold in the remaining cream. Spoon into ramekins or dessert dishes. Or, if you wish to turn out the mousse, fill large silicone muffin cups with the mixture. Place plastic wrap directly on the surface; refrigerate until firm, about 4 hours. (The mousse can be made ahead and refrigerated for up to 24 hours or frozen for up to 4 days; thaw in the refrigerator.)

Serve with some of the poached rhubarb, poaching liquid and some sliced strawberries.
Makes 6 servings.

HONEY-GRILLED PEARS *with* GINGER MASCARPONE CREAM

This is extremely easy and absolutely delectable. Mascarpone (an Italian cream cheese) mixed with sour cream is wonderful with the warm pears.

1 cup	mascarpone (8 oz/250 g)	250 mL
¼ cup	light sour cream	50 mL
2 tbsp	granulated sugar	25 mL
2 tbsp	slivered crystallized ginger	25 mL
8	firm, ripe pears, preferably Bartlett	8
2 tbsp	butter, melted	25 mL
2 tbsp	fresh lemon juice	25 mL
1 tsp	liquid honey	5 mL
•	Fresh mint sprigs	•

In a large bowl, beat together the mascarpone, sour cream and sugar until smooth. Stir in the ginger and transfer to a serving bowl. (The cream can be covered and refrigerated for up to 1 day.)

Slice the unpeeled pears in half lengthwise and remove the core neatly. (A melon baller works well.) In a large dish, stir together the butter, lemon juice and honey; add the pears and turn them to coat all surfaces; let stand at room temperature for at least 15 minutes or up to 2 hours.

Place the pears, skin side down, on the grill over medium-high heat; cook until the skin starts to brown lightly, about 10 minutes. Turn and cook until tender when pierced, about 5 minutes longer. Place the pears on individual dessert plates; place a dollop of mascarpone cream beside the pears and garnish with mint. *Makes 8 servings.*

TEA-INFUSED WINTER FRUITS *with* PRUNE BRANDY CREAM

My Welsh friend Aileen Yates inspired the creation of this interesting and delicious brunch dish, just another example of how Britain (behind many of our puddings) still influences our dessert traditions. Dried fruit fills the void when fresh local fruit is not available. Check out bulk stores for a good variety of fruits; or use what you have on hand.

2¼ cups	steeped tea	550 mL
¼ cup	finely diced preserved or crystallized ginger	50 mL
2 tbsp	granulated sugar	25 mL
1	lemon	1
3	whole cloves	3
1	cinnamon stick (1 inch/2.5 cm)	1
1 lb	mixed dried fruits (apricots, peaches, plums, pears, apples, etc.)	500 g
4 oz	pitted prunes	125 g
¼ cup	brandy	50 mL
1 cup	crème fraîche or a good sour cream	250 mL

In a medium saucepan, combine the tea, ginger and sugar. In small strips, remove the rind (just the outer yellow peel) from the lemon and add to the pan with the cloves and cinnamon stick. Bring to a boil, stirring to dissolve the sugar. Remove from the heat and stir in the mixed dried fruit. Transfer to a bowl, cool, cover and refrigerate overnight.

Place the prunes in a bowl and stir in the brandy; set aside to soak for at least 2 hours and up to overnight. Transfer to a blender and purée; spoon them back into a bowl and stir in the crème fraîche. Cover and refrigerate until serving time. Spoon some of the cream on each serving of fruit. *Makes 6 servings.*

LAVENDER CRÈME BRÛLÉE

Just outside Cambridge, Ontario, where I live, there's a field of lavender. It's very small, but I know the two women who have started the business can provide me with dried lavender any time. A much bigger field at the Okanagan Lavender Herb Farm near Kelowna, British Columbia, is a joy to see with its dozens of varieties. Dried lavender blossoms are also called culinary lavender buds, and if you can't get to one of the fields, they are available at some natural food stores or specialty shops. At the end of the meal, the only noise you will hear will be everyone scraping out his or her dessert dish to get every last taste of this easy dessert with its subtle hint of the herb.

2 cups	whipping cream	500 mL		⅓ cup	granulated sugar	75 mL
½ cup	milk	125 mL		2 tbsp	liquid honey	25 mL
2 tsp	dried lavender blossoms	10 mL		2 tbsp	raw (demerara) sugar	25 mL
6	egg yolks	6			or golden brown sugar	

In a large saucepan, bring the cream, milk and lavender to a boil. Remove from the heat, cover and let steep for 30 minutes. Strain into a small bowl.

In a medium bowl or large liquid measure, whisk together the yolks, granulated sugar and honey just to combine: do not let it foam. Very gradually whisk in the hot cream mixture. Divide among six ¾-cup (175 mL) heatproof ramekins or custard cups.

Place in a baking pan just big enough to hold them; pour hot water into the pan to come two-thirds up the sides of the ramekins. Cover with foil and bake in a 325°F (160°C) oven until the edges are set but the centres are still jiggly, about 50 minutes. Remove the ramekins to cool on a rack, then refrigerate, covered, until very cold, at least 6 hours or up to 2 days.

Before serving, place the ramekins on a large rimmed baking sheet. Sprinkle each with 1 tsp (5 mL) raw sugar. Broil on the rack nearest the element until the sugar is melted and golden brown, about 3½ minutes. Watch carefully. (Alternatively, brown the sugar with a kitchen blowtorch.) Chill, uncovered, for 30 minutes and up to 3 hours before serving. *Makes 6 servings.*

Pies

It was my good fortune to have been born into an Ontario farm family. When it came to harvest time, my father brought in the communal threshing machine before we owned our own harvest combine. The thresher travelled from farm to farm, and everyone helped his neighbour. Each farmer's wife would take her turn at providing meals for the hungry workers.

I can well remember helping with those noon meals when a crowd of men would come in from the fields to gather around our big, round kitchen table.

There was always pie. Although it may seem extraordinary to many young cooks, a pie was just about the easiest dessert a busy farm wife could make. It was also an economical method of making a few ingredients go a long way around a table of hungry diners. Pies had the advantage, too, of not demanding immediate attention. Farm men came in for dinner when they were ready, not when dinner was ready. And at harvest time, there was infinite choice, especially from the big garden my mother and I tended. We might make raspberry, plum, apple, squash, pumpkin, pear, peach (Mennonite cooks might even use the peelings left from making jam in a pie), currant, cherry, rhubarb, and even green tomato pie.

Pies were not just fuel for hungry workers. They could be the focus of a social event. In the 20th century, the Pie Social was popular in rural areas of Nova Scotia and other provinces as well. Each lady would bake a pie and pack it in a basket to share with a gentleman who won her pie in an auction. Not only would he share the pie, but also gain the privilege of escorting the pie maker home that night. Apparently, coconut cream, chocolate, lemon meringue and butterscotch were the preferred kinds of pie.

SPICED ROASTED ORCHARD FRUIT PIES

Julia Aitken is a British transplant who came to appreciate Ontario's bounty so much she co-authored a book called *The Ontario Harvest Cookbook* (Macmillan Canada, 1996). Her latest book is a guide to easy entertaining, *125 Best Entertaining Recipes* (Robert Rose, 2007), and this recipe reflects the best of both cookbooks. You can vary the fall fruits for these easy, free-form pies according to what's available in local stores and markets.

½	pkg (14 oz/397 g) frozen puff pastry, thawed	½	2 tbsp	butter, melted	25 mL
			1	apple, Spartan or Idared	1
1	egg	1	2	firm, ripe peaches	2
1 tbsp	cold water	15 mL	2	firm, ripe plums	2
¼ cup	packed brown sugar	50 mL	1	firm, ripe Bosc pear	1
2 tbsp	fresh lemon juice	25 mL	•	Icing sugar	•
½ tsp	five-spice powder*	2 mL			

Roll out the pastry on a lightly floured surface to a 12-inch (30 cm) square. Using a saucer or small plate as a guide, cut out four 5½-inch (13 cm) circles from the pastry and place on 1 or 2 baking sheets. In a small bowl, whisk together the egg and water; brush the pastry evenly with some of the mixture. Bake in a 400°F (200°C) oven until golden brown and puffed, 10 to 12 minutes. Remove from the oven, set aside and increase the temperature to 425°F (220°C). (The pastry can be baked up to 2 days ahead and stored in an airtight container.)

In a large bowl, whisk together the sugar, lemon juice and five-spice powder. Brush a 13- × 9-inch (3 L) baking dish with some of the melted butter. Whisk the remaining butter into the sugar mixture.

Do not peel the apple, but core it and cut it into 12 wedges, dropping them into the brown sugar mixture as you work. Spoon into the prepared dish and bake, uncovered, for 5 minutes. Meanwhile, cut each peach into 6 wedges, removing the pits. Cut each plum into 4 wedges, removing the pits. Core the pear and cut it into 8 wedges. Add the peaches, plums and pear to the apple mixture, stirring gently to coat with the sugar mixture; bake until the fruit is tender but not broken up, 12 to 15 minutes longer. Remove the dish from the oven, turn the oven off and place the pastry in the oven to freshen it, about 2 minutes.

With a slotted spoon, divide the fruit among 4 shallow bowls; drizzle evenly with the juices remaining in the baking dish. Top each portion with pastry and sift icing sugar over it. Serve at once. *Makes 4 servings.*

* Five-spice powder, usually comprised of equal amounts of ground Szechwan peppercorns, cloves, cinnamon, fennel seeds and star anise, is now available in most supermarkets.

ALMOND CHERRY GALETTE

Golden flaky pastry hugs a mound of shiny red cherries in this rustic summer pie. Serve with lightly sweetened whipped cream, Cheddar cheese or a good vanilla ice cream.

FLAKY PASTRY

2½ cups	all-purpose flour	625 mL		½ cup	cold butter, in bits	125 mL
1 tbsp	granulated sugar	15 mL		¼ cup	lard, in bits	50 mL
¼ tsp	salt	1 mL		⅔ cup	ice water	150 mL

FILLING

5 cups	pitted sour cherries	1.25 L		¼ tsp	almond extract	1 mL
¾ cup	granulated sugar	175 mL		¼ cup	finely crushed amaretti	50 mL
3 tbsp	quick tapioca	45 mL			cookies or coarsely	
3 tbsp	fresh lemon juice	45 mL			ground almonds	
1 tbsp	kirsch (optional)	15 mL				

TOPPING

1	egg white	1		2 tbsp	apple or red currant	25 mL
1 tbsp	cold water	15 mL			jelly, melted	
1 tbsp	granulated sugar,	15 mL				
	preferably coarse crystals					

FLAKY PASTRY: Place the flour, sugar and salt in a food processor; add the butter and lard; pulse until it forms large crumbs. With the machine running, add the ice water through the feed tube just until the dough starts to come together. (Do not overprocess.) Turn out onto a lightly floured surface and knead a few times to form a soft ball. Form into a flat disc and wrap tightly in plastic wrap. Refrigerate for at least 2 hours and up to 2 days.

To make the pastry by hand, combine the flour, sugar and salt in a large bowl. Cut in the butter and lard with a pastry blender or 2 knives until it forms coarse crumbs. Gradually sprinkle on the water and mash in with a fork or the tips of your fingers. (Be sure everything is kept cold.)

STRAWBERRY RHUBARB TART

FILLING: Stir together the cherries, sugar, tapioca, lemon juice, kirsch, if using, and almond extract.

On floured parchment paper with a floured rolling pin, roll the pastry into a 15-inch (38 cm) circle. Transfer the pastry with the paper to a pizza pan or baking sheet. Leaving a 3-inch (8 cm) border, sprinkle the centre with crushed amaretti cookies.

Spoon the filling over the cookies, mounding it slightly in the middle. Fold the pastry border up over the filling, gently pressing folds or pleats together.

TOPPING: Beat the egg white with the cold water and brush onto the pastry. Sprinkle with the sugar. Bake in a 425°F (220°C) oven for 15 minutes. Reduce the heat to 375°F (190°C) and bake until the pastry is crisp and golden and the filling is bubbly, another 45 to 50 minutes. Let cool on a rack for 30 minutes, then brush the filling with melted jelly. Serve warm or at room temperature. (The galette, like any pie, is best served the day it is baked.) *Makes 8 servings.*

Two of the season's first fruits team up for an elegant-looking but simple-to-make spring dessert. The tart can be assembled up to two hours ahead and left at room temperature.

•	Pastry for 10-inch (25 cm) single crust (see French Lemon Tart, page 232)	•
6 cups	diced rhubarb	1.5 L
1 cup	packed brown sugar	250 mL
2 tbsp	port or red wine	25 mL
½ cup	red currant jelly	125 mL
1 tbsp	water	15 mL
4 cups	fresh strawberries, hulled	1 L
•	Whipped cream (optional)	•

Line a 10-inch (25 cm) fluted tart pan with a removable bottom with pastry. Prick the bottom several times with a fork, cover with foil or parchment paper and fill with dry beans or rice. Bake in the bottom third of a 425°F (220°C) oven for 8 minutes. Remove the weights and foil; prick again. Drape a collar of foil over the edge and bake until the pastry is golden, another 5 to 8 minutes longer. Let cool on a rack.

Combine the rhubarb, brown sugar and port in a heavy saucepan. Cover and cook over low heat, stirring occasionally, for 10 minutes. Increase the heat to medium and cook, uncovered, stirring often, until the mixture is almost a purée but pieces of rhubarb still remain, about 10 minutes longer. Let cool.

Stir the jelly and water together in a small saucepan. Cook over low heat, stirring, until liquid.

Fill the baked shell with the rhubarb filling and smooth the top. Arrange the strawberries so they sit upright on top and brush with the jelly glaze. Just before serving, remove the pan edges and place the tart on a serving plate. Pass whipped cream with each slice, if desired. *Makes 8 servings.*

APRICOT TARTLETS

Eating fresh, ripe apricots is like eating candy, but they are also very good cooked, as in these easy tartlets that look as if you had swung by a French pastry shop. Puff pastry is often available in 1 lb (450 g) packages of two 10- × 10-inch (25 × 25 cm) sheets; you can also use half a 14 oz (398 g) package and roll it out to the same size). Serve the tartlets with whipped cream or vanilla ice cream.

½ cup	ground almonds	125 mL
⅓ cup	icing sugar	75 mL
2 tbsp	butter, softened	25 mL
¼ tsp	almond extract	1 mL
½ lb	puff pastry, thawed (1 sheet)	250 g
6	apricots (2-inch/5 cm), halved and pitted	6
2 tbsp	brown sugar	25 mL
1 tbsp	apricot jam	15 mL

Place a baking sheet in the centre of the oven and preheat the oven to 400°F (200°C).

In a small bowl, stir together the almonds, icing sugar, butter and almond extract; set aside.

Place the puff pastry on a parchment-lined baking sheet. Cut four 4½-inch (11 cm) circles. With a sharp knife, score (cut a line, but not right through the pastry) each circle ½ inch (1 cm) in from the edge. Spread the almond mixture inside the scored line. Arrange 3 apricot halves, cut side up, in each. Sprinkle the apricots with brown sugar. Place the baking sheet on top of the hot sheet in the oven and bake the tartlets until the pastry is brown, 30 to 40 minutes. Remove to a rack. Mince any big pieces of jam and melt the jam in the microwave or in a small saucepan over low heat. While still hot, brush the jam over the apricots. Let cool at least 5 minutes before serving warm, or serve at room temperature. *Makes 4 servings.*

COCONUT PUMPKIN PIE

A new taste enhances an old favourite in this traditional Thanksgiving dessert.

•	Pastry for 9-inch (23 cm) pie shell (see French Lemon Tart, page 232)	•
2	eggs	2
¾ cup	packed brown sugar	175 mL
1¾ cups	pumpkin purée (see page 206)	425 mL
	or	
1	can (14 oz/398 mL) pumpkin purée (not pie filling)	1
1 tsp	ground cinnamon	5 mL
½ tsp	ground ginger	2 mL
½ tsp	ground allspice	2 mL
¼ tsp	ground cloves	1 mL
¼ tsp	grated nutmeg	1 mL
¼ tsp	salt	1 mL
1⅓ cups	light cream	325 mL
¾ cup	unsweetened flaked coconut	175 mL
1 tbsp	rum or brandy	15 mL
•	Whipped cream	*

Line a deep 9-inch (23 cm) pie plate with pastry and flute the edges. Refrigerate while preparing the filling.

In a large bowl, beat together the eggs and sugar. Beat in the pumpkin, cinnamon, ginger, allspice, cloves, nutmeg and salt. Beat in the cream. Stir in ½ cup (125 mL) of the coconut and the rum. Pour into the pie shell, sprinkle the top with the remaining ¼ cup (50 mL) coconut and bake in the centre of a 450°F (230°C) oven for 10 minutes. Reduce the heat to 350°F (180°C) and bake until a knife inserted in the centre comes out clean, about 45 minutes longer. If the pastry gets too brown, cover the edge with a thin strip of foil. Serve cool with whipped cream. *Makes 8 servings.*

Apples

The heady fragrance of freshly picked apples on a sunny September day. The comforting aroma of an apple pie just out of the oven. It's no wonder this homegrown fruit has been such a favourite over the years and across the country—in the Okanagan Valley in British Columbia, along the Lower Great Lakes in Southern Ontario, in Quebec's St. Lawrence Valley, the Saint John River valley of New Brunswick and in Nova Scotia's Annapolis Valley, where French settlers planted our first orchards in 1632. Today, it is Canada's most important tree fruit crop.

Since the Collingwood and Meaford area near our farm in Ontario is such a huge apple-growing region, it was not surprising that we grew several varieties for our own use. Without the sophisticated storage facilities of today, my mother would extend the life of our apples by peeling and slicing, then drying them for use during the winter. Her pie made with dried apple slices was sweet with the concentration of natural sugars through drying, and it had an inviting texture unlike any found in fresh apple pie.

The tree I remember most was an old Snow apple tree sitting in a field north of our house. It was gnarled and misshapen, but it yielded fruit I have never been able to find again. Snow apples are not very common, and when I do see them at the farmers' market, I buy a basket just to see if I can re-create that taste of the past.

Although we find only a handful of varieties in the supermarket (those that are eye-appealing and hearty enough to withstand the hardships of travel and display), our ancestors probably enjoyed more than 600 types of apples.

Apple picking in Canada starts in late July or early August with the first non-storing varieties like Yellow Transparent, Paulared, Melba, Wealthy, St. Lawrence and Tydeman Red. These are often soft, not as sweet as later apples, but very good for something like applesauce. Many of these older varieties you may not find in a supermarket,

(continued on next page)

but these apples were very welcome to early farmers long after their winter supply of fruit had vanished.

Of the apples you might find in a supermarket, one of the most popular is the McIntosh, a truly Ontario variety named for John McIntosh, who discovered it as a seedling on a farm in Dundas County around 1811. This bright red apple is usually picked in September, has white, juicy, crisp flesh and is excellent for eating out of hand or mashed smoothly into applesauce. Some people who don't mind the apples losing their shape will use it for pies as well. Spartans and Gravensteins also cook smoothly into sauce, with Spartans a choice for pies too.

Northern Spy (my favourite cooking apple), Idared, Golden Delicious, Red Rome and Newton apples all hold their shape when cooked and are excellent for pies and baked apples.

On the other hand, Red Delicious with its showy dark red skin and sweet flavour is an eating, rather than a cooking, apple. Good for fresh eating too are Empire and Mutsu (Crispin), which is also good for baking. If you need an apple for salad, the best choice is Cortland, known as "the caterer's apple" because it stays white longer after being cut and is also good for fresh eating, baking, pies and sauces.

And, of course, the best place to look for any of these is the local farmers' market or orchards themselves, especially if you are looking for a taste of the past.

FRENCH APPLE TART

Golden Delicious, Idared or Spy apples are best for this easy take on a traditional French fruit tart. Serve it in small wedges with dollops of softly whipped cream.

•	Pastry for 9-inch (23 cm) tart or pie shell (see French Lemon Tart, page 232)		•	¼ tsp	almond extract	1 mL
				¾ cup	ground blanched almonds (about 3 oz/75 g)	175 mL
¾ cup	granulated sugar	175 mL		3	apples, peeled, cored and thinly sliced	3
¼ cup	butter, softened	50 mL				
1	egg	1		1 tbsp	fresh lemon juice	15 mL
2 tbsp	Calvados (apple brandy) or apple juice	25 mL		3 tbsp	apple jelly	45 mL

Line a 9-inch (23 cm) pie plate or tart pan with pastry. In a small bowl, stir together ½ cup (125 mL) of the sugar, 3 tbsp (45 mL) of the butter, the egg, 1 tbsp (15 mL) of the Calvados and the almond extract. Stir in the ground almonds until the mixture is smooth.

Spread the mixture over the bottom of the tart shell. In a medium bowl, toss the apples with the remaining ¼ cup (50 mL) of sugar. Spread half of the apples evenly over the almond mixture. Starting at the outer edge, arrange the remaining apple slices in overlapping concentric circles on top. Sprinkle with the lemon juice and dot with the remaining butter. Bake in a 400°F (200°C) oven for 15 minutes. Reduce the temperature to 350°F (180°C); bake until the apples are tender, 45 to 55 minutes longer. Remove to a rack.

In a small saucepan over medium-low heat, melt the jelly with the remaining Calvados, stirring until smooth. While the tart is still warm, brush the jelly mixture evenly over the apples. Let cool to room temperature before serving. *Makes 6 to 8 small servings.*

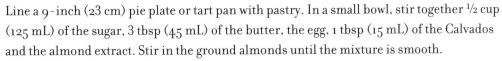

FRENCH LEMON TART

Elizabeth Baird is well known for seeking out the best of Canadian foods and sharing the knowledge with the rest of the country, especially in her position as food editor of *Canadian Living* magazine since 1987. When she helped me decide what should appear in *A Taste of Canada*, Elizabeth said I should include a lemon tart, a sophisticated version of the old-fashioned favourite, lemon meringue pie. This one is her choice, created in the Canadian Living Test Kitchen with Elizabeth sampling every step to make sure it was better than anything you could ever buy or order in a fancy restaurant. It is tangy and truly lemony. The pastry is my recipe.

PASTRY

1¼ cups	all-purpose flour	300 mL	2 tbsp	cold lard or shortening,	25 mL
2 tbsp	granulated sugar	25 mL		in bits	
¼ tsp	salt	1 mL	3 tbsp	ice water (approx)	45 mL
⅓ cup	cold unsalted butter, in bits	75 mL			

FILLING

5	eggs	5	¾ cup	fresh lemon juice	175 mL
3	egg yolks	3	2 tbsp	cold butter	25 mL
1 cup	granulated sugar	250 mL			

TOPPING

3 tbsp	apple jelly	45 mL	•	Assorted fruit (such as Cape gooseberries, blueberries and raspberries) or icing sugar	•

PASTRY: In a bowl, whisk together the flour, sugar and salt. Using a pastry blender or 2 knives cut in the butter and lard until it forms fine crumbs with a few larger pieces. Drizzle the ice water over the mixture, tossing with a fork until the dough clumps, adding up to 1 tbsp (15 mL) more water if the mixture is too crumbly.

Turn out onto a work surface and press into a smooth ball; flatten into a disc. On a lightly floured surface, roll the pastry out to an 11-inch (28 cm) circle. Fit it into a 9-inch (23 cm) fluted tart pan with a removable bottom. Trim to 1-inch (2.5 cm) overhang; fold the extra inside and press the pastry together. Refrigerate for 30 minutes or up to 24 hours, covered.

With a fork, prick the bottom at ½-inch (1 cm) intervals. Line with foil or parchment; fill with pie weights or dried beans. Bake in the bottom third of a 400°F (200°C) oven until the edge starts to turn golden, 15 to 20 minutes. Remove the weights and foil and prick the bottom again; bake until golden, about 10 minutes. Let cool on a rack.

(continued on page 234)

PLUM SORBET

FRENCH LEMON TART *(continued)*

For an elegant touch, drizzle each serving of this refreshing dessert with a little plum brandy.

1½ lb	purple plums	750 g
1¼ cups	granulated sugar	300 mL
1½ cups	water	375 mL
2 tbsp	fresh lemon juice	25 mL
2	egg whites	2

FILLING: In the top of a double boiler or large heatproof bowl over a saucepan of simmering water, whisk together the eggs, egg yolks, sugar and lemon juice. Cook, stirring often, until translucent and thick enough to mound on a spoon, 15 to 20 minutes.

Strain through a fine sieve into a bowl; stir in the butter until it melts. Place plastic wrap directly on the surface and refrigerate until cold, 2 hours. (The filling can be made up to 24 hours ahead.)

Spoon the lemon filling into the pie shell, smoothing the top. Bake in a 325°F (160°C) oven until the filling loses some shine and forms a thin skin, about 12 minutes. Let cool on a rack; then refrigerate until cold, about 2 hours.

TOPPING: In a small glass bowl, microwave the apple jelly on High for 30 seconds, or heat in a saucepan on the stovetop until melted. Spoon evenly over the filling. Refrigerate until set, about 30 minutes. (The tart can be refrigerated for up to 24 hours, covered with a large inverted bowl.) Garnish the centre with fruit or dust the edge of the pastry and a narrow border of filling with icing sugar. *Makes 8 to 10 servings.*

Pit and coarsely chop the plums. Measure out 2 tbsp (25 mL) of the sugar in a small bowl and set aside.

In a large saucepan, stir together the remaining sugar and water. Bring to a boil, stirring until the sugar is dissolved. Reduce the heat to low; cook, uncovered, for 5 minutes. Add the plums; return to a boil, stirring often. Remove from the heat; stir in the lemon juice. Cover and let cool completely.

With a slotted spoon, remove plums to a food processor or blender; process until puréed. Return the purée to the pan; stir until well mixed with the syrup. Pour into a 9-inch (2.5 L) square metal pan. Freeze, stirring often, until the mixture is mushy, about 4 hours.

Meanwhile, place a large bowl in the refrigerator. In a small bowl, beat the egg whites until foamy. Beat in the reserved sugar until soft peaks form.

Transfer the mushy plum mixture into the chilled bowl and beat with an electric mixer until very smooth. Quickly fold in the beaten egg whites. Spoon into a plastic container, cover and return to the freezer for at least 6 hours. *Makes about 6 cups (1.5 L).*

BLACK FOREST BROWNIES

International influences were strong during the 1970s, and sit-down dinner parties were popular. For such entertaining, I often made a European cake or torte, which my children would sample the next day, so instead of the simple chocolate cake with sprinkles most youngsters like for birthdays, my son usually requested either a Doboschtorte or a Black Forest Cake when his special day came around. These brownies are reminiscent of the latter, but they're easy to make and as one taster put it, "awesome."

1 cup	butter	250 mL		4	eggs	4
4 oz	unsweetened chocolate	125 g		1 tsp	vanilla	5 mL
2 cups	granulated sugar	500 mL		1 cup	all-purpose flour	250 mL
2 tbsp	kirsch (optional)	25 mL		½ tsp	salt	2 mL

TOPPING

1	can (14 oz/398 mL) pitted	1		1	egg	1
	sweet or sour cherries			1 cup	chocolate chips	250 mL
8 oz	cream cheese, softened	250 g				

In a heatproof bowl over a saucepan of simmering water, melt the butter with the chocolate. Remove from the heat; stir in the sugar and kirsch, if using. Let cool slightly, then beat in the eggs one at a time, stirring after each addition until the eggs are fully incorporated and the batter is shiny. Stir in the vanilla. Gradually add the flour and salt; mix until blended. Pour into a greased 13- × 9-inch (3.5 L) cake pan.

TOPPING: Drain the cherries well; chop coarsely and set aside. In a bowl, cream the cheese until smooth; beat in the egg until fluffy. Stir in the chocolate chips and cherries. Dollop the topping over the chocolate batter, then swirl it in with a kitchen knife.

Bake in the centre of a 350°F (180°C) oven until the edges are slightly puffed and the centre is just set, 30 to 35 minutes. Cool on a rack and refrigerate until cold before cutting into squares. Store in the refrigerator for up to 4 days. *Makes 32 brownies.*

RASPBERRY NANAIMO BARS

Not only is the origin of Nanaimo Bars a hot topic of debate; the bars themselves are still hot as a favourite Canadian treat. According to that wonderful book *A Century of Canadian Home Cooking* (Prentice Hall Canada, 1992), written by Carol Ferguson and Margaret Fraser, the *Women's Auxiliary to the Nanaimo Hospital Cook Book* (1952) included three similar recipes for what we now call Nanaimo Bars. The recipe appeared again under Nanaimo Bars in the *Vancouver Sun* in the early 1950s and in the British Columbia Women's Institute's *Centennial of British Columbia Cookbook* in 1958.

As well, test kitchens of several food companies developed various versions. Since the 1950s, endless variations have included Minted, Grand Marnier, Cherry, Pina Colada, Mocha, Peanut Butter and Orange Nanaimo Bars. I have not seen a Raspberry Nanaimo Bar, however, and found that raspberry liqueur added a touch of elegance to this familiar three-layered bar cookie.

BASE

1½ cups	graham cracker crumbs	375 mL		⅓ cup	unsweetened cocoa powder	75 mL
1 cup	unsweetened flaked coconut	250 mL		¼ cup	granulated sugar	50 mL
½ cup	finely chopped toasted walnuts	125 mL		1	egg, lightly beaten	1
⅔ cup	unsalted butter	150 mL		2 tbsp	seedless raspberry jam	25 mL

FILLING

2 cups	icing sugar	500 mL		2 tbsp	raspberry liqueur	25 mL
¼ cup	unsalted butter, softened	50 mL				

TOPPING

4 oz	semi-sweet chocolate	125 g		1 tbsp	raspberry liqueur	15 mL
2 tbsp	butter	25 mL				

Grease an 8-inch (2 L) square cake pan and line with parchment paper, leaving 1 inch (2.5 cm) extending over two edges for handles. Set aside.

BASE: In a large bowl, stir together the crumbs, coconut and walnuts; set aside.

In a saucepan, heat the butter, cocoa and sugar over low heat, stirring until the butter is melted. Remove from the heat and whisk in the egg. Add to the crumbs and stir until well mixed. Press evenly into the prepared pan and bake in a 350°F (180°C) oven for 10 minutes. Cool on a rack. Spread the raspberry jam in a thin layer overtop.

CRANBERRY GINGER OAT SQUARES

RASPBERRY NANAIMO BARS *(continued)*

FILLING: In a bowl, beat half the icing sugar with the butter. Beat in the liqueur along with the remaining icing sugar. Spread over the cooled base.

TOPPING: In a bowl over a saucepan of hot (not boiling) water, melt the chocolate (no need to chop) with the butter, stirring until smooth. Remove from the heat and stir in the liqueur. Spread over the filling. Refrigerate until the chocolate topping is firm. Let stand at room temperature for 5 minutes to soften slightly. Using the paper as handles, lift out of the pan and cut into bars. The bars can be stored in an airtight container in the refrigerator for 2 or 3 days or in the freezer for up to 2 weeks. *Makes 16 bars. (Pictured on page 23.)*

There was a date square recipe in every family collection in my mother's era. Date Squares in the eastern part of the country were Matrimonial Cake in Western Canada. Using fresh fruit instead of dried dates in this version is a refreshing modern twist. The tartness of cranberries provides a real surprise for those used to the extreme sweetness of traditional date squares and a real treat for anyone who is getting away from overly sweet desserts. Feel free to add another ¼ cup (50 mL) sugar when you cook the cranberries, but I think you will find most people prefer them tart.

12 oz	cranberries, fresh or frozen (about 3½ cups/875 mL)	375 g
⅔ cup	granulated sugar	150 mL
¼ cup	water	50 mL
2 tbsp	minced fresh ginger	25 mL
2¼ cups	rolled oats	550 mL
1¼ cups	all-purpose flour	300 mL
1 cup	packed brown sugar	250 mL
½ tsp	ground ginger	2 mL
¼ tsp	salt	1 mL
1 cup	cold butter	250 mL

In a saucepan, combine the cranberries, granulated sugar, water and fresh ginger. Cook over medium heat, stirring occasionally, until the berries burst, 6 to 8 minutes. Let cool.

In a large bowl, stir together the oats, flour, brown sugar, ground ginger and salt, being sure to press out any lumps in the sugar. With a pastry blender or 2 knives, cut in the butter until the mixture forms coarse crumbs. Press half evenly into a parchment-lined 9-inch (2.5 L) square cake pan; spread the cranberry mixture overtop. Sprinkle with the remaining oat mixture, patting it down evenly. Bake in the centre of a 350°F (180°C) oven until light golden, about 45 minutes. Let cool on a rack before cutting into squares. *Makes 16 squares.*

CHOCOLATE ALMOND BARS

A little candy, a little cookie—that's how to describe these chewy, decadent delights.

BASE

¼ cup	butter, softened	50 mL	½ cup	ground almonds	125 mL
⅔ cup	icing sugar	150 mL	¼ cup	all-purpose flour	50 mL
½ tsp	vanilla	2 mL	Pinch	salt	Pinch

TOPPING

⅓ cup	butter	75 mL	2 tsp	fresh lemon juice	10 mL
½ cup	packed brown sugar	125 mL	¾ cup	sliced almonds	175 mL
½ cup	corn syrup	125 mL	¼ tsp	almond extract	1 mL
1 tbsp	water	15 mL			

GLAZE

1 oz	semi-sweet chocolate, coarsely chopped	25 g

Line an 8-inch (2 L) square metal cake pan with parchment paper, leaving a 1-inch (2.5 cm) overhang at two edges; set aside.

BASE: In a bowl, beat the butter until creamy; gradually beat in the sugar until light and fluffy. Beat in the vanilla. Gradually stir in the almonds, flour and salt. Pat evenly into the prepared pan. Bake in the middle of a 350°F (180°C) oven until lightly coloured, about 12 minutes.

TOPPING: Meanwhile, in a small saucepan, melt the butter. Whisk in the sugar, corn syrup, water and lemon juice; bring to a boil over medium-high heat, whisking. Boil, continuing to whisk, until thickened, about 3 minutes. Remove from the heat. Stir in the almonds and almond extract. Spread over the base; bake until golden, about 15 minutes. Let cool slightly on a rack.

GLAZE: In a bowl over a saucepan of hot (not boiling) water, melt the chocolate, stirring occasionally. With a small spoon, drizzle over the topping. Let cool completely. Using the paper as handles, remove from the pan and cut into bars. The bars can be stored in an airtight container in the refrigerator for 1 week or frozen for up to 2 weeks. *Makes 16 bars, but you might want to cut them smaller since they are rich.*

CAPE BRETON PORK PIES

Through some curious quirk of language, these are not savoury meat pies but a favourite Cape Breton Christmas dainty—sweet and delicious date-filled tartlets. Leona MacInnis made them especially for the Glenora Inn and Distillery where I was delighted to sample them, but they are popular in other parts of the East, including Newfoundland.

∧ *Dates*

SHORTBREAD SHELLS

1 cup	butter, softened	250 mL	2 cups	all-purpose flour	500 mL
½ cup	icing sugar, sifted	125 mL	2 tbsp	cornstarch	25 mL
1	egg yolk	1	¼ tsp	salt	1 mL
1 tsp	vanilla	5 mL			

FILLING

2¼ cups	chopped dates	550 mL	¾ cup	boiling water	175 mL
	(12 oz/375 g)		¼ tsp	salt	1 mL
¾ cup	packed brown sugar	175 mL	1 tsp	vanilla	5 mL

ICING

⅔ cup	icing sugar, sifted	150 mL	1 tbsp	butter, softened	15 mL
2 tbsp	maple syrup	25 mL			

SHORTBREAD SHELLS: In a large bowl, cream the butter and sugar until fluffy; beat in the egg yolk and vanilla. In a separate bowl, stir the flour, cornstarch and salt together; gradually stir into the creamed mixture, gently kneading until smooth.

Working in batches, gently form the dough into ¾-inch (2 cm) balls; place one ball in each 1½-inch (4 cm) tart cup and press evenly over the bottom and up the sides of the cup to form a shell. Bake the shells in a 325°F (160°C) oven until crisp and pale golden, about 18 minutes. Let cool in the pan on a rack; loosen the shells with the tip of a knife.

FILLING: In a small saucepan, bring the dates, sugar, water and salt to a boil over medium heat; reduce the heat and simmer, stirring often, for 4 minutes or until thickened and smooth. Let cool; stir in the vanilla. Spoon the mixture into the shells.

ICING: Blend the icing sugar, maple syrup and butter together until smooth; place a dollop on each tart. (The tarts can be stored in an airtight container at room temperature for up to 4 days or frozen for up to 2 weeks.) *Makes 4 dozen.*

Christmas Dainties

A plate of fancy cookies and little cakes (Christmas cake or bars and squares) is known in the Prairies and northwestern Ontario as "dainties"—a lovely name for these special treats served at social gatherings, particularly during the Christmas season.

While our love of shortbread came with the Scots, many of our traditional Christmas cookies were brought here by German settlers, especially *Baseler Leckerli* (a chewy German cookie made with spices, honey, nuts and candied peel), some fruit cookies, sugar cookies and, of course, ginger creations. In the minds of Canada's German settlers, Christmas cookies were for children. Elaborately decorated cookies were hung on evergreen boughs, and later on Christmas trees, for children to enjoy and to eat.

The predominantly German custom of making cookies at Christmas caught on very quickly, so that despite the shortage of ingredients, most pioneer housewives made sugar cookies or gingerbread for the holidays.

Today, most Canadians still serve cookies during the Christmas season, perhaps making only one or two types or even buying them from a bakery. There are those who make dozens of kinds, and there are still cookie exchanges in which friends can make a few dozen of one kind of cookie and swap with friends so that each has a good variety of holiday "dainties."

LEMON SHORTBREAD STARS

Shortbread, brought here from Scotland, has long been a Canadian Christmas cookie favourite. These stars have a lovely lemony glaze to make them special.

1 cup	butter, softened	250 mL	1¾ cups	all-purpose flour	425 mL
¼ cup	cornstarch	50 mL	4 tsp	fresh lemon juice	20 mL
1 cup	icing sugar	250 mL	•	Strips of lemon zest or	•
1 tbsp	finely grated lemon zest	15 mL		silver balls (optional)	

Line two rimless baking sheets with parchment paper and set aside.

In a large bowl, beat the butter until fluffy. Gradually beat in the cornstarch; then beat in ⅓ cup (75 mL) of the icing sugar and 1 tsp (5 mL) of the grated lemon zest. With a wooden spoon, beat in the flour, ¼ cup (50 mL) at a time.

Divide the dough in half. Between 2 sheets of waxed paper, roll out each half to ¼-inch (5 mm) thickness, refrigerating the dough if it gets too soft. Using a floured 1½-inch (4 cm) star-shaped cookie cutter, cut the dough into stars, rerolling scraps and chilling the dough before cutting again.

Place the cookies 1 inch (2.5 cm) apart on the prepared baking sheets; freeze until firm, about 30 minutes, or refrigerate for 2 hours.

Bake in the top and bottom thirds of a 275°F (140°C) oven until firm and sandy-coloured on the bottom, 40 to 50 minutes, rotating and switching the pans halfway through. Let cool on the pans for 2 minutes before transferring the cookies to racks.

Meanwhile, stir together the remaining icing sugar, the remaining 2 tsp (10 mL) lemon zest and the lemon juice to make a glaze. Brush over the warm cookies and garnish the centre of each with strips of lemon zest or a silver ball if desired. Cool completely on the racks. (The cookies can be layered between waxed paper in an airtight container and stored for up to 1 week at room temperature or for up to 1 month in the freezer. Place waxed paper on top if freezing.) *Makes about 4 dozen cookies.*

ORANGE PECAN CRESCENTS

When my daughter-in-law, Cherrie, and I get together for our Christmas cookie-baking day, Pecan Crescents are always on our list at the request of my son, Allen. A hint of orange lifts these buttery crescents to entertaining proportions.

1 cup	unsalted butter, softened	250 mL
½ cup	icing sugar (approx)	125 mL
2 tbsp	orange liqueur	25 mL
2 tsp	grated orange zest	10 mL
2 cups	all-purpose flour	500 mL
½ tsp	salt	2 mL
1½ cups	finely chopped toasted pecans	375 mL

In a large bowl, beat the butter until light; gradually beat in the sugar until fluffy. Stir in the liqueur and orange zest. In a separate bowl, stir the flour with the salt; gradually stir into the butter mixture until blended. Stir in the pecans.

With lightly floured hands, shape rounded teaspoonfuls (5 mL) into crescents; place 1 inch (2.5 cm) apart on ungreased baking sheets. Bake in the centre of a 325°F (160°C) oven until light golden, about 25 minutes. Transfer to racks; dust lightly with more icing sugar. Let cool. *Makes 48 cookies.*

TIP: Toast the pecans in a 350°F (180°C) oven until fragrant, about 5 minutes, before chopping them.

COCONUT GINGER MACAROONS

This new spin on macaroons will appeal to ginger lovers. Crisp on the outside and chewy inside, this is one of the easiest cookies you'll ever bake.

2¾ cups	unsweetened flaked coconut (7 oz/200 g pkg)	675 mL
⅔ cup	granulated sugar	150 mL
⅓ cup	all-purpose flour	75 mL
¼ tsp	salt	1 mL
4	egg whites	4
¼ cup	finely chopped crystallized ginger	50 mL
1 tsp	vanilla	5 mL

In a large bowl, stir together the coconut, sugar, flour and salt. Whisk the egg whites until foamy; stir into the coconut mixture along with the ginger and vanilla.

Drop by tablespoonfuls (15 mL) about 1½ inches (4 cm) apart onto parchment-lined or greased baking sheets. Bake in the centre of a 325°F (160°C) oven until the edges are golden brown, 20 to 25 minutes. Transfer immediately to a rack; let cool. The macaroons can be stored in an airtight container at room temperature for up to 2 days. *Makes about 36 macaroons.*

NEWFANGLED HERMITS

Anne Lindsay is best known for her hugely popular series of cookbooks that are filled with delicious, light and nutritious recipes. This new take on a heritage cookie from *Anne Lindsay's New Light Cooking* (Ballantine Books, 1998) is a good example, with its reduced butter and wealth of fruit.

Over the years, Hermits have been called "Jumbo Raisin Cookies" or "Fruit Drops." Firmer versions were "Cookies for Soldiers or Miners" and even "Rocks" and "Door Stoppers." These, however, are not only big and soft, but also fast and easy to make. Use any combination of dried fruits you wish.

⅔ cup	packed brown sugar	150 mL	½ tsp	baking powder	2 mL
⅓ cup	butter, softened	75 mL	½ tsp	ground cinnamon	2 mL
1	egg	1	½ tsp	ground allspice	2 mL
⅓ cup	corn syrup	75 mL	½ tsp	grated nutmeg	2 mL
1 tsp	grated orange zest	5 mL	½ cup	dried blueberries	125 mL
1 tsp	vanilla	5 mL	½ cup	dried cranberries	125 mL
2 tbsp	fresh orange juice	25 mL	½ cup	dried cherries	125 mL
1¾ cups	all-purpose flour	425 mL	½ cup	raisins	125 mL
½ tsp	baking soda	2 mL			

In a large bowl, using an electric mixer, beat the brown sugar with the butter until mixed; beat in the egg, corn syrup, orange zest, vanilla and orange juice until light and fluffy.

In a separate bowl, combine the flour, baking soda, baking powder, cinnamon, allspice and nutmeg. Stir in the blueberries, cranberries, cherries and raisins. Stir into the butter mixture, mixing well.

Drop by rounded tablespoonfuls (15 mL) about 2 inches (5 cm) apart onto greased baking sheets; flatten the tops with the back of a spoon. Bake in the centre of a 350°F (180°C) oven until golden, 12 to 15 minutes. Let stand on the baking sheets for 2 to 3 minutes; transfer to racks and cool completely. (The cookies can be stored in an airtight container at room temperature for up to 1 week or frozen for up to 1 month.) *Makes 30 cookies.*

Blue Rocks harbour >
near Lunenburg, Nova Scotia

THE MARITIMES

THE FOOD TRADITIONS of Nova Scotia, New Brunswick and Prince Edward Island go back nearly four centuries to the French settlements of Acadia. These settlers prospered in their farming and learned the Micmac (*Mi'kmaq*) ways of using wild game, fish, fruit and maple syrup. However, such prosperity didn't last because the dispute between France and England forced them off their land in 1755, some going as far south as Louisiana, where they were called Cajuns. A few of these Acadians returned after 1763, but were forced to farm poorer land or to turn to fishing as a trade. They brought back with them, however, distinct dishes like Fricots (stews) and Râpure (grated potato and chicken or seafood pie) that became popular in parts of New Brunswick and Nova Scotia.

In 1783, United Empire Loyalists came north and brought along some New England food traditions, such as uses for corn and baked beans as Saturday night fare.

Black Loyalists contributed Southern American cookery methods like deep-frying and barbecued meat.

^ *French River, Prince Edward Island*

German farmers settled in Lunenburg and produced regional dishes like Dutch Mess (codfish and potatoes), Solomon Gundy (pickled herring), Kohl Slaw, homemade sausages and sauerkraut.

By the end of the 18th century, the garrison town of Halifax had become a centre of British social life, with elegant banquets and distinctive English dishes like meat pies, roast beef, trifle and gingerbread. The early English colonists were dependent on Great Britain for food, and these supplies grew into a thriving trade of tea, sugar, spices and dried fruits. Cargoes of salt cod and lumber left here and returned with sugar, molasses, spices, coffee, rum and fruit from the Caribbean.

Early in the 19th century, there were waves of Irish and Scottish immigration, with some Lebanese coming to Prince Edward Island. The Scots brought their oatcakes, scones, porridge bread and shortbread to Cape Breton, where they are still featured on many menus.

The mid to late 19th century was a prosperous age for the Maritimes, with logging, shipbuilding, farming and fishing. Although some of these activities have changed, especially fishing, we still relish lobster, Malpeque oysters and farmed mussels from Prince Edward Island; Digby scallops and dulse from Nova Scotia; and salmon, smelt, trout and shad from New Brunswick.

There are still wonderful land harvests throughout different regions—apples in the Annapolis Valley and wild blueberries in Nova Scotia; potatoes in Prince Edward Island; maple syrup, wild chanterelles and fiddleheads in New Brunswick.

The 20th century brought immigration from the Caribbean, Italy, Greece, the Middle East, Southeast Asia and India. Whatever ethnic twists young chefs add to the cooking in this part of Canada, the best food highlights these local ingredients and often reflects the traditions of the past.

A MARITIME
COMPANY BUFFET

Spicy Shrimp with Fresh
Coriander and Lime
(page 6)

Seafood Pot Pie
(page 68)

Steamed Fiddleheads Served Cold
with Mustard Vinaigrette
(pages 147 and 168)

Sesame Wheat Biscuits
(page 58)

Rhubarb Red Wine Mousse
with Poached Rhubarb
(page 221)

VIKING SETTLEMENTS HERE DATE BACK to A.D. 1000, but John Cabot officially "discovered" Newfoundland in 1497.

Canada's first onshore industry was in Newfoundland with the catching, drying and salting of cod. By the early 1500s, ships from England, France, Portugal and Spain were sailing to its cod-fishing banks and taking back the salt "flakes" to feed Europe.

English colonists formed the first official settlement in 1610 at Conception Bay, followed in the 17th and 18th centuries by harbour towns for fishing, whaling, trading and pirating. Outports were established by the English in the north and west, the Irish in St. John's and the east coast and the French along the south shore.

Because of the harsh climate and lack of arable land, traditional Newfoundland fare was quite limited. Salt cod, salt beef, fatback salt pork, molasses, root vegetables, dried peas and beans were the basic ingredients. Their still popular Jigg's Dinner of boiled salt beef and root vegetables and pea soup (thick yellow split peas with diced turnips, carrots and potatoes) can be traced back to the daily diet of 16th-century fishermen. Game such as moose, deer, rabbit and partridge, along with wild fruit like blueberries, partridgeberries and bakeapples, add variety even today.

In 1992, cod stocks crashed and a moratorium was placed on fishing, but locals can still jig for cod and the fish along with cod tongues and cheeks remains a favourite.

Because of the long, cold winters in this part of the world, Canadians welcomed the respite that came with the preparations for Christmas. Before the 19th century, however, Christmas passed with a meal mostly of wild game and fish at manor houses and forts (see

NEWFOUNDLAND
AND LABRADOR

^   *Town of Rose Blanche-Harbour le Cou in Newfoundland*

Paul Kane's account of a Christmas dinner at Fort Edmonton, page 59), with little importance given to the day. It wasn't until the middle 1800s that December 25 was made a legal holiday and became a time of celebration and visiting, especially in early times when roads were more easily accessible by sled when they were frozen in the winter.

The West Coast cities followed the British Christmas food tradition of fruitcakes and puddings while in Quebec, Christmas Eve dinner or Réveillon might include tourtière, baked beans, cipaille and Bûche de Noël. The Acadians in Nova Scotia and New Brunswick followed a quiet French tradition as well. In Manitoba and Saskatchewan, Canadians of Ukrainian origin celebrated Christmas Eve on January 6 (see page 133). Early settlers in Ontario tried to duplicate their British Christmas and were more apt to roast a goose than a turkey.

Christmas markets in cities like Vancouver and Toronto in the 19th century were amazing sights, with all manner of meats and poultry displayed in outrageous ways.

In Newfoundland and Labrador, the Irish and English followed their home traditions. Newfoundlanders are known for their love of food, music and fun, and this is no more evident than at Christmas. Years ago, all business in small towns would shut down between December 23 and January 6 so that people could visit from village to village, including the mummers, who did their visiting in costume.

Wherever they settled, early Canadians tried to make the holiday as special as possible, and the menu has not changed much across the country since the 19th century. This one is traditional, perhaps with a few little modern twists.

CHRISTMAS DINNER

Cod and Potato Ovals with Spicy
Lemon Mayonnaise
(page 4)

Roast Turkey (and Gravy)
(page 91)

Wild Mushroom and Leek Stuffing
(page 90)

Mashed Potatoes

Rutabaga and Pear "Crisp"
(page 155)

Shredded Sprouts Sautéed
with Pancetta
(page 149)

Individual Mincemeat Cheesecakes
(page 197)
Or
White Christmas Pudding
(page 214)

Chocolate Pecan Fruitcake
(page 212)

OTHER MENUS

TWO EASY FESTIVE DINNERS FOR CLOSE
    FRIENDS ~ 251

A CROSS-CANADA THANKSGIVING ~ 252

CANADA'S BIRTHDAY PARTY ~ 252

TWO EASY FESTIVE DINNERS FOR CLOSE FRIENDS

These classic Canadian dinner party menus are within anyone's budget or skill and are based on long-time favourite dishes with a twist. In the first, the combination of roast beef and Yorkshire pudding stems from our British roots, but it's still a winner. Add a colourful starter, a few easy sides and a fabulous make-ahead dessert for a dinner that would be welcome right across the country. The second features pork, that meat that has been popular since the time of the very first settlers. Scalloped potatoes just seem to go along with pork.

Menu I	Menu II
Smoked Salmon and Cheese Brochettes with Citrus Greens *(page 3)*	Parsnip and Pear Soup with Five-Spice Powder *(page 32)*
Mustard-Herb Roast Beef *(page 105)*	Slow-Roasted Pork Shoulder with Spiced Apple Relish *(page 95)*
Mushroom Yorkshire Puddings *(page 158)*	Do-Ahead Scalloped Potatoes with Gruyère Crust *(page 142)*
Mashed Potatoes	Steamed Green Beans or Brussels Sprouts
Buttered Baby Carrots	Caramelized Squash Rounds *(page 157)*
Broccoli Slaw *(page 169)*	Lavender Crème Brûlée *(page 223)*
Chocolate-Hazelnut Bombe with Raspberry Sauce *(page 193)*	Coconut Ginger Macaroons *(page 242)*

^ *Lavender field (top)*
^ *Teepee smokehouse used to smoke fish and game, in Deline, Northwest Territories (bottom)*

A CROSS-CANADA THANKSGIVING

Canadian Thanksgiving is probably my favourite holiday in the year. For much of the country, it usually comes with brisk air, sunny skies and bright autumn leaves. I've collected the best of Canada's ingredients to create a real holiday feast. Each dish celebrates a different region, and together they're as rich and varied a spread as the country itself.

Stilton and Pecan Shortbread
(The Prairies)
(page 5)

Montebello Curried Beet Soup
(Quebec)
(page 26)

Roast Pheasant with Honey-Fig Sauce
(The North, where game birds are prized, especially geese, partridge and pheasant)
(page 85)

Creamy Potato-Parsnip Mash
(The Atlantic provinces)
(page 141)

Roast Plum and Sweet Onion Salad
(British Columbia's Okanagan Valley, where tree fruits flourish)
(page 176)

Coconut Pumpkin Pie
(Ontario)
(page 228)

CANADA'S BIRTHDAY PARTY

Where we live in Ontario, strawberries are in season, I can catch the last of the local asparagus, and it's usually a bright, sunny day on July 1.

What better reasons for an outdoor party? For as long as I can remember, we have celebrated Canada's birthday by having friends for dinner. Once we welcomed a couple of young new citizens into the country and another time we had 56 guests for a charity pig roast. Since we moved into a smaller house, our numbers have decreased to below 20 people, but I still go out to the farms to buy a flat of strawberries and many pounds of asparagus. I stretch one long table across our tiny yard, drape it with white cloths and decorate it with many colourful bouquets of flowers and herbs my friend Sharon Boyd magically puts together from her garden.

Guests bring treats we nibble on to start—perhaps a plate of smoked salmon, fresh seasonal vegetables like raw sugar snap peas and steamed fingerling potatoes with a dip, or crackers and pâté, sometimes cretons from our French-Canadian friend.

Deluxe Roasted Beef Tenderloin
(variation on page 104)

Pink Peppercorn–Mustard Sauce
(page 160)

Horseradish Potato Salad
(page 170)

Lentil and Hazelnut Salad
(page 174)

Roasted Asparagus with Tarragon Vinaigrette
(page 148)

Strawberry Shortcake
(page 202)

Chocolate Pavlova with Minted Strawberries
(page 192)

INDEX

Aa

almonds
    Almond Cherry Galette, 226–27
    Apricot Almond Bread, 53–55
    Chocolate Almond Bars, 238
    Chocolate Almond Torte, 198
    Layered Almond-Plum Trifle, 217
    Light Orange Almond Fruitcake, 211
appetizers, 1–19
apples
    about, 229–30
    Apple Butter Cinnamon Rolls, 52
    Apple Thyme Grilled Pork Chops, 96
    Cheddar Apple Soup, 31
    French Apple Tart, 231
    Slow-Roasted Pork Shoulder with Spiced
      Apple Relish, 95
    Spiced Roasted Orchard Fruit Pies, 225
apricots
    Apricot Almond Bread, 53–55
    Apricot Coffee Cake with Butterscotch
      Walnut Filling, 200
    Apricot Tartlets, 228
arugula
    Baked Chèvre on Mesclun with Fig
      Vinaigrette, 177
    Baked Penne with Mushrooms and Arugula,
      128
    Beet and Stilton Salad, 176
    Fresh Peach, Gorgonzola and Prosciutto
      Salad, 172
    Grilled Melon and Arugula Salad, 177
    Roasted Beet and Barley Salad with Walnut
      Vinaigrette, 175
    Roast Plum and Sweet Onion Salad, 176
    Warm Potato and Arugula Salad, 170
asparagus
    Creamy Penne with Asparagus, Mushrooms
      and Prosciutto, 127
    Hint of Spring Soup with Cumin Croutons, 25
    Poached Eggs on Asparagus with Yogurt
      Hollandaise, 44
    Roasted Asparagus Soup, 27
    Roasted Asparagus with Tarragon
      Vinaigrette, 148

Bb

bacon
    Bean Soup with Parsley and Bacon Garnish, 34
    Maple-Glazed Grilled Peameal Bacon, 98
    Pickerel BLT, 73
    Wild Mushroom and Back Bacon Risotto, 19
baked beans
    Chipotle Maple Baked Beans, 101
Baked Chèvre on Mesclun with Fig
    Vinaigrette, 177
Baked Penne with Mushrooms and Arugula, 128
barley
    Roasted Beet and Barley Salad with Walnut
      Vinaigrette, 175

Wild Rice and Barley Pilaf, 157
bars. See squares and bars
beans
    about dried beans, 100
    Bean Soup with Parsley and Bacon Garnish, 34
    Chipotle Maple Baked Beans, 101
    Fiesta Three-Bean Salad, 169
    Spicy Dark and Delicious Beef Chili, 106
    Squash and Bean Stew with Chipotle
      Cream, 137–39
beef
    Baked Penne with Mushrooms
      and Arugula, 128
    Beef and Tomato Curry, 107
    Braised Beef with Caramelized Root
      Vegetables, 110–12
    Caesar Burgers, 112
    Deluxe Roasted Beef Tenderloin, 104
    Game Filet with Wild Mushrooms, 113
    Lamb Koftas with Tomato Yogurt Sauce, 122
    Mustard-Herb Roast Beef, 105
    Oven-Braised Short Ribs with Chinese
      Greens, 108
    Peppered Roast Tenderloin with Red Wine
      Sauce, 103–4
    Simple Beef Stew with Orange-Walnut
      Gremolata, 109
    Spicy Dark and Delicious Beef Chili, 106
beets
    Beet and Stilton Salad, 176
    Montebello Curried Beet Soup, 26
    Quick Pickled Beets, 162
    Roasted Beet and Barley Salad with Walnut
      Vinaigrette, 175
biscuits
    Sesame Wheat Biscuits, 58
blackberries
    about, 218
    Peach-Blackberry Upside-Down Cake, 203
    Pear and Blackberry Hazelnut Crunch, 219
Black Forest Brownies, 235
blueberries
    Blueberry and White Chocolate Muffins
      with Sugar Sprinkle, 48
    Blueberry Bread Pudding with Whisky
      Sauce, 216
blue cheese
    Beet and Stilton Salad, 176
    Fresh Peach, Gorgonzola and Prosciutto
      Salad, 172
    Gorgonzola Focaccia, 13
    Homemade Tomato Soup with Blue Cheese
      Garnish, 28
    Stilton and Pecan Shortbread, 5
bocconcini
    Tomato and Marinated Bocconcini Salad, 179
bok choy
    Glazed Hot and Sweet Salmon with
      Bok Choy, 64
    Oven-Braised Short Ribs with Chinese
      Greens, 108

Braised Beef with Caramelized Root
    Vegetables, 110–12
Braised Veal Shanks with Wild Mushrooms
    and Potatoes, 115
bread. See also bread pudding; quick breads
    about bread-making, 51
    Apple Butter Cinnamon Rolls, 52
    Chorizo and Scrambled Egg Breakfast Pizza, 46
    Whole Wheat Pizza Dough, 46
bread pudding
    Blueberry Bread Pudding with Whisky
      Sauce, 216
    Brie and Prosciutto Bread Pudding, 43
brie
    Brie and Prosciutto Bread Pudding, 43
Broccoli Slaw, 169
brownies
    Black Forest Brownies, 235
Brussels sprouts
    Shredded Sprouts Sautéed with Pancetta, 149
burgers
    Caesar Burgers, 112
    Chicken Tortilla Wraps, 84
    Lamb Koftas with Tomato Yogurt Sauce, 122
butternut squash. See squash
Butter Tarts in Phyllo, 190

Cc

cabbage
    Maple Cabbage Slaw, 168
Caesar Burgers, 112
cakes and tortes. See also fruitcake
    Apricot Coffee Cake with Butterscotch Walnut
      Filling, 200
    Chocolate Almond Torte, 198
    Chocolate Chip Coffee Cake, 199
    Chocolate Molten Cakes, 194–95
    Individual Mincemeat Cheesecakes, 197
    Lemon Mousse Cakes with Raspberry
      Sauce, 201
    Peach-Blackberry Upside-Down Cake, 203
    Pumpkin Roll with Praline Filling, 207–8
    Strawberry or Peach Shortcake, 202
    Summer Plum Cake with Cognac Cream, 204
Cape Breton Pork Pies, 239
Caramelized Onion and Prosciutto Tart, 47
Caramelized Onion and Pumpkin Varenyky
    (Perogies), 135–36
Caramelized Onion Pizza with Anchovies
    and Black Olives, 11
Caramelized Squash Rounds, 157
Caramel Sauce, 195
carrots
    Creamed Fiddleheads and Carrots, 146
    Cumin-Roasted Carrots, 146
cheddar
    Cheddar Apple Soup, 31
    Cheddar Jalapeño Cornbread, 55
cheese. See also blue cheese; bocconcini; brie;
    cheddar; chèvre; Gruyère
    Grilled Tomato and Cheese Quesadillas, 9

cheese (*continued*)
Honey-Grilled Pears with Ginger Mascarpone Cream, 222
Roasted Tomato and Cheese Tart, 12
Smoked Salmon and Cheese Brochettes with Citrus Greens, 3
Two-Cheese Veal Loaf, 116
Zesty Three-Cheese Macaroni, 130
cherries
Almond Cherry Galette, 226–27
chèvre
Baked Chèvre on Mesclun with Fig Vinaigrette, 177
Quick Chèvre and Roasted Pepper Tarts, 10
chicken
Chicken Piri Piri, 84
Chicken Tortilla Wraps, 84
Curried Chicken Pot Pie with Phyllo Crust, 78
Greek Grilled Chicken, 81
Green Curry Chicken, 80
Jerk Wings, 11
Moroccan Chicken Stew with Saffron Dumplings, 82
New World Coq au Vin, 79
Roast Chicken with Garlic, 77
chicken liver
Quick Brandied Chicken Liver Pâté, 15
Warm Chicken Liver Salad with Parsley, 180
Chicken Piri Piri, 84
Chicken Tortilla Wraps, 84
chili
Spicy Dark and Delicious Beef Chili, 106
Chinese-Style Roast Duck, 86
Chipotle Maple Baked Beans, 101
chocolate
Black Forest Brownies, 235
Blueberry and White Chocolate Muffins with Sugar Sprinkle, 48
Chocolate Almond Bars, 238
Chocolate Almond Torte, 198
Chocolate Chip Coffee Cake, 199
Chocolate-Hazelnut Bombe with Raspberry Sauce, 193
Chocolate Molten Cakes, 194–95
Chocolate Pavlova with Minted Strawberries, 192
Chocolate Pecan Fruitcake, 212
Chocolate Raspberry Pavlova, 192
Hot Chocolate Soufflé, 196–97
Individual Hot Chocolate Soufflés, 197
Raspberry Nanaimo Bars, 236–37
Chorizo and Scrambled Egg Breakfast Pizza, 46
chowder
Fennel-Roasted Seafood Chowder, 41
Harvest Corn Chowder, 36
Christmas desserts
about Christmas dainties, 240
about fruitcake, 209–10
Cape Breton Pork Pies, 239
Lemon Shortbread Stars, 241
White Christmas Pudding, 214
chutney
Small-Batch Spicy Peach Chutney, 164
Tomato-Currant Chutney, 164

cinnamon rolls
Apple Butter Cinnamon Rolls, 52
Citrus-Glazed Roast Goose, 89
clams
Fennel-Roasted Seafood Chowder, 41
Oyster Stew, 73
coconut
Coconut Ginger Macaroons, 242
Coconut Pumpkin Pie, 228
Raspberry Nanaimo Bars, 236–37
Cod and Potato Ovals with Spicy Lemon Mayonnaise, 4
coleslaw
Broccoli Slaw, 169
Maple Cabbage Slaw, 168
cookies. *See also* squares and bars
Coconut Ginger Macaroons, 242
Lemon Shortbread Stars, 241
Newfangled Hermits, 243
Orange Pecan Crescents, 242
corn
about, 150
Corn-Crusted Roast Salmon, 64
Harvest Corn Chowder, 36
New-Fashioned Corn Roast, A, 151
Stir-Fried Corn and Sweet Peppers, 152
cranberries
about, 159
Cranberry Ginger Oat Squares, 237
Cranberry Streusel Muffins, 50
Cranberry Walnut Loaf, 53
Jewel Jam, 162–64
Pumpkin Bisque with Cranberry Oil Swirl, 33
Spiced Cranberry Port Sauce, 158
Wild Rice and Cranberry Salad, 172
Creamed Fiddleheads and Carrots, 146
Cream of Fiddlehead Soup, 27
Cream of Wild Rice and Mushroom Soup, 35
Creamy Penne with Asparagus, Mushrooms and Prosciutto, 127
Creamy Potato-Parsnip Mash, 141
crème brûlée
Lavender Crème Brûlée, 223
cucumbers
Cucumber Raita, 160
Rice Noodle Cucumber Salad, 182
Summer Tossed Sushi Salad, 181
Cumin-Roasted Carrots, 146
curried main dishes, soups and sauces
Beef and Tomato Curry, 107
Cheddar Apple Soup, 31
Curried Chicken Pot Pie with Phyllo Crust, 78
Green Curry Chicken, 80
Lamb Koftas with Tomato Yogurt Sauce, 122
Montebello Curried Beet Soup, 26
Spicy Lamb Turnovers with Curried Yogurt, 8–9

Dd

Deluxe Roasted Beef Tenderloin, 104
desserts. *See* bread pudding; cakes; cookies; fruitcake; pies and tarts; puddings; squares and bars
dessert sauces
Caramel Sauce, 195

Cognac Cream, 204
Ginger Mascarpone Cream, 222
Prune Brandy Cream, 222
Raspberry Sauce, 201
Whisky Sauce, 216
Do-Ahead Scalloped Potatoes with Gruyère Crust, 142
Dried Pear and Poppy Seed Bread, 57
duck
Chinese-Style Roast Duck, 86

Ee

East Coast Lobster Rolls, 63
eggplant
Penne with Grilled Vegetables, 132
eggs
Chorizo and Scrambled Egg Breakfast Pizza, 46
Poached Eggs on Asparagus with Yogurt Hollandaise, 44

Ff

Fennel-Roasted Seafood Chowder, 41
fiddleheads
about, 147
Creamed Fiddleheads and Carrots, 146
Cream of Fiddlehead Soup, 27
Fiesta Three-Bean Salad, 169
figs
Baked Chèvre on Mesclun with Fig Vinaigrette, 177
Lamb Shanks Braised with Figs and Root Vegetables, 119
Roast Pheasant with Honey-Fig Sauce, 85–86
fish and seafood. *See also* clams; lobster; mussels; oysters; shrimp
Cod and Potato Ovals with Spicy Lemon Mayonnaise, 4
Corn-Crusted Roast Salmon, 64
East Coast Lobster Rolls, 63
Fennel-Roasted Seafood Chowder, 41
Glazed Hot and Sweet Salmon with Bok Choy, 64
Grilled Arctic Char with Orange-Onion Salsa, 69
Mussels in Coconut Broth, 70
Oven-Roasted Halibut with Caper-Herb Vinaigrette, 63
Oyster Stew, 73
Pickerel BLT, 73
Quick Seafood Stew, 67
Seafood Pot Pie, 68
Smoked Salmon and Cheese Brochettes with Citrus Greens, 3
Spicy Shrimp with Fresh Coriander and Lime, 6
Thai Tom Yum Shrimp Soup, 39
Wine-Pickled Salmon, 5
focaccia
Gorgonzola Focaccia, 13
French Apple Tart, 231
French Lemon Tart, 232–34
Fresh Peach, Gorgonzola and Prosciutto Salad, 172
Fresh Pineapple Sweet and Sour Pork, 97

fruitcake
about, 209–10
Chocolate Pecan Fruitcake, 212
Light Orange Almond Fruitcake, 211

Gg

game
Game Filet with Wild Mushrooms, 113
Garlicky Portobello Mushrooms, 154
Garlic Potato Wedges, 145
Glazed Hot and Sweet Salmon with Bok Choy, 64
goose
Citrus-Glazed Roast Goose, 89
Game Filet with Wild Mushrooms, 113
Gorgonzola. *See* blue cheese
Greek Grilled Chicken, 81
Green Curry Chicken, 80
gremolata
Simple Beef Stew with Orange-Walnut
Gremolata, 109
Grilled Arctic Char with Orange-Onion Salsa, 69
Grilled Melon and Arugula Salad, 177
Grilled Tomato and Cheese Quesadillas, 9
Gruyère
Do-Ahead Scalloped Potatoes with Gruyère
Crust, 142

Hh

Harvest Corn Chowder, 36
hazelnuts
Chocolate-Hazelnut Bombe with Raspberry
Sauce, 193
Lentil and Hazelnut Salad, 174
Pear and Blackberry Hazelnut Crunch, 219
Hint of Spring Soup with Cumin Croutons, 25
Homemade Tomato Soup with Blue Cheese
Garnish, 28
Honey-Grilled Pears with Ginger Mascarpone
Cream, 222
Horseradish Potato Salad, 170
Hot and Sour Soup, 38
Hot Chocolate Soufflé, 196–97
hummus
Lemon-Parsley Hummus, 12

Ii

Individual Hot Chocolate Soufflés, 197
Individual Mincemeat Cheesecakes, 197
Irish Soda Bread, 58
Italian Escarole Soup, 26

Jj

jam
Jewel Jam, 162–64
Small-Batch Honey-Plum Jam, 162
Jerk Wings, 11
Jerusalem artichokes
about, 14
Jerusalem Artichoke and Wild Rice
Pancakes, 15
Jewel Jam, 162–64

Kk

kale
Stir-Fried Kale, 154

Ll

lamb
about, 118
Lamb Koftas with Tomato Yogurt Sauce, 122
Lamb Shanks Braised with Figs and Root
Vegetables, 119
Lemon-Rosemary Grilled Lamb, 120
Mint-Chili Lamb Racks, 120
Spicy Lamb Turnovers with Curried Yogurt, 8
Lavender Crème Brûlée, 223
Layered Almond-Plum Trifle, 217
leeks
Wild Mushroom and Leek Stuffing, 90
lemons
Cod and Potato Ovals with Spicy Lemon
Mayonnaise, 4
French Lemon Tart, 232–34
Lemon Anise Loaf, 56
Lemon Mousse Cakes with Raspberry
Sauce, 201
Lemon-Parsley Hummus, 12
Lemon-Rosemary Grilled Lamb, 120
Lemon Shortbread Stars, 241
Lentil and Hazelnut Salad, 174
lettuce greens, about, 166–67. *See also* arugula
Light Orange Almond Fruitcake, 211
lobster
East Coast Lobster Rolls, 63

Mm

macaroni
Zesty Three-Cheese Macaroni, 130
Maple Cabbage Slaw, 168
Maple-Glazed Grilled Peameal Bacon, 98
maple syrup
about, 188–89
Cape Breton Pork Pies, 239
Chipotle Maple Baked Beans, 101
Maple Cabbage Slaw, 168
Maple-Glazed Grilled Peameal Bacon, 98
Maple Yogurt Mousse, 187
meat loaf
Two-Cheese Meat Loaf, 116
Mint-Chili Lamb Racks, 120
Montebello Curried Beet Soup, 26
Moroccan Chicken Stew with Saffron
Dumplings, 82
mousse
Lemon Mousse Cakes with Raspberry
Sauce, 201
Maple Yogurt Mousse, 187
Rhubarb Red Wine Mousse with Poached
Rhubarb, 221
muffins
Blueberry and White Chocolate Muffins with
Sugar Sprinkle, 48
Cranberry Streusel Muffins, 50
Spiced Pumpkin-Date Muffins, 48
mushrooms
Baked Penne with Mushrooms and Arugula, 128

Braised Veal Shanks with Wild Mushrooms
and Potatoes, 115
Cream of Wild Rice and Mushroom Soup, 35
Creamy Penne with Asparagus, Mushrooms
and Prosciutto, 127
Game Filet with Wild Mushrooms, 113
Garlicky Portobello Mushrooms, 154
Hot and Sour Soup, 38
Mushroom Yorkshire Puddings, 158
New World Coq au Vin, 79
Thai Tom Yum Shrimp Soup, 39
Wild Mushroom and Back Bacon Risotto, 19
Wild Mushroom and Leek Stuffing, 90
Wild Rice and Barley Pilaf, 157
mussels
Mussels in Coconut Broth, 70
Quick Seafood Stew, 67
Mustard-Herb Roast Beef, 105
Mustard Vinaigrette, 168

Nn

Nanaimo bars
Raspberry Nanaimo Bars, 236–37
Newfangled Hermits, 243
New-Fashioned Corn Roast, A, 151
New World Coq au Vin, 79
nuts. *See* almonds; hazelnuts; pecans; walnuts

Oo

onions, caramelized
Caramelized Onion and Prosciutto Tart, 47
Caramelized Onion and Pumpkin Varenyky
(Perogies), 135–36
Caramelized Onion Pizza with Anchovies
and Black Olives, 11
oranges
Citrus-Glazed Roast Goose, 89
Grilled Arctic Char with Orange-Onion
Salsa, 69
Light Orange Almond Fruitcake, 211
Orange Pecan Crescents, 242
Simple Beef Stew with Orange-Walnut
Gremolata, 109
Oven-Braised Short Ribs with Chinese
Greens, 108
Oven-Roasted Halibut with Caper-Herb
Vinaigrette, 63
oysters
Oyster Stew, 73

Pp

Pad Thai, 129
pancetta
Harvest Corn Chowder, 36
New World Coq au Vin, 79
Shredded Sprouts Sautéed with Pancetta, 149
Two-Cheese Veal Loaf, 116
Warm Potato and Arugula Salad, 170
Pan-Seared Veal Chops with Balsamic Glaze, 116
parsnips
Braised Beef with Caramelized Root
Vegetables, 110–12

parsnips (*continued*)
 Creamy Potato-Parsnip Mash, 141
 Lamb Shanks Braised with Figs and Root
  Vegetables, 119
 Parsnip and Pear Soup with Five-Spice
  Powder, 32
 Roasted Harvest Vegetables with Sesame-Sage
  Sauce, 156
pasta. *See also* pasta salad
 Baked Penne with Mushrooms
  and Arugula, 128
 Creamy Penne with Asparagus, Mushrooms
  and Prosciutto, 127
 Italian Escarole Soup, 26
 Penne with Grilled Vegetables, 132
 Spaghetti Puttanesca with Cherry Tomato
  Sauce, 130
 Zesty Three-Cheese Macaroni, 130
pasta salad
 Lentil and Hazelnut Salad, 174
 Wild Rice and Cranberry Salad, 172
pastry. *See also* pies and tarts
 Almond Cherry Galette, 226–27
 Cape Breton Pork Pies, 239
 Flaky Pastry (Seafood Pot Pie), 68
 French Lemon Tart, 232–34
pâté
 Quick Brandied Chicken Liver Pâté, 15
pavlova
 Chocolate Pavlova with Minted
  Strawberries, 192
 Chocolate Raspberry Pavlova, 192
Peach-Blackberry Upside-Down Cake, 203
peaches
 Fresh Peach, Gorgonzola and Prosciutto
  Salad, 172
 Peach-Blackberry Upside-Down Cake, 203
 Small-Batch Spicy Peach Chutney, 164
 Spiced Roasted Orchard Fruit Pies, 225
 Strawberry or Peach Shortcake, 202
pears
 Dried Pear and Poppy Seed Bread, 57
 Honey-Grilled Pears with Ginger Mascarpone
  Cream, 222
 Parsnip and Pear Soup with Five-Spice
  Powder, 32
 Pear and Blackberry Hazelnut Crunch, 219
 Rutabaga and Pear "Crisp," 155
pecans
 Blueberry Bread Pudding with Whisky
  Sauce, 216
 Butter Tarts in Phyllo, 190
 Chocolate Pecan Fruitcake, 212
 Orange Pecan Crescents, 242
 Pumpkin Roll with Praline Filling, 207–8
 Stilton and Pecan Shortbread, 5
Penne with Grilled Vegetables, 132
Peppered Roast Tenderloin with Red Wine
 Sauce, 103–4
peppers, sweet
 Fiesta Three-Bean Salad, 169
 Lentil and Hazelnut Salad, 174
 Penne with Grilled Vegetables, 132
 Quick Chèvre and Roasted Pepper Tarts, 10
 Stir-Fried Corn and Sweet Peppers, 152

perogies
 Caramelized Onion and Pumpkin
  Varenyky (Perogies), 135–36
pheasant
 Roast Pheasant with Honey-Fig Sauce, 85–86
Pickerel BLT, 73
pies and tarts (savoury)
 Caramelized Onion and Prosciutto Tart, 47
 Quick Chèvre and Roasted Pepper Tarts, 10
 Roasted Tomato and Cheese Tart, 12
 Seafood Pot Pie, 68
 Spicy Lamb Turnovers with Curried
  Yogurt, 8–9
 Tourtière Turnovers, 16
pies and tarts (sweet)
 about, 224
 Almond Cherry Galette, 226–27
 Apricot Tartlets, 228
 Butter Tarts in Phyllo, 190
 Cape Breton Pork Pies, 239
 Coconut Pumpkin Pie, 228
 French Apple Tart, 231
 French Lemon Tart, 232–34
 Spiced Roasted Orchard Fruit Pies, 225
 Strawberry Rhubarb Tart, 227
pineapple (fresh and candied)
 Chocolate Pecan Fruitcake, 212
 Fresh Pineapple Sweet and Sour Pork, 97
 Light Orange Almond Fruitcake, 211
 White Christmas Pudding, 214
Pink Peppercorn-Mustard Sauce, 160
pizza
 Caramelized Onion Pizza with Anchovies and
  Black Olives, 11
 Chorizo and Scrambled Egg Breakfast Pizza, 46
 Whole Wheat Pizza Dough, 46
plums
 about, 205
 Layered Almond-Plum Trifle, 217
 Plum Sorbet, 234
 Roast Plum and Sweet Onion Salad, 176
 Small-Batch Honey-Plum Jam, 162
 Spiced Roasted Orchard Fruit Pies, 225
 Summer Plum Cake with Cognac Cream, 204
Poached Eggs on Asparagus with Yogurt
 Hollandaise, 44
pork. *See also* bacon; pancetta; prosciutto
 about, 94
 Apple Thyme Grilled Pork Chops, 97
 Chipotle Maple Baked Beans, 101
 Fresh Pineapple Sweet and Sour Pork, 97
 Hot and Sour Soup, 38
 Maple-Glazed Grilled Peameal Bacon, 98
 Slow-Roasted Pork Shoulder with Spiced
  Apple Relish, 95
 Sticky-Crisp Barbecued Ribs, 101
potatoes. *See also* sweet potatoes
 about, 143
 Braised Veal Shanks with Wild Mushrooms
  and Potatoes, 115
 Cod and Potato Ovals with Spicy Lemon
  Mayonnaise, 4
 Creamy Potato-Parsnip Mash, 141
 Do-Ahead Scalloped Potatoes with Gruyère
  Crust, 142
 Garlic Potato Wedges, 145

 Horseradish Potato Salad, 170
 Roasted Harvest Vegetables with Sesame-Sage
  Sauce, 156
 Sage New Potato Kabobs, 141
 Warm Potato and Arugula Salad, 170
 Wasabi Mashed Potatoes, 142
pot pies
 Curried Chicken Pot Pie with Phyllo Crust, 78
 Seafood Pot Pie, 68
pot roast
 Braised Beef with Caramelized Root
  Vegetables, 110–12
preserves, 162–64
 about preserving, 161
prosciutto
 Brie and Prosciutto Bread Pudding, 43
 Caramelized Onion and Prosciutto Tart, 47
 Creamy Penne with Asparagus, Mushrooms
  and Prosciutto, 127
 Fresh Peach, Gorgonzola and Prosciutto
  Salad, 172
 Grilled Melon and Arugula Salad, 177
 Italian Escarole Soup, 26
 Sautéed Sugar Snaps with Prosciutto
  Chips, 148
puddings. *See also* bread pudding;
 Yorkshire pudding
 Lemon Mousse Cakes with Raspberry
  Sauce, 201
 Raspberry Pudding, 213
 White Christmas Pudding, 214
pumpkin
 about, 206
 Caramelized Onion and Pumpkin Varenyky
  (Perogies), 135–36
 Coconut Pumpkin Pie, 228
 Pumpkin Bisque with Cranberry Oil Swirl, 33
 Pumpkin Roll with Praline Filling, 207–8
 Spiced Pumpkin-Date Muffins, 48

Qq

Quick Brandied Chicken Liver Pâté, 15
quick breads
 about bread-making, 51
 Apricot Almond Bread, 53–55
 Cheddar Jalapeño Cornbread, 55
 Cranberry Walnut Loaf, 55
 Dried Pear and Poppy Seed Bread, 57
 Irish Soda Bread, 58
 Lemon Anise Loaf, 56
 Tangerine Date Loaf, 55
Quick Chèvre and Roasted Pepper Tarts, 10
Quick Pickled Beets, 162
Quick Seafood Stew, 67

Rr

Rapini Sautéed with Walnuts and Anchovies, 152
raspberries
 Chocolate Raspberry Pavlova, 192
 Jewel Jam, 162–64
 Raspberry Nanaimo Bars, 236–37
 Raspberry Pudding, 213
 Raspberry Sauce, 201

red currants
    Jewel Jam, 162–64
rhubarb
    about, 220
    Rhubarb Red Wine Mousse with Poached
        Rhubarb, 221
    Strawberry Rhubarb Tart, 227
ribs
    Oven-Braised Short Ribs with Chinese
        Greens, 108
    Sticky-Crisp Barbecued Ribs, 101
rice. *See also* risotto, wild rice
    Summer Tossed Sushi Salad, 181
rice noodles
    Pad Thai, 129
    Rice Noodle Cucumber Salad, 182
risotto
    Wild Mushroom and Back Bacon Risotto, 19
Roast Chicken with Garlic, 77
Roasted Asparagus Soup, 27
Roasted Asparagus with Tarragon
    Vinaigrette, 148
Roasted Beet and Barley Salad with Walnut
    Vinaigrette, 175
Roasted Harvest Vegetables with Sesame-Sage
    Sauce, 156
Roasted Sweet Potato Soup with Cardamom
    Cream, 31
Roasted Tomato and Cheese Tart, 12
Roast Pheasant with Honey-Fig Sauce, 85–86
Roast Plum and Sweet Onion Salad, 176
Roast Turkey with Wild Rice and Sausage
    Stuffing, 91–92
rutabaga
    Roasted Harvest Vegetables with Sesame-Sage
        Sauce, 156
    Rutabaga and Pear "Crisp," 155

Ss

Sage New Potato Kabobs, 141
salad dressings
    Fig Vinaigrette, 177
    Mustard Vinaigrette, 168
    Tarragon Vinaigrette, 148
salad greens, about, 167–68. *See also* arugula
salads, 165–82
salmon. *See also* smoked salmon
    Corn-Crusted Roast Salmon, 64
    Fennel-Roasted Seafood Chowder, 41
    Glazed Hot and Sweet Salmon with
        Bok Choy, 64
    Grilled Arctic Char with Orange-Onion
        Salsa, 69
    Seafood Pot Pie, 68
    Wine-Pickled Salmon, 5
sandwiches
    Grilled Tomato and Cheese Quesadillas, 9
    Pickerel BLT, 73
sauces. *See also* dessert sauces
    Cherry Tomato Sauce, 130
    Chipotle Cream, 139
    Curried Yogurt, 9
    Honey-Fig Sauce, 85–86
    Orange-Onion Salsa, 69
    Pink-Peppercorn Mustard Sauce, 160

    Red Wine Sauce, 103–4
    Sesame-Sage Sauce, 156
    Spiced Cranberry Port Sauce, 158
    Spicy Lemon Mayonnaise, 4
    Tomato Yogurt Sauce, 122
    Yogurt Hollandaise, 44
Sautéed Sugar Snaps with Prosciutto Chips, 148
seafood. *See* fish and seafood
Sesame Wheat Biscuits, 58
shellfish. *See* clams; fish and seafood; lobster;
    mussels; oysters; shrimp
short ribs. *See* ribs
Shredded Sprouts Sautéed with Pancetta, 149
shrimp
    Pad Thai, 129
    Quick Seafood Stew, 67
    Seafood Pot Pie, 68
    Spicy Shrimp with Fresh Coriander
        and Lime, 6
    Thai Tom Yum Shrimp Soup, 39
Simple Beef Stew with Orange-Walnut
    Gremolata, 109
Slow-Roasted Pork Shoulder with Spiced Apple
    Relish, 95
Slow-Roasted Tomatoes, 149
Small-Batch Honey-Plum Jam, 162
Small-Batch Spicy Peach Chutney, 164
smoked salmon
    Smoked Salmon and Cheese Brochettes
        with Citrus Greens, 3
soufflés
    Hot Chocolate Soufflé, 196–97
    Individual Hot Chocolate Soufflés, 197
soups, 24–41. *See also* chowders; stews
Spaghetti Puttanesca with Cherry
    Tomato Sauce, 130
Spiced Cranberry Port Sauce, 158
Spiced Pumpkin-Date Muffins, 48
Spiced Roasted Orchard Fruit Pies, 225
Spiced Sweet Potato Purée, 145
Spicy Dark and Delicious Beef Chili, 106
Spicy Lamb Turnovers with Curried Yogurt, 8–9
Spicy Shrimp with Fresh Coriander and Lime, 6
spinach
    Split Pea Soup with Smoked Turkey and
        Spinach, 29
    Warm Chicken Liver Salad with Parsley, 180
Split Pea Soup with Smoked Turkey
    and Spinach, 29
squares and bars
    Black Forest Brownies, 235
    Chocolate Almond Bars, 238
    Cranberry Ginger Oat Squares, 237
    Raspberry Nanaimo Bars, 236–37
squash (winter squash)
    Caramelized Squash Rounds, 157
    Curried Chicken Pot Pie with Phyllo Crust, 78
    Squash and Bean Stew with Chipotle
        Cream, 137–39
stews
    Braised Veal Shanks with Wild Mushrooms
        and Potatoes, 115
    Lamb Shanks Braised with Figs and Root
        Vegetables, 119
    Moroccan Chicken Stew with Saffron
        Dumplings, 82

    Oven-Braised Short Ribs with Chinese
        Greens, 108
    Oyster Stew, 73
    Quick Seafood Stew, 67
    Simple Beef Stew with Orange-Walnut
        Gremolata, 109
    Squash and Bean Stew with Chipotle
        Cream, 137–39
Sticky-Crisp Barbecued Ribs, 101
stilton. *See* blue cheese
Stir-Fried Corn and Sweet Peppers, 152
Stir-Fried Kale, 154
strawberries
    Chocolate Pavlova with Minted
        Strawberries, 192
    Rhubarb Red Wine Mousse with Poached
        Rhubarb, 221
    Strawberry or Peach Shortcake, 202
    Strawberry Rhubarb Tart, 227
stuffing
    Roast Turkey with Wild Rice and Sausage
        Stuffing, 91–92
    Wild Mushroom and Leek Stuffing, 90
sugar snap peas
    Sautéed Sugar Snaps with Prosciutto
        Chips, 148
    Summer Tossed Sushi Salad, 181
Summer Plum Cake with Cognac Cream, 204
Summer Tossed Sushi Salad, 181
sweet potatoes
    about, 144
    Braised Beef with Caramelized Root
        Vegetables, 110–12
    Roasted Sweet Potato Soup with Cardamom
        Cream, 31
    Spiced Sweet Potato Purée, 145

Tt

Tangerine Date Loaf, 53
tarts. *See* pies and tarts
Tea-Infused Winter Fruits with Prune Brandy
    Cream, 222
Thai Tom Yum Shrimp Soup, 39
Toasted Garlic Soup, 33
Tomato and Marinated Bocconcini Salad, 179
Tomato-Currant Chutney, 164
tomatoes
    Beef and Tomato Curry, 107
    Grilled Tomato and Cheese Quesadillas, 9
    Homemade Tomato Soup with Blue Cheese
        Garnish, 28
    Lamb Koftas with Tomato Yogurt Sauce, 122
    Penne with Grilled Vegetables, 132
    Roasted Tomato and Cheese Tart, 12
    Slow-Roasted Tomatoes, 149
    Spaghetti Puttanesca with Cherry Tomato
        Sauce, 130
    Tomato and Marinated Bocconcini Salad, 179
    Tomato-Currant Chutney, 164
tourtière
    about, 18
    Tourtière Turnovers, 16
trifle
    Layered Almond-Plum Trifle, 217

turkey
Roast Turkey with Wild Rice and Sausage
Stuffing, 91–92
Split Pea Soup with Smoked Turkey and Spinach, 29
turnip. *See also* rutabaga
Lamb Shanks Braised with Figs and Root Vegetables, 119
Two-Cheese Veal Loaf, 116

Uu

Ukrainian Christmas Eve, 133

Vv

veal
Baked Penne with Mushrooms and Arugula, 128
Braised Veal Shanks with Wild Mushrooms and Potatoes, 115
Pan-Seared Veal Chops with Balsamic Glaze, 116
Two-Cheese Veal Loaf, 116
vegetarian
Caramelized Onion and Pumpkin Varenyky (Perogies), 135–36
Squash and Bean Stew with Chipotle Cream, 137–39
Zesty Three-Cheese Macaroni, 130
vinaigrettes. *See* salad dressings

Ww

walnuts
Apricot Coffee Cake with Butterscotch Walnut Filling, 200
Beet and Stilton Salad, 176
Cranberry Walnut Loaf, 53
Pumpkin Roll with Praline Filling, 207–8
Rapini Sautéed with Walnuts and Anchovies, 152
Roasted Beet and Barley Salad with Walnut Vinaigrette, 175
Simple Beef Stew with Orange-Walnut Gremolata, 109
Warm Chicken Liver Salad with Parsley, 180
Warm Potato and Arugula Salad, 170
Wasabi Mashed Potatoes, 142
White Christmas Pudding, 214
Whole Wheat Pizza Dough, 46
Wild Mushroom and Back Bacon Risotto, 19
Wild Mushroom and Leek Stuffing, 90
wild rice
about, 171
Cream of Wild Rice and Mushroom Soup, 35
Jerusalem Artichoke and Wild Rice Pancakes, 15
Roast Turkey with Wild Rice and Sausage Stuffing, 91–92
Wild Rice and Barley Pilaf, 157
Wild Rice and Cranberry Salad, 172
Wild Rice Pancakes with Sour Cream and Caviar, 15
Wine-Pickled Salmon, 5

Yy

Yorkshire pudding
Mushroom Yorkshire Puddings, 158

Zz

Zesty Three-Cheese Macaroni, 130

PHOTO CREDITS

MAUVE PAGÉ ~ ix, x, 6, 14, 19, 24, 28 (bottom), 29 (top), 34, 35, 36, 38, 39 (top and bottom), 41, 42, 57, 62, 68, 70, 80, 81, 85 (top), 93, 94, 95, 100, 102, 103, 106, 107, 115 (bottom), 117, 119, 122, 126, 127, 129 (bottom), 132 (top and bottom), 139, 143, 144, 147, 156 (top and bottom), 165, 166, 167, 171, 174, 175 (top), 182, 186, 189, 192 (bottom), 198, 202, 209, 210, 218, 220, 224, 231, 232, 235, 240, 250, 251 (top)

GRACE YAGINUMA ~ vi–vii (middle), 13, 25, 28 (top), 32, 108, 115 (top), 128, 180 (top and bottom), 192 (top), 193, 223

MICHELLE MAYNE ~ 8, 27, 29 (bottom), 47, 79, 151, 179, 201, 229, 230

LEIGH MCGLONE ~ 43, 52, 67, 90, 104, 118, 200, 207, 243

DARWIN WIGGETT (www.darwinwiggett.com) ~ ii–iii, 59, 60, 124, 183, 184–85, 245, 246, 248–49

CHRIS MASON STEARNS ~ xii (left), 20–21, 76, 137, 140, 161, 205, 206

ISABELLE BOISCLAIR xii–xiii (middle), xiii (right), 69 (bottom), 113 (bottom), 251 (bottom)

PAMELA KENNY ~ vi (left), vii (right), 44, 51, 109

ANDREW BEIERLE ~ 69 (top), 175 (bottom)

CHRIS CHIDSEY ~ 239

SUZANNA DIEBES ~ 4

ELENA ELISSEEVA ~ 150

MARJA FLICK-BUIJS ~ 105

RICHARD GOERG ~ 133

ADRIANA HERBUT ~ 219

VALENTINA JORI ~ 1

BRIAN LARY ~ 226

WAYNE LYNCH (www.waynelynch.ca) ~ 74

JERRY MAYO ~ 18

KEVIN MILLER ~ 159

PATRICK NIJHUIS ~ 194

KARUNAKAR RAYKER ~ 10

PETER SZUSTKA ~ 113 (top)

YUCEL TELLICI ~ 85 (bottom)

NADINE WEGNER ~ 129 (top)

JOE ZLOMEK ~ 188